15.95

The Babe Didn't Point . . .

. . . and Other Stories about
Iowans and Sports by *Bill Bryson*

To My friend
Bill Bryson
Sincerely
Babe Ruth

The Babe

and Other Stories about Iowans

Didn't Point

and Sports by Bill Bryson

COMPILED AND EDITED BY
Michael G. Bryson, Sr.
AND
Michael G. Bryson, Jr.

Iowa State University Press/Ames

All photos from the collection of Bill Bryson and
reprinted courtesy of Michael G. Bryson, Sr.
and Michael G. Bryson, Jr. Material appearing originally in
the *Des Moines Register* or the *Des Moines Tribune* is reprinted
with the permission of the *Des Moines Register.*

Composed by Iowa State University Press
Printed in the United States of America

First edition, 1989

Library of Congress Cataloging-in-Publication Data

Bryson, Bill, 1915–1986.

The Babe didn't point and other stories about Iowans and
sports / by Bill Bryson; compiled and edited by
Michael G. Bryson, Sr. and Michael G. Bryson, Jr. — 1st ed.

p. cm.

ISBN 0-8138-0044-7

1. Sports — United States.   2. Sports — Iowa.   3. Athletes —
United States.   4. Athletes — Iowa.

I. Bryson, Michael G., 1942–

II. Bryson, Michael G., 1969–

III. Title.

GV583.B74 1989
796′.0973 — dc19   88–9103
                                                                        CIP

TO MARY BRYSON,
an extraordinarily
wonderful wife,
mother, grandmother

Contents

Bob Feller and Cap Anson

Stories about Iowa's Two Greatest Baseball Players

The Storm Lake Frost Bowl
Sporting Firsts in Iowa

The Boo Is New
Unusual Stories behind the Birth of Some Sporting Traditions

The Wild Horse of the Osage

Stories and Anecdotes about "Temporary Iowans"

The Spit That Split Iowa and Iowa State

A Potpourri of Anecdotes and Amusing Stories

There's a Gorilla on the Green
Putting Around with Some Golfing Stories

Mom Was Upset because Musial Wouldn't Wear His Uniform
Little-known Stories about Sports Greats

The Unsung Relatives behind the Heroes
The Parents and the Wife of the Football Star and the Coach

The President Made a Drunk a Hero
And Other Columns of Comments and Observations

Award Winners and Favorites
Some Great Moments in Sports

Acknowledgment

THE EDITORS would like to acknowledge the help of those who assisted in producing this book: Sherry Bryson, wife and mother of the editors, and Mary Bryson, mother and grandmother of the editors, put in countless hours helping with proofing and editing. Bill Silag, managing editor of the Iowa State University Press, in addition to helping with the editing, provided the much-needed enthusiasm that made completion of this project not only a labor of love, but also a joy.

Introduction

Bill Bryson was Iowa's premier baseball writer and was nationally known for his award-winning writing for the *Des Moines Register* in a career that spanned nearly fifty years.

"There was not a baseball park in the country where Bill was not known and respected," said E. R. Saltwell, a former Chicago Cub general manager and executive.

Bill, a warm and witty man, wrote about virtually every sport in every season, but baseball was his specialty — indeed, his greatest love. He brought to his baseball stories a depth of knowledge about the game and a command of the language that was unrivaled.

His peers often referred to him as a "walking encyclopedia of baseball knowledge," and major league stars, managers, and executives on the national level knew Bill on a first-name basis.

"And he *knew* writing," said Michael Gartner, a former editor of the *Des Moines Register* and later president of NBC News. "The beauty of a smooth double play was matched only by the clarity and grace of Bill's description of that play in the next morning's *Register.*

"He was a self-educated man who quickly came to know more about writing than professors did and more about sports than professionals did," said Gartner.

Bryson, who died unexpectedly of a heart attack in January of 1986, contributed a chapter to H. L. Mencken's *The American Language Supplement II* and was coauthor of a baseball dictionary.

He also was a contributor to a half-dozen other books and author of literally thousands of articles about baseball for national magazines. His stories were included in the *Best Sports Stories — 1953 Edition, Best Sports Stories — 1957 Edition, Best Sports Stories — 1961 Edition, Best Sports Stories — 1963 Edition,* and *Best Sports Stories — 1966 Edition.* Bryson also was a contributor to the *Best of Baseball,* to *The Annotated Casey at the Bat,* and to a number of college textbooks on how to write sports.

One of his major baseball stories was included in the *Fireside Book of Baseball II,* which also featured contributions from such illustrious writers as Sherwood Anderson, Jacques Barzun, Jim Bishop, Bennett Cerf, Bob Considine, Bergen Evans, Ring Lardner, and Grantland Rice.

Bryson was such a prolific writer — it's estimated that he wrote an astonishing 40,000-plus sports stories during his career — that one national baseball magazine had several pseudonyms reserved exclusively for Bill's stories, to avoid the impression that he was writing most of the publication.

Because of his vast knowledge of baseball history and its lore, he also was quoted as a source of information in literally scores of books, newspaper stories, and magazines, including such publications as *Saturday Review* and *The New Yorker.*

It was quite a feat for a man to develop such a national reputation in sports, considering that he spent the greater portion of his career living in a city that was four hundred to five hundred miles from the nearest major league baseball park.

Although Bill lived in a state without a major league team, the *Register* regularly dispatched him to major league parks during the summer months and to the spring training camps late each winter. He covered thirty-two consecutive World Series, starting in 1942, and more than a dozen All-Star games until his retirement in 1978.

Bill, who had a penchant for puns and loved a play on words, held no one in awe — and no one in disdain. He loved people — all kinds of people. At a major league park, it wasn't unusual for him to talk with a Joe DiMaggio, a Mickey Mantle, a Ted Williams, or a Casey Stengel, then wander over and strike up a conversation with the groundskeeper about the condition of the field that day. En route to his seat in the press box, he might engage in another bit of banter with a guy selling hot dogs or programs.

And, once the game started, Bryson knew everything that was going on. "Sitting with Bill in the press box was an experience," said

Gartner. "Bill could tell you who was out of position on which play, who seemed to be favoring his right leg, who was a bit sluggish because of the party the night before, who seemed to be using a different bat, and who was sitting in the boss's box seat last night."

It wasn't unusual for major league managers, executives, and scouts to seek out Bill's advice on the big league potential of a particular player. Once, the head man of a major league club hurriedly called Bryson long distance to ask if the club should shell out a particularly high bonus a prospect was asking. "You'll eventually get your money's worth," Bryson replied — and the player was signed within an hour.

One of Bill's favorite pastimes was telling the thousands of sports anecdotes that he had picked up over the years. He loved to talk. But at the same time, he loved to listen — and he had an uncanny ability to get others to open up, to reach back and recall that almost-forgotten anecdote or that unusual event that had occurred decades ago.

He always sought the different, the unusual, the unexpected to add a special touch to his columns and stories — and most of the time he succeeded by using a previously unearthed anecdote to illustrate a point here or an example there.

Even when he tackled the toughest of interviewees — the gruff manager or the obstinate player ignored by other sportswriters — Bill's warmth and good humor would soon have his subject laughing and recalling anecdotes and stories with wreckless abandon, fodder for a Bryson story the next day.

Bill had a phenomenal memory for events associated with baseball, hence his "walking encyclopedia" tag. Someone would come up with an obscure question, such as Who were the three best shortstops for the Tigers during the 1930s and '40s? and Bill without hesitating would reel off a slew of statistics, then enthrall his listener with a half-dozen anecdotes about the players just mentioned. He could tell you that by 1885 baseball writers had dreamed up more than 100 synonyms for the word *hit* — and then from memory could recite the words. For nearly three decades, Bryson wrote a popular *Sunday Register* column, "Information Pleas," in which he would answer questions from fans and readers. Most of the time he was able to answer the questions simply from memory.

He was a prodigious worker. It wasn't unusual for him to attend a game of Des Moines's minor league baseball team, write a game story for the next morning *Register,* then a feature story or column for the afternoon *Des Moines Tribune,* before coming home to his office-den to work on a story or two for a national magazine.

After that, he might dash off a poem or two (few of his contemporaries or even closest friends realized that he was an extraordinarily talented poet), before reading—for pleasure—a scholarly tome on some aspect of the English language.

(Bill was a night person most of his life. Although he spent at least part of his career working for an afternoon paper, which meant early morning deadlines, Bryson preferred to work late at night at the office or at home, then sleep when others worked so-called regular hours.)

Bryson was born in 1915 in Hillsboro in Henry County in southeastern Iowa and grew up across the county in the little community of Winfield. His love of baseball was nurtured early, after watching his father, a rural mail carrier, pitch in some pickup games in the area. By age eleven, Bryson was the official scorer for the Winfield town team—and he was only fourteen when he began writing sports stories for the *Winfield Beacon*.

After graduating from high school, he served a brief stint with the now defunct *Tri-City Star* in Davenport, then joined the *Register* in 1937 and quickly became the paper's baseball expert. He later was a columnist for the *Register*'s afternoon paper, the *Tribune,* which folded in 1982, four years after Bryson's retirement.

Bill and the late Garner (Sec) Taylor, longtime sports editor of the two Des Moines papers, teamed to cover World Series and All-Star games that spanned the careers of such greats as Joe DiMaggio, Bob Feller, Willie Mays, Stan Musial, Jackie Robinson, Ted Williams, and others.

Thus Bill was a witness to such famous World Series moments as Don Larsen's perfect game for the New York Yankees, Bill Mazeroski's dramatic ninth-inning homer in the 1960 Series, the incredible victory of the New York Mets in the 1969 Series, and Willie Mays's sensational over-the-shoulder catch for the New York Giants. Bill also reported the famous Bobby Thomson home run against the Brooklyn Dodgers in the 1951 National League playoff game that gave the Giants a pennant.

But Bill said his biggest thrill was the time he saw Babe Ruth slug a home run in the first All-Star game in Chicago in 1933.

His favorite athlete was the Yankees' Lou Gehrig, and one of his most cherished mementos was a handwritten letter that Gehrig wrote to Bryson in response to a letter twelve-year-old Bill had written to the famous slugger.

His wife of forty-five years, Mary, was the longtime home-furnishing editor for the *Des Moines Register and Tribune* who continues to write occasionally for the paper years after her retirement. The Brysons had three children—Michael, Betty, and William, Jr.—and six grandchildren.

Selecting the stories for this book wasn't an easy task for the editors, considering Bryson's copious production over the years. Bill witnessed many of the greatest moments of sports during his long career. But only a few of these events are included in this collection, because these activities have been thoroughly covered in scores of other anthologies, books, and articles.

Instead, the editors concentrated on selecting Bryson's stories that have not been reprinted elsewhere, and the type of stories that Bill enjoyed the most—interviews with people, from the loftiest of stars to the wife of a basketball coach or the mother of a football star; the debunking of long-accepted sporting myths; how many sporting traditions and customs were born; generally unknown stories about athletes from Iowa or "temporary Iowans"; and sporting firsts in the Hawkeye State.

One chapter features many of Bryson's favorite anecdotes, while another contains a selection of his sometimes biting, sometimes witty, tongue-in-cheek columns. The last chapter includes several of Bryson's prize-winning stories, along with stories from two events that he particularly enjoyed covering—the thrilling 1975 World Series and the improbable victory of the New York Mets in the 1969 Series.

The Babe Didn't Point

The Babe Never Called His Famous Homer

SPORTS LEGENDS, distorted in the memory or magnified in the retelling, die hard. None is more hardy than the fable that Babe Ruth, in the 1932 World Series against the Chicago Cubs, pointed with his bat to the flagpole in the centerfield stands at Wrigley Field. And, on the next pitch, whaled a home run to the exact spot.

Charlie Root, who managed Des Moines's baseball team in 1950, was Babe's victim—and the point of the legend always made the old pitcher furious.

Root always gave Ruth credit for getting two fly balls up into the jet stream blowing toward the bleachers. He admitted that Babe, before his second homer, made certain gestures in answers to hecklers in the Cub dugout. Ruth held up one finger after the first strike and two after the second—both called. Also, Root said, Babe had a habit of swinging his bat out with one hand as he took his stance.

"But," Charlie explained, "he did this before every pitch. If he had really pointed, everybody who knows me knows that Ruth would have been on the seat of his pants on a knockdown pitch."

And Charlie's clincher was: "Ruth himself never said he pointed."

In a 1944 interview with John Carmichael of the *Chicago Daily News,* Babe said: "Right now I want to settle all arguments. I didn't

7

Charley Root in 1938

exactly point to any spot, like the flagpole. . . . I just sorta waved at the whole fence."

If anything was said in the Yankee dressing room afterward about Ruth's warning point, it escaped *New York Times* sportswriter William E. Brandt. The only quote from the Babe came after Brandt told him their mates praised Ruth and Lou Gehrig for hitting two homers each in the 7–5 victory. "Aw, go on, now," Ruth was quoted. "The wind was with us, that's all. Any time they let us hit into the air, zowie—the wind did the rest."

> EDITOR'S NOTE: Any gesturing that the Babe made to the outfield that fateful day was to alert park personnel that part of a temporary wooden railing atop the outfield wall had broken loose and was in danger of falling onto the field, according to confirmed research that was found among Bryson's personal papers after his death. Park attendants correctly interpreted the Babe's "pointing" and quickly rushed to repair the fence.

Jim Thorpe Really Was a Prc

MANY ARE THE LEGENDS about the athletic might of Jim Thorpe. There are the track and field records, and the memoirs of his dazzled opponents, to put the stamp of truth on them. But there is also one myth about this Sac and Fox Indian who was voted "the greatest athlete of the half-century" in a 1950 Associated Press poll. It comes up every time there's a hint that any Olympic gold medal winner may have to surrender the trinket because his or her amateur heart, or purse, is not pure.

It was always said that Thorpe had to give back his prizes for the decathlon and pentathlon in the 1912 Olympics "because he had accepted money for playing semiprofessional baseball." The implication was that Jim picked up a buck or two for playing on Sundays for some obscure town team.

As a matter of harsh fact, Thorpe was a full-salaried professional player for three years before King Gustav V of Sweden, in 1912 Olympic victory ceremonies at Stockholm, proclaimed Jim "the world's greatest athlete." Thorpe was to add emphasis to this royal decree with his second selection as a collegiate all-American halfback at Carlisle that fall.

While Thorpe was winning all this amateur acclaim, he was under a professional baseball contract to Beaumont of the Texas League. There was nothing "semi" about Beaumont, nor about the three clubs Thorpe played for in 1909, 1910, and 1911: Wilmington, Rocky Mount, and Fayetteville, North Carolina. They were members of the Eastern Carolina League, part of the professional minor league structure in Class D.

Thorpe never made a secret of his pro connection. The evidence was there for anybody who consulted the Spalding or Reach baseball guides.

Jim was first with Wilmington, then with Rocky Mount in 1909 as a pitcher-outfielder. The official averages showed that he hit .253. The next year, Thorpe's batting added even less to his all-around distinctions. His average slipped to .236. Pitchers aren't supposed to hit, though, and Jim was almost exclusively a pitcher. He won ten, lost ten for Rocky Mount. How Jim hit or pitched for Fayetteville in 1911 has been lost to history. The league folded in midseason, and no averages were issued.

Thorpe signed with Beaumont for the 1912 season, but took a leave of absence to prepare for his Olympic triumphs.

More than a half-century after he was rightfully stripped of his honors, the International Olympic Committee in 1982 restored Jim's gold medals—thus ending years of battling by his family and friends to have the medals returned.

Ironically, Thorpe was either too honest or too naive to mark his pro pursuits with an assumed name. That was a common practice in Jim's era, and even up into the early 1930s, for summer pros who wanted to keep their college eligibility.

At least three members of baseball's Hall of Fame hid behind pseudonyms as pro novices. Two of them took the name of King. Mickey Cochrane, also a football quarterback at Boston U., was "Frank King" when he caught for Dover, Delaware, of the Eastern Shore League in 1923. Joe Medwick was "Mickey King" as a nineteen-year-old rookie who hit .419 for Scottsdale, Pennsylvania, of the Middle Atlantic League in 1931. It was a protection Joe never needed. He stayed in pro ball and passed up a passel of college football scholarships.

Eddie Collins wanted to keep his eligibility at Columbia if he didn't make it as a second baseman with the Philadelphia Athletics in 1906. He made it, under his own name, after one season as "Eddie Sullivan."

One *nom de sport* wasn't enough for Ed Reulbach, later a great Cub pitcher, in his four amateur years (1901–04) at Notre Dame. For three summers, he was "Lawson" at Sedalia, Missouri, of the Missouri Valley League. Then he was "Sheldon" for Montpelier-Barre, Vermont, of the Northern League.

Don't Keep Your Eye on the Bal

THE ADVICE most frequently shouted from the stands to the Little League batter is "Keep your eye on the ball!"

Fond parents or other volunteer counselors should yell something like: "Sharpen up your mental computation," according to Dr. Creighton J. Hale. Advising a batter to keep his eye on the pitch as it nears the plate is asking for the impossible, said Dr. Hale, who at one time served as a research director of Little League baseball.

Eyesight was always believed to be the most important factor in getting the bat on the ball, but Dr. Hale disagreed on the basis of years of scientific studies. Little League abilities weren't the only ones Dr. Hale measured. He also probed major leaguers with machine and camera.

What does the trick in batting, said Dr. Hale, is "the most marvelous computing machine in the world—the human mind. In fact," he explained, "the batter can't see the ball at all during its final fifteen feet of flight from pitcher to catcher. Batters hit according to computation by the brain. The instant the ball leaves the pitcher's hand, the hitter's brain begins plotting the projected line of flight. It takes 23/100 of a second for the brain to make this computation—and the batter is guided by it. A big leaguer's pitch takes an average of 43/100 of a second to reach the plate.

"When the batter swings, he isn't even looking at the ball, as high-speed cameras have proved. He swings at the spot his computer designated—or he doesn't swing because his brain has told him the ball will land outside the strike zone.

"Computing errors, of course, account for his missing the pitch. Practice sharpens the computing apparatus."

Stengel Was a Flop during Most of His Career

IN THE WANING YEARS of his life, it wasn't unusual for sportswriters and sportscasters to refer to gnarled old Casey Stengel as the "professor" or as a "baseball genius." And, in the summer of 1966 he reached the pinnacle of baseball success when he was inducted into the Hall of Fame.

But it will come as a surprise to many to know that after his first thirty-nine years in the profession, the reformed southpaw dentist was about as strong a candidate for baseball's hallowed shrine as Phyllis Diller is for Miss Universe.

Casey wouldn't have made it as a player, though he lasted fourteen years in the majors as an outfielder who hit .284. That was hardly enough to put him in the first rank of batters, especially since he averaged only thirty-seven runs-batted-in per year.

Baseball writers of Stengel's playing days laughed at his antics, but his comedy also made them cry about his waste of talent.

"I know Casey rather well," Jack Kofoed, a New York sportswriter, once reported. "He is a good-hearted comedian who always looks on the sunny side. Apparently nothing in the world is serious to him. . . . He never really achieved the heights that he should have gained . . . simply because of that careless attitude. He had a lot of fun, and that was enough for him. He did not aspire to become a Cobb, and though he possessed speed, batting ability, and a great arm, he never rose to stardom."

Stengel was traded by Pittsburgh to the Phillies in 1918 for George Whitted, and the deal, said Kofoed, "was severely criticized in Philadelphia. Whitted was an excellent player, a brainier one than Stengel, and one who took his profession seriously. . . . Stengel did not play for most of the season because he disapproved of the deal. He did not want to be on the Philadelphia payroll. When he did report, his work was lackadaisical. He had a lot of fun, but he loafed, and brought down a lot of wrath on his head. . . .

"McGraw (manager John of the Giants), who thoroughly understood Stengel, was glad to take him, and Casey justified the deal by playing the finest game of his life.

"A man of his disposition has to be with a winner to play winning ball." (The Giants won pennants in 1921, '22, and '23 with Casey as a part-time outfielder.)

This aged analysis by Kofoed held true for Stengel the manager. The big league phase of Casey's career as a manager began in 1934 at

Brooklyn, when he established this code of behavior for the Dodgers: "Drink all the beer you want, and if you have a toothache, take a shot of grog—it won't hurt you. But don't let me catch any of you guys sneaking out of the hotel at three o'clock in the morning to mail a letter."

Casey's record as a National League manager was hardly a passport to the Hall of Fame. In nine years, his percentage was .403. The Dodgers fired him after he finished sixth-fifth-seventh, paying him to sit out the 1937 season (and paying him more not to manage than they paid successor Burleigh Grimes to manage). Casey managed the Boston Braves for six years and his finishes were 5–7–7–7–7–6. Stengel missed two months of the 1942 season after he suffered a broken leg when struck by a taxicab. A Boston columnist declared the cab driver "the man who did most for baseball in Boston in 1943."

Stengel skidded back to the minors. When the Yankees unexpectedly resurrected him in 1949, the general reaction was: "Ol' Case better be good—or funny." He was both. Besides laughs, he gave the Yanks ten pennants and seven world championships in twelve years—and that was his passport to the Hall of Fame.

The Yankees fired Stengel after the 1960 season because management felt that he was simply too old. (Stengel died in 1975 at the age of eighty-five.) Even though the Yankees had prospered mightily under his leadership, it was no secret that many of his players considered him a grumpy and intolerable man and were delighted at his departure.

The Yankees were one of the last teams to use black players and Stengel openly expressed his dislike for blacks: he called Elston Howard, the first black to make the Yankees, "Eightball" to his face.

Stengel returned to managing in 1962 when the expansion New York Mets were added to the National League—and under his tutelage the team was a tribute to futility. The Mets were 40–120 in 1962, 51–111 in '63, and 53–109 in '64.

The Mets had a 31–64 mark—in dead last place for the fourth straight year—when Stengel broke his hip in an accident in 1965 and was forced to retire from baseball forever.

An Obscure Iowan's Bat Wound Up in the Hall of Fame

YOU SAY that a bat Babe used with the Yankees is in the baseball Hall of Fame, and the reaction is either a ho-ho or a ho-hum.

After all, it would be ridiculous (ho-ho) to have a baseball Hall of Fame without at least one cudgel that helped Babe Ruth hit 714

Loren Babe, 1976

home runs. It would be like having an aviation Hall of Fame without at least a propeller or a strut made by the Wright brothers.

And so (ho-hum) what? Everybody knows there's bound to be a bat of Babe's in the Hall of Fame.

Loren Babe's?

It's there, all right, on display as the weapon that blasted the longest home run, by actual measurement, in big league history—a bat stamped with the autograph of Loren Babe, who was born and grew up in Pisgah, near Iowa's western border.

Neither that historic home run, nor even any unhistoric ones, will be found in Loren Babe's record, however. Singles, and not too many of them, were Loren's specialty in a New York career that sent him to bat just thirty-nine times as a third baseman late in 1952 and early in 1953. His average was .205.

"It was my bat that hit the longest homer—but it was his muscles," said Babe, referring to the bundle of brawn known as Mickey Mantle. "I often wonder what people think when they visit the Hall of Fame (at Cooperstown, New York) and see the sign that says this was the bat that hit a 565-foot homer—and then look up and see my signature on it."

How did it happen that Mantle scorned his own bat and selected one branded for an obscure reserve infielder on that April night in 1953 in Washington?

Babe, who later served as a Yankee coach and minor league manager, could give no enlightenment. "I guess I hadn't been hitting with my own bat and was ready to try anything—just grabbed the first bat I came to in the rack. . . . I don't really remember," Mantle later recalled.

Anyway, in Mantle's hands, Babe's bat made such violent contact with a pitch from Chuck Stobbs that the ball flew far into the parking lot behind the left-field wall in old Griffith Stadium.

Arthur (Red) Patterson, then the Yankee publicity director, left the pressbox, dashed out to the parking lot and found a ball-shagging youngster who had marked the point of descent.

Colorful, Gaudy Baseball Uniforms Are Nothing New

BASEBALL TRADITIONALISTS rose in indignation during the early 1970s when several teams such as the Oakland A's and Houston Astros began wearing gaudily colored uniforms. It was the most startling sports fashion news since Gussie Moran wore lace panties at Wimbledon, and many fans felt it was darn near blasphemous to casually cast aside baseball's ancient tradition of wearing white uniforms at home and grays on the road.

But gaudy and vivid-colored uniforms, surprisingly, have been around baseball for eons. In the late 1940s, for example, the Dodgers wore bright blue satin pants for their home night games in Brooklyn.

And they were copycats. The Cincinnati Reds had capered in shiny red bloomers for years after putting big league ball under lights for the first time in 1935. In fact, the Oakland A's, who wore soft gold and loud green uniforms in the 1970s, weren't much different from the Dodgers of 1937. Brooklyn's "daffiness boys" went abroad that year in tan uniforms with kelly green caps, socks, lettering, and trim. (The colors have since been changed to blue and white or gray.)

Even the radiance of the '37 Dodgers didn't much excite old-timers once accustomed to seeing visiting clubs in costumes of dark blue, red, brown, or even black. Both Chicago clubs wore dark blue on the road for years, the Cubs until 1922, the White Sox until 1930.

"Ya can't tell the players without a scorecard," the vendors yell. There was once a time when you couldn't tell 'em without a color chart. That was when the Cincinnati Reds of the American Association, then a major league, decided to identify their players vividly by position in 1883.

There was a different colored shirt for each position. Pop Snyder, the catcher, wore scarlet. Pitcher Will White's shirt was blue. The other two pitchers took turns in a red and white blouse. Biddy McPhee, the second baseman, was dressed in orange and black. Third baseman Hick Carpenter wore black and white. And so it went through the line-up.

A year before, the National League had decidedly distinctive uniform hues for all clubs, both home and away: Chicago, white; Boston, red; Providence, light blue; Cleveland, navy blue; Troy, New York (the club was moved to New York City the next season), green; Buffalo, gray; Worcester, brown; Detroit, old gold.

In 1883, the color rule was changed to apply only to the socks. Ironically, after a decade or so of the brightly colored uniforms in the

1970s and 1980s, many major league teams began changing back to the traditional whites and grays during the middle 1980s.

Orange Baseballs Were a Lemon

ORANGE TENNIS BALLS have become fairly common these days, but when Charles O. Finley, baseball's restless rebel, suggested in the 1970s that baseballs be colored orange, he colored his fellow American League tycoons an irate red.

Charles O. argued bright orange would make the flight of the ball more vividly visible than the traditional white ball. It might, indeed. Color engineers agree that an orange ball could be followed easier than the standard white.

But the baseball traditionalists, already aghast by the bright green and yellow uniforms in which Finley had clad his Athletics, balked loudly, arguing that baseballs have always been white and white they should remain. What many people didn't realize, however, was that Charles O.'s proposal was by no means an innovation — not by a matter of decades in both the minor and major leagues.

In 1938, an orange baseball was used in an exhibition game between Bellingham, Washington, of the Western International League and Seattle of the Pacific Coast League. The colorful experiment was so successful that the Western International League approved the orange ball for regular season play. It made a hit with the spectators. Unfortunately, it also made a hit with the person of Bee Mandish, a Bellingham outfielder, in a game with Yakima. Mandish said he was wounded because he had lost the flight of the ball from the pitcher. So back came the white baseballs.

Baseball's so-called centennial year, 1939, marked not only the first televised game in the majors, but also the first played with an orange ball.

Ebbets Field in Brooklyn, long since destroyed to make room for an apartment building, was the scene of both firsts. There were no complaints from the Dodgers, nor the opposing Pirates, about the visibility of the orange ball. Onlookers said they could follow it better, too.

The players, especially the pitchers, did complain, though, that the ball had "a strange feel." Manufacturers admitted they hadn't yet found a yellow or orange dye that was really satisfactory for horsehide. The dye used then would rub off on sweaty fingers.

Babe Ruth Wasn't a Lumbering Lummo

THE EMPHASIS on Babe Ruth's home run records has tended to make people think of him as a large, scarcely mobile power plant. Often neglected are his uncommon skills in everything else, from pitching to baserunning.

One sportswriter mentioned in a story about glue-footed sluggers that "Babe Ruth couldn't catch a bus." Old-time Ruth admirers surely rose from their rocking chairs to protest that this was a base — or baserunning — canard.

Ruth was no greyhound, compared with the likes of Ty Cobb, Maury Wills, or Lou Brock. There was a time, though, when Babe would have had no trouble catching a Greyhound bus — and not just when it was crawling out of the terminal. He might have caught it when it was up to full throttle on the highway.

The most significant evidence of baserunning speed, it is generally agreed, is found in the statistics on steals and triples. Only a handful of American Leaguers manage to steal more than seventeen bases each season. Ruth swiped seventeen in two different years and was in double figures in three other seasons before age and growing girth slowed him down.

And not many of today's American Leaguers have the rare combination of speed and power to produce sixteen triples in a season. Ruth raced to sixteen triples in 1921, one of the years in which he had seventeen steals. Babe also had three-base productions of thirteen, twelve, and eleven. The eleven came in only ninety-five games in 1918, when he also had a pitching record of 13–7.

It's doubtful that any batter ever did everything as well as Babe did in 1921, when he was twenty-six years old. His 1921 assortment would have made him not merely a triple-crown winner, but a quintuple champion by today's standards. Ruth hoisted fifty-nine homers, a total exceeded only by himself (sixty in 1927) in a 154-game schedule. He also pounded forty-four doubles and sixteen triples. He batted in 170 runs and his average was .378.

Of course, Ruth's fielding wasn't bad, either. His range was vast, at least until his appetite, just as vast, brought an excess cargo about the midriff in later years.

Babe had the extra difficulty of playing in the sun field for the Yankees, but his errors were few. His hands were sure and his instincts were pure. Old-timers say Babe never threw to the wrong base. Ruth threw to the right base quite a few times in adding to his all-around accomplishments of 1921. He had seventeen assists.

You Can Score before the Opening Tip-off in Basketball

ONE OF THE PRIMITIVE GAGS of sports begins with the cocky declaration: "I'll bet I can tell you what the score of the game will be before it starts."

If any chump was ever gullible enough to say, "I'll bet you can't," then came the snapper: "It will be 0 to 0 before the game starts, stupid."

In football, yes, or baseball, or almost any other sport. In basketball, it's not necessarily so. A basketball team can be ahead, 1–0, before the opening tip-off — before the clock is ever started. This actually happened in a game between two high school teams in northern Kentucky during the early 1960s.

The coach of one team neglected to give his starting line-up to the official scorer before the specified deadline. The referee called a technical foul on the remiss coach. The opponents made the free throw before the game.

It could happen in college basketball, too. The rules make it possible for the team to be ahead by 1–0 or 2–0, or even tied, 1–1, before the official forty minutes of action begins.

At least ten minutes before the scheduled starting time, the code dictates, each team shall "supply the name and number of each squad member who may participate." The starting line-ups must be given to the official scorer at least three minutes before tip-off time. "Failure to comply with either of these provisions," the rule specifies, "is a technical foul." The resulting free throw, or throws, would be attempted before the tipoff.

There's no way a team can score in football before the clock is started on the opening kickoff. But it is possible to score after time has expired. The commonest way, of course, is on a play that begins before time runs out. The half, or the game, isn't over until the play in progress at the gun is completed.

Bill Stern: The Greatest Mythmaker of Them All

BILL STERN was once considered the dean of American sportscasters. Unfortunately, that urgent, distinctive theatrical voice of his spun some of the biggest sports lies ever told. It will take historians a hundred years to expunge the myths Stern created from 1939 to 1951 in his "Sports Newsreel" show.

His audience rating was among the highest in network radio. Bill used the suspense method to tell the wondrous deeds of some young athlete, keeping the identity a secret until the punchline: "And that man was. . . ." Here would come the name of any celebrity from Einstein to Eisenhower.

Stern never let a fact stand in the way of a dramatic climax. He wrenched history out of shape to fit his script.

Those closely associated with sports all have their favorite Stern myth, and this is one of the favorites.

When Abraham Lincoln lay dying, Stern related, he sent for General Abner Doubleday, the man who was supposed to have invented baseball. And the president's last words were addressed to the general: "Keep baseball alive. In the trying days ahead, the country will need it."

Aside from the facts that Lincoln never recovered consciousness after he was shot, and that Doubleday was nowhere around the death scene, the story is absolutely true.

Another Stern story had a youngster in Cincinnati pleading with his father to be allowed to sign a contract offered by the original Cincinnati Red Stockings of that city. "But, Dad," the youth told his disapproving parent, "this is *major league* baseball!" and that man was . . . William Howard Taft.

The Red Stockings did not sign their players to contracts. There was no such thing as a major league then . . . and when the club disbanded in November of 1870, Taft was only thirteen years old.

Stern loved to use the names of presidents as climactic stringers. He said William McKinley (who didn't know a bat from a pogo stick) passed up a pro baseball opportunity to go into politics.

Thomas Edison's deafness, said Stern, was the result of being hit in the head by a pitch when he was a semipro player — which he never was.

He once told how Grantland Rice saw a young fighter get knocked out, then heard him singing in the shower afterward. Rice, according to Stern, advised the young man to give up boxing and make singing his profession.

And that man was . . . Frank Sinatra.

It was one of the few times the easygoing Rice blew his stack.

Stern's autobiography was published in 1959. It included the poignant story of his escape from drug addiction, brought on by the use of opiates to ease the pains of injuries and illness. It also included the defense of his whoppers: that his sports program, which brought him $1,800 a week, "was strictly entertainment and being such was one in which I was entitled to unlimited dramatic license."

"Tinker to Evers to Chance" Owes Its Fame to a Poem

THE PHRASE "Tinker to Evers to Chance" has long been synonymous with success, cooperation, and teamwork. In reality, it was a poem that gave these three notoriety, not success on the ball field.

Shortstop Joe Tinker, second baseman Johnny Evers, and first baseman Frank Chance were, indeed, a crack infield for the Chicago Cubs from 1902 until the start of World War I. And they did help the Cubs to National League pennants in 1906, '07, '08, and '10.

But their abilities to pull off double plays have been exaggerated over the years. For instance, between 1906 and 1909, they executed a total of only fifty-four double plays among them. Compare that with the major league record of two hundred seventeen pulled off by the Philadelphia Athletics during the 1949 season. The National League record is two hundred fifteen by Pittsburgh in 1966.

Actually, what gave the trio its overrated reputation was a poem — "Baseball's Sad Lexicon" — written in 1910 by columnist Franklin P. Adams of the *New York Evening Mail*:

> These are the saddest of possible words —
> "Tinker to Evers to Chance."
> Trio of bear Cubs and fleeter than birds —
> "Tinker to Evers to Chance."
> Ruthlessly pricking our gonfalon bubble,
> Making a Giant hit into a double,
> Words that are heavy with nothing but trouble —
> "Tinker to Evers to Chance."

As for teamwork and cooperation, Tinker and Evers didn't much care for each other and once got into a fight and didn't speak a word to each other for years.

The Best Darn Onion-Thrower in the Majors

Tossing Onions Led Zuber to the Big Leagues

BILL ZUBER only had to see an onion to be reminded how he became a professional baseball player.

The odds against Zuber becoming a pro, let alone pitching eight full seasons in the big leagues, must have been the greatest ever faced by an Iowa youngster with baseball yearnings. Kids nowadays consider themselves underprivileged if they don't have coaching and organized competition from the age of nine. Manicured fields, full uniforms, and big league-type equipment are taken for granted.

Zuber didn't even know what a baseball looked like until he was in his teens. The game wasn't encouraged in the Amana Colonies, where Zuber grew up. In fact, it was expressly forbidden, along with all other pastimes. "If Cy Slapnicka hadn't seen me throwing onions," Zuber once recalled, "I'd have been a farmer and a cooper." His winter job as a youngster was in the colonies' barrel factory.

"A bunch of us kids were harvesting the onions. When nobody was looking, we'd see how far we could throw them. One day this man was watching us, but he was a stranger and we didn't think he'd tell on us. He came over to me and, before I knew what was happening, I was a pro baseball player."

The stranger was Slapnicka, the Cleveland scout who, a few years later, was to sign Bob Feller. "Slap" used to drive over from his

21

Bill Zuber, age 23, with the Cleveland Indians

home in Cedar Rapids to buy bread and hams and cheese in the Amanas. "The man picked out a round onion, about the size of a baseball," said Zuber. "He pointed to a barn about a hundred yards away. He says, 'Let's see you hit that barn.' I threw it clear over the barn.

"The man says, 'I'm a scout for Cleveland. How would you like to be a pro baseball player? I'll give you a contract with Cedar Rapids and we'll try you out as a pitcher.' I said, 'Don't you want to see me throw a baseball?' He said, 'No. Anybody who can throw an onion that far ought to be able to throw a baseball.' "

This was like a bumpkin playing tunes through a paper on a comb being invited to play with the Cedar Rapids symphony orchestra.

The year was 1930 and Zuber had just turned seventeen. Bill wasn't ready for even the Class D Mississippi Valley League competition at Cedar Rapids.

Indeed, what young man, no matter how strong an arm, would be after a childhood sternly directed away from fun and games? The Amana Society was changing from a church-controlled commune to a corporation in 1932. Members were beginning to work for wages instead of allotments of commodities.

Except for prospective doctors and dentists going away to study, young men were discouraged from leaving the colonies. Yet here was one leaving just to play games. Unthinkable.

Since the German-founded Society moved to twenty-five thousand rolling Iowa acres in 1855, all forms of amusement had been *verboten*. Even to possess any kind of ball or toy was forbidden.

Bill learned to pitch in a Cedar Rapids semipro league his first year under contract to Cleveland.

His right arm had all the zing that Slapnicka anticipated, but a woeful lack of direction. Wildness kept him in the minors for seven years except for two brief trials with the Indians. "The trouble," said Zuber, "was there weren't any handles on a baseball like on an onion."

Bill, who later operated a popular restaurant in Homestead until his death in 1982, never became a big winner in the majors. But he helped the Yankees win pennants in 1943 and '44. His 5–1 record assisted in the Red Sox's 1946 championship.

No other onion-thrower ever did as well.

*Hal Trosky in 1953, with sons Hal Jr., Jim, and Lynn,
at the State Legion Junior Baseball tourney*

Headaches Cut Short Trosky's Brilliant Future

THE BEST BALLPLAYER to ever come out of the eastern Iowa village of
Norway was a cross-handed batter when he was playing there. He also
was a pitcher then, that big kid named Harold Troyavesky.

There were a lot of changes made when the youngster got into the
professional world in 1931 — in name, position, and manner of holding the bat.

His name became Hal Trosky. Nearby Cedar Rapids of the Mississippi Valley League tried him as a pitcher, but released him, and
Dubuque of the same league signed Hal.

When Trosky became accustomed to an orthodox left-handed
grip, Dubuque used him in the outfield in twenty-nine games and he
hit .302 with three homers. He was 2–2 as a pitcher.

By 1934, Trosky was a rookie first baseman with the Cleveland Indians and he whaled thirty-five home runs, a record for rookies then, and knocked in a rookie-record 142 runs. He went on to cause headaches for enemy pitchers as the Indians' first baseman until 1941.

Trouble was, baseball also was causing headaches for Hal — terrible migraines that forced him to give up baseball and go back to the farm near Norway in 1942.

He twice tried comebacks with the Chicago White Sox, in 1944 and 1946, but the old ability was gone and he added only a dozen homers to the 216 he had crashed for Cleveland. "I never really did get rid of those migraines till I got out of baseball," Trosky recalled before his death in 1979 at the age of sixty-seven.

One of Trosky's rookie batting records remains untouched, and he still shares two others for a 154-game schedule. No freshman in either league has ever whacked more extra base hits (eighty-nine) than Hal did on his way to his .330 average in 1934. Besides his thirty-four homers, Trosky drilled forty-five doubles and nine triples.

His two-base total, matching a record set by Roy Johnson of Detroit in 1929, hasn't been approached.

Trosky's 374 mark for total bases, the combined value of all hits (four for a homer, three for a triple, and so on), stood alone until Tony Oliva equaled it in 1964. Oliva netted his in a 162-game schedule, however, missing only one contest. Trosky played in all 154 games.

In 1936, he hit .343 and slammed forty-two homers, his best season for the Indians. Twice — on May 30, 1934, and on July 5, 1937 — he smacked three consecutive homers. He hit well over .300 four seasons and, despite his poor showing with the White Sox, finished with a lifetime career of .302.

Bing Miller Had an Embarrassing Start to a Mighty Career

EDMUND (BING) MILLER had the unusual distinction of being a major leaguer who was born in an Iowa log cabin.

Miller earned other distinctions in a major league career that began with about as much embarrassment as an outfielder can have: The first fly ball he tried to catch for the Detroit Tigers hit him on the head.

Bing Miller

Brighter days were ahead—fifteen seasons of them in the majors—aglitter with a .312 batting average. Only two Iowans hit better in the big leagues. Both are in the Hall of Fame: Cap Anson (.334) and Fred Clarke (.315).

Miller was born in the log cabin in Lynn County, in eastern Iowa, on August 30, 1894. "We moved to another farm with a more modern house when I was just a little tyke," Bing recalled a few years before his death in 1966. "But there wasn't anything very modern about our life. We were eleven miles from Vinton and I had to ride a horse to and from high school there."

If Miller was underprivileged in other respects as a youth, he had unusual baseball advantages. Just as Bill Feller was to do later for his son Bob on their farm near Van Meter, Norman Miller took a few acres out of production to lay out a ball field so sons Edmund and Ralph (also a big leaguer, but for just one game) would have a place to play with neighbor boys.

Norman Miller's ambition was to have a son who was a star big league pitcher. "That was my hope, too," Bing once said, "and I always pitched when I was a kid, with my brother catching. I was a pitcher my first two years in pro ball—1914 and '15 with Clinton of the old Central Association. I won nineteen straight in 1915, but then I hurt my arm, so I was forced to go to the outfield."

Two years later, Miller's .337 batting average for Clinton and Waterloo persuaded Detroit to buy Bing for a midseason trial.

"First thing the Tigers did in practice," said Bing, "was send me out to the sun field (right) and have Jimmy Burke, the coach, hit me some fly balls. He only hit me one. It was a mile high and I lost it in the sun. It hit me right square on the top of the head and knocked me down.

"I can still hear Burke roaring with laughter while I staggered to my feet. Some of the boys helped me off the field. That night, the Tigers shipped me out to Peoria."

With him went a new and strange possession—a pair of sunglasses. "I'd never ever heard of outfielders wearing dark glasses, until Harry Heilmann (a veteran Tiger outfielder) took pity on me and gave me a pair of his," said Bing.

Miller didn't get back to the majors until after three more years in the minors, plus time out for service in France in World War I.

The Tigers had given up on him. So did the Senators, despite his .288 rookie season for them in 1921. But the Athletics found him useful for a dozen seasons, including pennant years of 1929, '30, and '31.

Bing banged the winning hit in the '29 series—a double that rounded out a .368 average—after the Cubs purposely walked Jimmie Foxx to get at the Iowan. "It's a good thing, though, that the umpires didn't examine my bat or they wouldn't have allowed the winning hit," Bing recalled. Before the game, Miller said he found his favorite old bat while rummaging in his locker. "The barrel was all chipped and splintered," he said. "The rules won't let you use a bat with nails in it, but I got by with it. I got some brads and fastened down the splinters. Then I put a lot of tobacco juice on my repair work. Nobody ever noticed."

The Checkbook War To Sign Bancroft's Denis Menke

BASEBALL SCOUTS and executives were lined up in the streets in 1958 in a checkbook war to sign Bancroft's teenage phenom Denis Menke.

Ironically, if a Baltimore lieutenant hadn't picked the wrong time to go to dinner one evening, without leaving a message, Menke would have signed with the Orioles, the team he originally wanted to play for.

It was in '58 that Denis was pitching, shortstopping and batting St. John's of Bancroft to the championship in the state high school baseball tournament in Mason City. The fans were all but outnumbered by the scouts and other big league emissaries lured by the quiet, unassuming youngster who played the game of baseball with more exciting promise than any Iowan since Bob Feller.

Every big league club had at least one scout in the stands. There also were managers, general managers, even club presidents on hand, checkbooks at the ready, to add prestige to the rich bids for Menke.

Checking in at a Mason City hotel the first day of the tournament, I remember that the offer had reached $30,000—a handsome figure in those preinflated bonus days. At the ballpark that night, $50,000 was mentioned—and scoffed at by some listeners.

Next day at lunch, a couple of Chicago Cub scouts told me: "We've been cut off at $70,000. We might as well go home. It's going to take $100,000 to get this boy."

It took even more than that, as it turned out. One club willing to go as high as anybody else, even higher, was Baltimore. But, as mentioned, the Oriole negotiator chose the wrong time to go to dinner.

Menke and his dad, a former pro with Des Moines's minor league

*Mr. and Mrs. Walter Menke with son Denis in Cedar Rapids,
soon after Denis signed with the Milwaukee Braves*

team, decided they would give careful consideration to all offers.
"But," Denny once told me, "I had already made up my mind that
there were two clubs I didn't want to sign with—the Braves and the
Yankees. They were the champions and they were so well-stocked with
players, I thought I'd have a better chance to reach the majors with
some other club."

Hounded and harassed by scouts and officials everywhere, including their farm near Bancroft, the Menkes sought the peace that
prompt action would bring. They got the word around that Denis was
ready to sign. But one who didn't get the word was Baltimore's Jimmy
Adair, acting for Paul Richards, then the Oriole manager and general
manager.

Richards already had inspected Menke with approval in several
games and had departed, leaving the final dickering to Adair.

"I thought then I would sign with the Orioles," said Denny. "They asked me not to take an offer from anybody else until they had a chance to match it — or better it.

"Then Dad and I set the deadline. We tried to phone Mr. Adair at his hotel, but they told us he had gone out to dinner. He didn't leave word where he could be reached. We tried a few restaurants, but still couldn't find him, so we decided to go ahead with our final negotiations. The Braves' offer was the best and Eddie Dancisak, their scout, convinced me I'd have a chance to reach the majors as quickly with them as with anybody else."

The Braves gave Menke his big league opportunity after four seasons in the minor leagues, when he was twenty-one. But Denny was sent back to the minors — at his own request. "They were using me as a utility man — all over the infield and sometimes in the outfield," Menke recalled of that 1962 season. "But mostly they were using me on the bench. I still had a lot to learn and I figured I needed to go down where I could play every day for experience."

A half season at Toronto and Menke was back to stay — as a regular.

His twelve-year major league career also included stints with Houston and Cincinnati, which enabled him to crack a homer for the Reds in the 1972 World Series. He finished with a .250 lifetime average, then took a job as a coach for the Houston Astros.

Clarke Had Only One Pitcher
He Could Trust in the First World Series

FRED CLARKE, the greatest baseball player Des Moines ever produced, saw his last World Series a few years before his death in 1960. The stocky, time-mellowed old warrior found all the talk about "pitching depth" and "bench strength" a little confusing.

Clarke said he had seen in the paper where one manager "says his pitching strength isn't so good because he hasn't got more than five men he can trust. Well, by golly," Clarke went on, "I didn't have that many pitchers on my whole staff when we went into the World Series against the (Boston) Red Sox in 1903. In fact, I just had one I could trust."

Clarke, who doubled as a very trustworthy left fielder, was then Pittsburgh's manager, as he had been since 1900 (with two previous

years as Louisville's skipper before that club merged with the Pirates) and would be through 1915.

The Pirates had agreed to play Boston's American League champions in the first modern World Series—but wished they hadn't after what befell the Pittsburgh pitching staff.

"Up until late in the season," said Clarke, "I had three crackerjack pitchers. But then Ed Doheny went—well, I guess you'd say he had a nervous breakdown—and he was in a mental institution when we played the Red Sox.

"That was tragic. But what happened to Sam Leever was just plain ridiculous. The day after the season ended, Sam went out and shot two hundred clay pigeons. It made his shoulder so sore, he could hardly throw. Leever did pitch two games in the World Series, but he wasn't himself and he lost both of them."

Sad Sam's recoil damage left Clarke with one able-bodied pitcher who also could be called reliable. Fred still had veteran William (Brickyard) Kennedy, "but he wasn't reliable," and a couple of green youngsters—Gus Thompson, who had appeared in just five big league games, and Bucky Veil, an operator in twelve games.

That's why Deacon Phillippe pitched five complete games for the Pirates, a World Series record that is likely to stand for an even longer period than it has already stood.

One reason five starts were possible was that the Series was best-of-nine (though only eight games were needed) and postponements stretched the event over thirteen days. A layoff from October third to the sixth enabled Deacon to win two successive starting assignments. He had just one day of rest after winning the opener, 7–3. Overwork finally caught up with Phillippe, a thirty-one-year-old who by then was ready to retreat to his native Rural Retreat, Virginia.

Clarke tried his other pitchers in the fifth and sixth games and they were mangled. Deacon lost the seventh, 7–3, then tried again with one day's vacation and dropped the clincher to Bill Dinneen, 3–0.

If Clarke had only possessed a second reliable pitcher, he might have won. The Red Sox prevailed with two dependables. Dinneen and Cy Young pitched every inning for Boston.

*   *   *

Clarke earned his next championship chance in 1909, when he had a pitching staff headed by three highly skilled veterans: Lefty

Babe Adams, baseball's most accurate pitcher, doing chores
on his farm after retiring from baseball

Leifield (19–8), Vic Willis (22–11), and Nick Maddox (13–8). Still around, but somewhat worn, was the indestructible Phillippe (8–3).

Fred stunned everybody, though, by pitching a big Missouri rookie in the opening game against the favored Tigers. "Babe Adams was his name," said Clarke, "and he didn't know he was going to pitch until it was time for the warm-up. Then I handed him a new ball and his hands started to shake so much, he almost dropped it. I gave him a look of contempt and said, 'What's the matter, kid, you yellow? Haven't you got any stuff in you?'

"For two or three innings, I kept riding him the same way and he really did some pitching. Then I switched tactics and started to praise him. He just held 'em to six hits and beat 'em, 4–1.

"When it was over, I shook his hand and I said, 'Tell me, Babe, what were you thinking about when you went out there to pitch?' And he said, 'I was thinkin' you were the meanest so-and-so I ever saw and, as soon as I won that game, I was coming in and punch you right in the nose.' "

Adams didn't need any such psychology in his next two starts. The rookie won the sixth game, 6–4, and, with two days' rest, wrapped up the championship, 8–0.

Clarke had to apply psychology again before Adams's third victory wrapped up the championship—this time to the whole club. The Pirates had lost the sixth game of perhaps the roughest, rowdiest World Series ever played. Several players of both clubs were spiked and there were a couple of fistfights. "I knew I had to do something the night before the final game," said Clarke. "My boys were so wrought-up and shaky, I just had to get 'em into a calm mood."

Clarke stocked his Detroit hotel room with tubs of iced pop and beer, hired a quartet to sing, and invited a couple of fellows who had a reputation as tellers of funny stories. Then he informed the players there would be a meeting in his room that night.

"They all came in expecting a lecture," he said. "You never saw such surprised looks as when I began handing out beer and pop and the quartet started to sing. Well, we sat around two or three hours, talking and laughing and listening to the singing, never mentioning the next day's game. Finally, I told 'em: 'All right boys, let's go to bed now. We've got a ballgame tomorrow. If we win, all right. If we don't, well that's all right, too. We've already had a good season.'

"You know, everybody showed up next day just as loose and relaxed, and the Tigers were tight as a drum. We scalped 'em, 8–0."

And rookie Babe Adams, the subject of two different types of psychology, breezed to his third six-hit victory.

*   *   *

Clarke, who wound up a twenty-two-year playing career (much of it combined with managing) in 1915, was the last big league regular developed in Des Moines until Dick Bertell moved into a Chicago Cub job in 1961.

Clarke's family brought him to Des Moines at a tender age and he bought his first ball glove with earnings as a newspaper carrier. Fred's first boss, as supervisor of the newsboys for the paper, was Ed Barrow, who was to found the Yankee dynasty as general manager in 1921.

Clarke, who was eighty-seven when he died in 1960, once told me he wasn't the city's best baseball prospect as a youth. "Nobody made me any pro offers," he said. "Several clubs, though, were interested in a boy named McKibben. Hastings of the Nebraska State League invited him to play with them in 1892. But McKibben decided he didn't want to go that far from home. So I went in his place. The manager at Hastings wasn't too happy about getting me instead of the player he wanted, but he agreed to give me a trial. I hit pretty good and he kept me."

Two years later, Clarke was in the big leagues with Louisville. It was a start at the bottom. The National had twelve clubs then and Louisville was a sad twelfth.

Clarke, who was later to become a millionaire from the wheat and oil on his ranch near Winfield, Kansas, demonstrated his financial acumen on his first day in the big leagues.

Clarke reported to Louisville from the Savannah, Georgia, club in midseason of 1894, clutching an undersized bat and a telegram promising him a $100 bonus when he reported.

The manager told him to get into his uniform and that he'd receive his $100 next morning. "No, sir," Clarke insisted. "I get it right now or I don't play." The manager had to go to the box office for the money. Clarke got into his uniform then, pinning the bills into his hip pocket.

As for his little bat, his new mates scoffed that National League pitchers would knock it right out of his hands. Instead, Fred's small weapon knocked five hits against Gus Wehying, one of the league's better pitchers. It's a first game record that still stands.

Mace Brown Will Always Be
Remembered for One Pitch

MACE BROWN'S seventy-six big league pitching victories don't put him within candle-holding range of Bob Feller's 266. Still, Mace's total ranks among the highest ever by an Iowan.

Brown's victory opportunities were limited because he was one of the first relief specialists. His forte was preserving victories for other pitchers.

The native of North English reached his high mark in 1938, when he won fifteen games, besides saving many more, in Pittsburgh's challenge. "But I'm afraid," Mace recalled once, "that I'll be remembered for just one pitch—the one that Gabby Hartnett hit to knock us out of the pennant."

It has been called "the home run in the dark," that historic shot by Hartnett that killed the Pirates after Brown had two out and two strikes on Gabby with the score tied in the ninth inning.

It has been written, I reminded Mace, that perhaps the game should have been called at the end of the eighth. That's when Gabby connected, and onlookers lost sight of the ball in the gloaming, and didn't know it was a homer until they heard it crash in the bleachers. "Oh, no, it wasn't that dark," said Brown. "There's no doubt the game would have been called if I could have gotten Gabby out. But I saw the ball go in the bleachers. . . . In fact, I've seen it every day of my life since then."

Brown's memory, so poignantly sharp on that one disastrous pitch, slips a cog when he tries to remember the name of the Iowa town whose $15 offer turned him from catching to pitching. "I'd been a catcher all my life, and it was the summer of '29, just after I'd finished my first year as a varsity catcher at Iowa," said Mace. "I got a job painting houses and barns in Corwith during vacation, catching for their town team on Sundays. One day the fellow I was painting with remarked that a little town nearby—I can't think of the name of it—was looking for a pitcher to play for them at a county fair. He said they'd pay a good pitcher $15. That was a lot of money in those days. I'd never pitched before, but I said, 'You tell 'em I'll take that job.'

"I won the game and never did go back to catching. Otto Vogel (the University of Iowa's long-time baseball coach) taught me some of the fine arts of pitching at Iowa the next season, then I went into pro ball."

Mace Brown in 1937

Brown, so close to a World Series in 1938, finally got into one in 1946, his last season as a pitcher.

Mace earned his way, too. At the age of thirty-seven, he relieved in eighteen games for the Red Sox, won three against a single loss, and saved several others. He later served the Red Sox as a minor league manager, scout and pitching coach.

Both Manning and Carroll Claimed Ken Henderso

THERE WAS A TIME when some Manning residents were upset because the southwest Iowa community failed to receive due credit as an early haven in the life of baseball star Ken Henderson.

Amos Misselhorn, then secretary of the Manning Chamber of Commerce, once wrote the *Des Moines Register* in a letter: "Every article in your paper that mentions Ken has him being from Carroll, Iowa, and this is not true, so would appreciate it if you change this as it should be Manning." Manning was underlined.

Sure enough, the last place Henderson was from in Iowa was Manning. The place he arrived in Iowa, however, was Carroll. Unfortunately, Manning was thus always omitted in the hometown information given on big league rosters.

But, indeed, it was undoubtedly in Manning that Henderson, throwing his rattle out of the crib, first showed the aptitude for a baseball career with San Francisco, the Chicago White Sox, Atlanta, Texas, the New York Mets, Cincinnati, and the Chicago Cubs from 1965–80.

Henderson had family roots in Manning. His mother grew up there. His maternal grandparents, Mr. and Mrs. Labert Stahl, Sr., were lifetime residents. "I asked Ken to have the Giants list him from Manning instead of Carroll on their roster, but I guess he forgot," Stahl once said.

There were no ballplayers in the Stahl family, said Labert. "I guess Ken got all his ability from his dad's side of the family. His dad, Joe, was quite a semipro player down in Fredericksburg, Missouri, before the war, and the Red Sox wanted to sign him."

But he went into the navy for the war and, by the time it was over, he decided he was too old to start in pro ball. So he made a career of the navy—twenty-two years before he retired in the early 1960s.

It was because Joe was on long cruise duty in 1946 that Ken became an Iowa native. "Our daughter came home to have him," said Stahl. "We took her to a hospital in Carroll for the birth, then she and the baby stayed with us here in Manning for about a year."

Joe decided early, said Stahl, that Ken wasn't going to miss the baseball opportunity that escaped the elder Henderson.

"Joe worked with that boy from the time he was big enough to swing a bat and throw a ball. He spent hour after hour teaching him everything he knew and making him into a switch-hitter."

Joe didn't have long to wait for the lessons to pay off. As a seventeen-year-old graduate of Claremont High in San Diego in 1964, Ken had offers from most big league clubs.

"The Giants gave him a bonus of $50,000–$60,000," said Stahl. "He could have got more money from the Dodgers, but for some reason his dad was partial to the Giants."

As a novice pro, Henderson was shuttled about from Fresno to Magic Valley to Tacoma in 1964. Hometown pride didn't run too high then. Ken's combined average was .191 and he smote just one homer in sixty-three games.

He was a big leaguer in 1965 only because the bonus rule of the time forced the Giants to keep him on their roster the entire season. He looked great in brief trials on defense, but hit only .192 in seventy-three at-bats.

The experience Ken needed came finally at Phoenix in the Pacific Coast League, when he spiked a .272 average with robust slugging. He came back up to the Giants in mid-September of 1966 to insert a .310 batting average and strong defense into the Giants' unsuccessful stretch drive.

He wound up with a .257 lifetime batting average.

Whimsy and Laughter Were Lamson's Key to Success

BOB LAMSON was perhaps the worst singer of his era, especially when he could be persuaded — which wasn't hard — to raise his gravelly voice in a syrupy-sentimental Parsons College song of his undergraduate days there.

But Bob earned high marks in all the other aspects of life that make for zest and gusto and laughter. Nobody could do more than Lamson to keep athletes relaxed with a quip or a bit of whimsy. But only when the situation demanded it. Otherwise he was a serious and conscientious coach, and a successful one.

Lamson was in his fortieth year as a coach, Iowa State's assistant in basketball and the head man in golf, when he died in 1967. Twenty of those years were devoted to turning out well-coached teams in Webster City, first in the high school, then in the junior college.

Bob often marveled that Webster City was willing to hire him after his first contact with an official of the high school there.

Bob thought he was being made the goat of a practical joke and the answers he gave the Webster City official were, Lamson recalled, "exactly the kind to scare off a prospective employer."

Lamson transferred from Parsons to Iowa State for his last two years of college. Bob and some of his fraternity brothers stayed over a few days after graduation for relaxation. "Some of the fellows at the frat house," said Bob, never admitting that one might have been named Lamson, "made phone calls to brothers who had already gone home. They'd disguise their voices and pretend to be a superintendent calling up to offer a job as a teacher and coach.

"I went home to Cedar Rapids, where my folks were living then, and I had been there just a little while when I got a long distance call. Right away, I thought about those phony calls from the frat house."

The caller identified himself as "John Smith of Webster City High School," and Lamson thought he recognized the voice of a fraternity brother.

"I said: 'John Smith, eh? And how is Pocahontas?' " Bob related. "Then he wanted to know if I could teach certain subjects to high school students. So I went along with the gag and said, 'I can learn 'em anything that's wrote in books.' " Lamson recalled that there was a long pause after that. "Finally," he said, "the man told me perhaps a personal interview would be better and that he would be at my house the next day.

"I didn't give it another thought till a man came to the door next day and said he was John Smith of Webster City. He never referred to that phone call—then or later. And you know darned well I didn't either. But he had a contract with him and I signed it fast."

Any boasting by Lamson was always of the disarming kind that directed laughter at himself. He once bragged that he had shown more foresight than any other man who had ever taken a flying spill from a runaway golf cart.

It was during an Iowa Masters tournament on the Iowa State course, with Bob in his customary role as starter. A slowdown in the competitors' progress was reported and Bob zoomed away in the golf cart to check.

Pell-melling down a hill, the cart hit a bump and Bob found himself separated from his conveyance in a midair flight. He landed hard near a foursome waiting to tee off. He looked up at the golfers rushing to his aid and dazedly sorting out identities, said: "I picked out the right foursome, didn't I?" Three of the four were doctors.

Emil (Dutch) Levsen plays for the Cleveland Indians

Levsen Was Last Pitcher To Win
Both Ends of a Doubleheader

NO BIG LEAGUE PITCHER has pitched all the way in a doubleheader and won both games since Dutch Levsen of Wyoming, Iowa, did it for Cleveland on August 28, 1926.

Iowans own two of the last three ironman sweeps in the majors. Herman (Hi) Bell of Sibley won only three games for the St. Louis Cardinals in 1924 — and two of them came on July 19. Urban Shocker was twice a route-going winner for the Browns on September 6 the same year.

The real endurance marvel was the original Ironman — Joe McGinnity, who missed being an Iowan by the breadth of the Mississippi River. McGinnity, from Rock Island, Illinois, won three daily doubles — all in the month of August of 1903.

Walt O' Connor: The Small Wonder Had a Tough Batting Star

WALT O'CONNOR, the small wonder of Melrose High and Drake basketball teams, also put in a stretch as a professional baseball player. Not many have started against tougher pitching.

O'Connor once recalled his first game after the St. Louis Cardinals signed him in 1941. "The Cards sent me to Decatur of the Three-I League," said Walt, "and my first game was at Evansville. I was a catcher and they sent me down to the bullpen with the relief pitchers. When I saw this pitcher humming the ball for Evansville, I was glad I wasn't playing.

"Along in the late innings, the manager was looking for a pinch-hitter. I scrunched down on the bullpen bench and pulled my cap down over my eyes. He spotted me anyway and in I went.

"I didn't even see the first pitch," said Walt. "The umpire said it was a strike. I made up my mind I was going to swing at the next one, no matter where it was. It was just a blur, but my bat was swinging in the right place and I got a single.

"Dain Clay (later a big league outfielder) was my roommate and I told him, 'If all the pitchers in the league are that good, I'll never make it.'

" 'Don't worry,' Dain told me. 'He's by far the best.' Then I asked him what the guy's name was. 'Warren Spahn,' he said." (Spahn, of course, later became one of the greatest National League pitchers of all time.)

Otto Vogel: The Man Who Guided Hawkeye Baseball for Forty Years

BASEBALL MEMORIES always got a good workout when friends and former players talked about Otto Vogel, better known as "Otts," who served as Iowa's baseball coach for some forty years starting in 1925.

Like: "Do you remember the time Otts jumped up to go protest a decision and knocked himself groggy on the ceiling of the dugout?"

Or: "That time," said Dale Erickson, one of Otts' former players, "when we had this big rhubarb with Minnesota here? . . . everybody milling around the umpires . . . and all at once there's that old vendor, still with his basket of peanuts and popcorn, standing right alongside Otts, arguing with the umpires."

Vogel also had fond memories of hundreds of players who came under his direction. He had better players than Jack Bruner and a great many, certainly, who were less exasperating than the left-hander from Waterloo who came to Iowa after narrowly missing death in World War II.

Jack had suffered a broken neck when he was knocked off a gun turret and into the South Pacific in a Japanese attack.

Yet it was Bruner who figured vividly in one of the stories Vogel loved to recall of his coaching days. "We called him a screwball then," Otts once said, "or said he was wacky. The term for it nowadays is flaky. But Jack was a competitor."

There was the game at Indiana one year; the temperature was ninety-four degrees and the Hawkeyes went wearily into the ninth inning in a 1–1 tie on Bruner's pitching. "Jack was leading off for us," said Otts. "He was drenched with sweat and looked like he was about ready to drop. 'I don't care if you get on,' I told him. 'But, if you do, take it easy running the bases. Save yourself for pitching—that's the important thing.'

"So what does he do? He drags a bunt past the pitcher and runs like mad to beat it out. 'Now take it easy,' I yell at him. On the next pitch, he steals second.

"Now the batter flies out to right. There's only an outside chance that Bruner can make it to third after the catch—even if he's fresh. But Jack tags up and races away. He's in with a furious slide."

The next thing, Vogel said, "I figure that crazy fool would try to steal home. I yelled for him to stay close to the bag. Well, he didn't try to steal—but he did make a big break down the line. A quick throw might have got him going back into third. But the catcher threw the ball away and Jack breezed home. The next two batters went out.

"Now I had all my relief pitchers warming up. Jack was so exhausted, I was sure he'd collapse before he got one batter out. All he does is drag himself out there to the mound, strike out two batters and get the other one on a pop-up!"

*   *   *

Bruner's distinctions didn't end in college. Jack became probably the only big league pitcher ever put out of action by falling off a bullpen bench. "I was with the White Sox in Yankee Stadium," Bruner recalled. "Joe DiMaggio hit one a mile and everybody else jumped up off the bullpen bench. I was at one end. The bench tilted and I slid off, landing on my left elbow.

"It didn't hurt much at the time. But a little later, the order came for me to warm up. I found I had a knot on my elbow, and I couldn't throw at all. It was a week or more before I could pitch again."

Vogel's Argument Ruined Twogood's Pitching Career

ON THE SUBJECT of Otto Vogel stories, Forrest (Toogy) Twogood recalled that although "Otto's coaching helped me a lot, I wish he hadn't been so doggoned entertaining as a debater. If Otto hadn't put on such a wonderful show in an argument at Michigan, I wouldn't have hurt my arm, and I'd have realized my greatest ambition — to be a big league pitcher."

Twogood came down from Sioux City to become Vogel's first outstanding pitcher in the mid-1920s. Toogy later became an assistant athletic director at Southern California after long terms as head coach, first in baseball and then in basketball. He was one of the few Hawkeye athletes to play on Big Ten championship teams in two different sports: basketball in 1926 and baseball in 1927.

"I had high hopes of becoming a big league pitcher," said Toogy, "but my arm never recovered after I hurt it at Michigan.

"Otto had taught me a quick move to first for a pickoff — a kind of half balk. I picked a runner off first, but the umpire said I balked and he waved the man on to second.

"Otto came roaring out to debate the point. He stormed around for at least ten minutes. And there was stupid old Toogy just standing there enjoying it. It was such a great performance that I forgot all about tossing the ball to somebody to keep my arm warm. It was a bitterly cold day, too. When Otto finally gave in, my arm had stiffened up. I'll never forget that next pitch.

"The batter was Ernie McCoy — later the Michigan basketball coach and athletic director at Penn State. On my first pitch to him, something snapped in my arm. It never did heal."

Despite his crippled wing, Twogood pitched a half-dozen years in the higher minors and had two spring trials with the Cleveland Indians.

Dizzy Dean, 1938

Twogood also pitched on a staff that, on the basis of what the members did later in the majors, was one of the greatest ever assembled in the minors. That was at St. Joseph of the Western League in 1930. Foremost was Dizzy Dean. There also were Bill Lee, who became an all-time Cub great; Mace Brown, Twogood's old Iowa teammate; Fritz Ostermueller; and Jim Winford.

They won the pennant by how many games? Toogy laughed. "Would you believe last place?" he asked. "We even finished ten-eleven games out of seventh."

Dean was a rookie that year, Twogood recalled, "but already so great that he had an 18-7 record, as miserable as his support was — poor hitting and worse fielding. Dizzy was a big fun-loving hillbilly, but there was no meanness in him," said Toogy. "He shared an apartment in St. Jose with me and two other players. But that didn't mean he always slept there. He also had a room at a hotel and another at the YMCA. He'd stop off at the handiest one when his night of fun was over."

Iowan Was Mickey Mantle's High School Coach

FRANK NOGEL, a principal of Canary Lake and Cornell grade schools in the Saydel school district, was the high school coach of Mickey Mantle. Football was the first of three sports in which Nogel coached Mantle at Commerce (Oklahoma) High School — and the one sport he thought Mickey would pass up. "Mickey's dad, Mutt Mantle, had been grooming him to be a big league baseball player ever since Mickey was big enough to throw a ball," said Nogel. "He wouldn't let Mickey go out for football when he was a freshman.

"The next year — the year before I went to Commerce — Mutt gave in to Mickey's pleading to let him play football. Then, in one of the early scrimmages, he got kicked in the ankle and that brought on osteomylitis.

"I knew he had come back to play basketball and baseball, but I didn't think Mutt would let him try football again, but he did."

Except for lack of experience, said Nogel, Mantle would have become a regular back right away. "If his leg ever bothered him, he certainly didn't show it," said Frank. "He never favored it. I never had anybody who drove harder for that extra yard.

"It's hard to believe now, as big and strong as Mickey was, but he was one of the smallest players on my squad—not very tall and maybe 160 pounds. There were a lot of big veteran backs, so I put Mickey on the 'B' squad as a quarterback. Before the season was over, he'd worked his way up to a halfback job on the first string.

"The next year, he was our best running back—and a good passer, too. He set up the winning touchdown and then smashed it across to give us the championship of the Lucky Seven Conference."

Football, basketball, or baseball, Mantle was the hardest worker Nogel ever coached—and one of the most frequently angry. "He was always such a perfectionist," said Frank, "that he was constantly pressuring himself to do better. He'd get mad every time he'd make a mistake, but always at himself. His anger never hurt the team morale. He never got on another player for making a mistake. Instead, he would encourage the other boys and settle them down.

"He was our leader in basketball—the playmaker. He could score from anyplace, too. Mickey passed off a lot, but sometimes he'd get twenty or more points in a game."

Even in baseball, Mickey practiced harder than anyone else. "After regular workouts, or after games," said Nogel, "Mickey would persuade three or four boys to stay around for extra hitting. He'd bat until it was too dark to see the ball."

Mantle didn't work that hard on his lessons, Frank recalled. "Mickey was no scholar," he said. "But he did well enough that he was never in danger of being ineligible."

Mickey and Frank left Commerce at the same time: Mantle en route to the big leagues, Nogel for Iowa to become high school principal at Carlisle.

The Out-of-Stater Who Played in Two Iowa Championships

BILL BURBACH probably is the only fellow who never lived in Iowa yet played in Iowa state championship high school tournaments in two different sports.

The first time Burbach ever pitched in organized competition was in the game for the Iowa prep championship at Des Moines in 1963, when Bill was a fifteen-year-old sophomore at Wahlert of Dubuque.

"I'd been a third baseman up till then," said Burbach. "Our starting pitcher was hit hard early, so the coach had me pitch the last six innings. I can't even remember who beat us, but I know we lost."

Bill had no style, no finesse, and not a whole lot of control in that pressurized debut. But he had a fastball that made scouts sit up and take notice. They still were taking notice the next two years, although Burbach, as a full-time pitcher, wasn't able to return Wahlert to the state tournament.

The rangy blond did help Wahlert get into another state meet, but that was in basketball. "We got beat in the semifinals the year I was a junior," said Bill, who reached the major leagues with the New York Yankees in 1969, '70, and '71. He had a 6–11 record during that span.

"I was born in Cuba City in Wisconsin," said Bill, "but lived most of my life in Dickeyville (Wisconsin). "That's only about twelve miles from Dubuque. I wanted to go to a Catholic high school and Wahlert was the nearest and best."

Broken Jaw Gave Johnny Brigl
a New Outlook on Lif

EDITOR'S NOTE: In 1951, an Oklahoma State football player deliberately slugged Johnny Bright, shattering the jaw of one of Drake University's greatest football players. The foul blow was captured in photographs that later won the Pulitzer Prize and touched off one of the most bitter racial incidents in sports history. Eleven years after the incident, Bright reflected in an interview with Bryson on how the slugging incident had changed his outlook on life. This column appeared in May of 1962.

JOHNNY BRIGHT clenched a big cigar and reflectively rubbed his jaw that, maliciously broken in a football game, gave him a new philosophy of life. Bright, with a personality to match his name, had been chatting amiably with friends in his hotel room, bantering on the phone with others who learned he had arrived in Des Moines to play with the alumni against the Drake varsity.

Inevitably, someone mentioned the jaw-breaking at Oklahoma State in 1951, a piece of malevolence captured in Pulitzer Prize fashion by Des Moines Sunday Register photographers.

"I have a copy of that picture series," said Johnny, and the

Johnny Bright, 1950

bushiest set of eyebrows west of John L. Lewis knitted together in a frown. "Every year before the football season starts, I get it out to remind me never to get careless.

"That incident gave me a new philosophy of life," Bright said. He stopped there until he was nudged with the necessary question. "Never trust anybody," he said.

"The bitterness is gone," Johnny added. "I didn't hold a grudge against Wilbanks Smith very long." (Smith was the Cowpoke lineman who slugged Bright.) But the lesson has remained.

Johnny said the shattering of the jaw also shattered his faith in a lot of things, or at least stirred grave doubts.

"I wasn't even sure what they meant when they talked about democracy in this country," said the man who has been one of the best backs in Canadian football for ten years. "Even in a northern state like Kansas, I wasn't able to stay in the same hotel with the Drake team when we played at Wichita U."

Bright gave only scant consideration to playing in the National Football League when his record-smashing career ended at Drake in 1951. "The Philadelphia Eagles drafted me," he said, "and I would have been their first Negro player. But there was a tremendous influx of southern players into the NFL at that time and I didn't know what kind of treatment I could expect."

Philadelphia tried to lure him from Canada a few years ago. So did Denver after that city helped launch the American Football League. "I might have been interested," said Johnny, "if the offers could have matched what I was making from both football and teaching."

By that time Bright was well established in the school system at Edmonton, teaching, coaching football and basketball, and heading the physical education department.

Then, of course, there were the handsome wages for running the ball for the Edmonton Eskimos.

Iowa Race Driver Once "Rode" His Helmet 150 Fee

ONE OF DAVE OSTREM'S TROPHIES for victories in sportscar races throughout the Midwest is a dented, grass-stained helmet that he once "rode" for 150 feet or more.

It was an upside-down ride for the Des Moines man after his machine was bumped by another car on a curve and did a terrifying backflip.

"The rollbar helped some, of course," said Dave, referring to the curved pipe over the driver's head. "But my hands were wrenched from the steering wheel and my head must have bumped the ground a dozen times. The helmet took every jolt and all I got out of the accident was a slight headache.

"It was a practice spin," for the annual race at Elkhart Lake, Wisconsin, said Ostrem, "and they wouldn't let me in the race until I'd had a checkup at the hospital.

"I told the mechanic, 'Get the car ready, I'll be back for the race.' I got back in time, all right. But no mechanic could have repaired that car. It was a pile of junk."

What does a driver think about when, hitting a wicked curve at eighty miles per hour, he suddenly finds himself jouncing along on his head?

"I remember," he said, "I didn't even think of getting hurt. All I could think was, 'I've got to get my hands back on the wheel.' But I never did. Luckily, the seat belt held and the helmet absorbed the punishment."

The Eighty-Year-Old Volunteer Coach at Iowa

MAURY KENT was pushing eighty years of age when he was still helping out as a volunteer freshman football coach at the University of Iowa during the mid-1960s. He regularly reported to the freshman practice field every day there was activity.

Maury first came onto the football scene at Iowa in 1904, arriving from Marshalltown to win a letter as a freshman quarterback.

Kent was an expert punter and a kicker of field goals, including one of forty-five yards and a few game-winners. He was also the first Hawkeye player ever to throw what was then a new-fangled weapon — the forward pass.

The 1960s sessions were Kent's second era as a volunteer assistant at Iowa. The other was way back in 1907.

"That was the year," Maury said, "when the Big Ten put in the rule limiting athletes to three years of varsity play. They made it retroactive, so I lost my senior year of sports. It was an awful blow then, but it helped get me an early start in coaching. They let me help out."

When spring came, Maury was a full-fledged coach at the age of twenty-two. He was appointed boss of the Hawkeye baseball team. It was a job he could have kept for many seasons. He served only one. When it came to baseball, Kent preferred playing — and there were lots of pro clubs willing to pay him for it.

Maury was good enough to pitch in 1912 and 1913 with the Brooklyn Dodgers and to put in several years in the high minors.

Kent was Iowa's head basketball coach in 1914–18 and held the same job at Northwestern in 1923–27, although he had never played the game as a prep or collegian.

"I always used the winters to work in the gym on my pitching," said Maury. "My ambition was to get to the big leagues and I wanted all the practice I could get."

Kent didn't have a uniform for his indoor workouts. All the baseball suits already were in use — by basketball players. "Basketball was just getting a good start at Iowa in those days," Maury recalled. "They didn't have any basketball suits—they wore our baseball shirts and pants for practice and for games."

Kent was once in the rare position of being able to trade college football players and fortify his team at a few weak spots.

That was after Maury left Iowa in 1918 to become head coach at Haskell Institute in Kansas, which ranked with Carlisle Institute in Pennsylvania (Jim Thorpe's alma mater) as a major college for American Indians. "The Indian students of these two institutes could transfer back and forth without hurting their standing either scholastically or athletically," said Kent.

When Maury took over at Haskell, he found he had no capable quarterbacks. "But," he said, "I learned that Carlisle had several good quarterbacks, so we worked out a trade. They sent me a quarterback and I swapped them a player for a position where they needed one."

Fright Prompted Iowan To Pay Baseball Fi

JACKIE COLLUM, one of the better pitchers Iowa has produced, said Andy Seminick and Del Rice were the two best catchers who handled his serves in sixteen pro seasons.

Seminick managed Des Moines in 1960 and at the time was considered a mild, mellow, and soft-hearted leader.

"Mild?" said Collum. "Hah!"

"I've heard that Andy got mellow after he quit playing," Jackie went on. "But he sure wasn't when we were together on the Reds in the mid-1950s."

"I only got fined once by a manager, and Seminick was responsible—because I was scared of him."

The Reds were in a ninth-inning tie with the Giants, then of New York, in the Polo Grounds, said Collum, when Manager Birdie Tebbetts came out to the mound. "Seminick stayed behind the plate," said Jackie, "while Birdie told me how he wanted me to pitch to Hank Thompson. 'Don't give him anything but breaking stuff,' Birdie told me.

"Andy called a curve and it was a strike. Then he gave me the sign for a fast ball. I kept shaking him off and he came charging out.

"I told him what Birdie had said. Andy says, 'I don't care what

Birdie said. You throw that fast ball or I'll punch you in the nose.' "

The 160-pound Collum recalled how many fights Seminick had won around the league, including one memorable afternoon when, on behalf of the Phils, Andy knocked three Giants out of commission. "So," said Jackie, "I threw the fast ball. Thompson hit it out of the park.

"Tebbetts fined me fifty bucks before I got to the clubhouse. When we got inside, he fined me fifty more.

"Next day, I met Birdie in the hotel lobby. He says, 'The fines are off, kid. Andy told me what happened.' "

The Third Baseman Who Wore a Catcher's Mask

THE CHICAGO WHITE SOX never had much confidence in the fielding ability of Dick Kenworthy, who grew up in Grant, Iowa. In fact, the first time Dick tried fielding at third base he wore a catcher's mask for self-protection.

Shortstop, Kenworthy's position in high school, was beyond his limited talents in pro baseball. Second base was ruled out because Dick flunked school—dancing school! Kenworthy lacked the fancy footwork for the essential double-play business in the middle of the diamond. "They even had me take dancing lessons, figuring it would help my coordination," said Dick. "But it didn't work. I still couldn't make the double play."

A trial in the outfield wasn't promising. At a bit under five-feet, nine-inches, Kenworthy was considered too short for first base. That left third base.

The mask was never actually part of Kenworthy's game equipment. He wore it in practice during spring training of 1963 until he learned to get his hands up quickly enough on the sudden smashes that steam toward a third baseman.

Kenworthy was good enough to play for the Sox from 1962 to 1968. He had a .215 lifetime average.

Dick Bertell, 1957

Dick Bertell Literally Had a Painful Care

DICK BERTELL, the only Iowa big league player to hit .300 since 1939, literally had a painful baseball career. At the age of thirty-two in 1967, Dick was forced to end his five-year major league career because of the latest in his long series of injuries. In addition to the damaged knee that brought a premature end to his big league catching, Dick had such mementos as several false teeth, replacing the ones knocked out by a pitcher's bouncing warmup throw; a right index finger gnarled by six different fractures; two sets of stitches in his scalp, another set in his mouth, and yet another vestige of hemstitching on one leg where he was spiked by Joe Adcock.

Occupational hazards also cost him fractures of the thumb, ring finger, and little finger on his throwing hand, a few broken ribs, fractured toes, a shoulder separation, and assorted other injuries.

Injuries weren't the only handicaps Bertell had to overcome in 1962 when he hit .302 in seventy-seven games for the Chicago Cubs, the first Iowan to rise above .300 since Hal Trosky stroked .335 for Cleveland in 1939. Dick spent much of that season in the army. On weekend passes from Fort Knox, Kentucky, he would fly to wherever the Cubs were playing, usually arriving very short of sleep.

"It was one of my biggest years for injuries too," Bertell recalled. "It started off when Joe Adcock came in without sliding and stepped on my leg. That took eight stitches. Later on I broke both big toes."

From the time Cap Timm, the former Iowa State baseball coach, converted Bertell from a pitcher–third baseman into a catcher at Iowa State, Dick showed a reckless defiance in blocking the plate. "I liked to get down the line when I had a tag play coming up," Dick once explained. "Then, even if the runner knocked the ball out of my hand, I had a chance to pick it up and tag him again before he got to the plate."

This disregard for personal safety cost Bertell many of his injuries.

When Alex Karras Became a Movie Star

EDITOR'S NOTE: In 1968, Alex Karras—until then known primarily as an outstanding college football player at the University of Iowa and a fearsome pro with the Detroit Lions, launched his acting career with a role as himself in a movie called *Paper Lion*. The star of the movie was Alan Alda, then a relative unknown. Both, of course, went on to bigger and better acting duties. Karras even made a guest appearance on Alda's highly popular "M*A*S*H" series a few years later. Bryson attended the premier of *Paper Lion,* then talked extensively with Karras and Alda in preparing this column, which appeared in October 1968.

THE MIDDLE-AGED, scholarly looking man in the row ahead had been telling his wife what a fearsomely violent gladiator Alex Karras is. Then Alex came down the aisle past us, with some of his Detroit Lion teammates who were in the St. Louis theater for the world premier of *Paper Lion.* Alex was neatly dressed in somber hues. He had on the black-framed glasses he wears away from the football arena.

"That's the big, mean monster?" the woman ahead asked when Karras was pointed out. "Why, he looks like an overly large, intellectual philosophy professor!"

All 255 pounds of Karras quivered with laughter when he was told about the remark after the movie.

Alan Alda didn't laugh. Alda is the thirty-two-year-old actor who plays, and very well, the punishing role of author George Plimpton. He is an unathletic man trying to get the "real feel" of pro sports for his books. "You know," said Alda, "Alex really is a philosopher. And there's a real intellectual quality to those fantasies of his about reincarnation.

"He did more than anyone else to prepare me for this role with the discussions of the philosophy of pro football—the pride and the ambition, beyond money, that motivate the players."

Alda was impressed by the "naturalness of Karras, John Gordy, and coach Joe Schmidt," who have most of the lines among the Lions who play themselves in the movie.

"That was the hardest part of all—being myself," said Alex. "When they get the bright lights on you and the camera is grinding, it's hard to keep from posturing and posing and—well, trying to be an actor."

"Alex could have a career as an actor if he wanted it," Alda put in. Karras only tilted his cigar and grinned.

Later, when the former Iowa tackle had drifted away, Alda added: "He's one of the greatest put-on artists I've ever known. He reminds me of W. C. Fields—a buffoon, but a master of satire, too."

Karras's fantasies about reincarnation, especially those concerning Hitler and Eva Braun, made up a long passage in Plimpton's book. They get only a quick scene in the movie, with a too-brief buildup, winding up with Alex saying: "Hitler was really my mother-in-law in Clinton, Iowa."

And what did Alex think his mother-in-law's reaction to that would be? "Oh, she won't mind," he said. "I promised her I'd get her into the movie somehow, and that was the only way I could think of."

What Watt Got Was Not Naug

WHAT WATT GOT, when his arm was bought, was not a lot—but it wasn't naught.

It was, rather, three naughts, tucked behind a number between twelve and fifteen, that persuaded Eddie Watt to forsake his amateur standing at then State College of Iowa and become a pitching apprentice of the Baltimore Orioles. Or, in simple prose and arithmetic, the former Iowa City prep received between $12,000 and $15,000 for his signature on a baseball contract in 1962.

That's not a lot? Well, it isn't if it's measured alongside other gigantic baseball bonuses. That's the way Watt measured it and that's why it has sometimes been written that Eddie received no bonus to sign with the Orioles, for whom he became an established relief expert.

If somebody gave me twenty cents for my signature, I'd call it a bonus—which puts Watt and me $19,999.80 apart on what we consider a bonus.

Eddie admitted once that he had unintentionally misled the sportswriters who have written that he was paid nothing to join the Orioles. "I didn't say I signed for nothing," said Eddie. "But I can see where the writers would think that, because what I said was that I wasn't a bonus baby. I don't consider a fellow a bonus player unless he gets at least $20,000."

Eddie wouldn't be pinned down on the exact size of his non-bonus, but conceded it was "something over $12,000," an approximation confirmed by Jim Russo.

Russo, later an assistant personnel director of the Orioles, was a scout when he made his offer to Watt—after seeing him pitch just three-and-a-third innings.

"I was really amazed," said Eddie, "when I found out Mr. Russo would give me the money to sign after seeing me just once, and in such a short relief job."

That was in the Basin League, a summer amateur circuit manned mostly by collegians in Nebraska and the Dakotas.

What Russo saw in that brief look, he recalls, was "a young man who came into a tough situation with a lot of poise and confidence and, most important, good control. I had heard that Watt wouldn't sign then, because he wanted to go back to college and play basketball and baseball. But I found out differently when I sounded Eddie out on it."

"Sure, I'd have liked to play my last two years of college sports," said Watt. "But I was too broke to go back to school that fall—my junior year—until the Orioles made it possible. Besides, I wanted to get married, and the baseball money made that possible, too."

Watt continued as a scholar in the off season and received his degree in education in January 1966.

Watt's pitching was seldom on display in his one collegiate season. State College had plenty of veteran pitchers. Besides, Eddie was too valuable as a .354-hitting third baseman.

"The White Sox and Reds offered to sign me as a pitcher after my sophomore year," said Eddie, "but not for any extra money. The Pirates wanted me as an infielder or an outfielder, but not for a bonus.

"I knew I'd have to make it as a pitcher, though. I can't run, I can't throw—not for distance—and I can't field. And I can't hit the curve."

Watt also pitched for Philadelphia and the Chicago Cubs in a career that extended from 1966–75. He had a 38–36 lifetime record.

Stories about Iowa's Two Greatest Baseball Players

Bob Feller
and Cap Anson

The Big Event:
Welcoming "Our Bobby" Home Each Fall

EDITOR'S NOTE: Life was pretty gloomy for many Iowans during the autumn of 1941: farm prices were still at minuscule levels, the Great Depression continued to hold a gnarled grip on most residents, and the war was raging in Europe — a war into which the United States would be drawn only a few months later with the savage, unexpected attack on Pearl Harbor.

But there was one event each fall from 1936 to 1941 that buoyed the spirits of disheartened Iowans — the annual pilgrimage home by Bob Feller from his summer-long duties as the greatest baseball pitcher Iowa has ever produced.

The annual return of Feller — or "Our Bobby" as he was affectionately called — to his hometown of Van Meter just outside of Des Moines was no small affair. Thousands of people flocked to the tiny community, which took on a carnival atmosphere that rivaled the Iowa State Fair.

And, for most Iowans talk of the sadder aspects of daily life — money problems, the war, farm prices — was replaced with jubilant chit-chat about "Our Bobby" coming home.

Bryson, who had known Feller since the days of Bob's amazing sandlot exploits, wrote the following story early in the fall of 1941. It is being reprinted exactly as it appeared then, because it provides an intriguing insight into the Feller phenomenon, the unique personality behind the then twenty-two-year-old young man with the blazing fastball and the captivating effect he had on his fellow Iowans.

Bob Feller, 1938

OUT AROUND VAN METER, it seems that every other person you meet is either a relative of Bob Feller or else claims the personal glory of "discovering" the most precious sports gem ever found in Iowa. There are at least twenty members of the "I-Found-Feller-Club" in Van Meter, in nearby Des Moines, and throughout central Iowa, where Bob's early-developed smoke ball was fired on behalf of six or seven different teams, ranging from high school and American Legion Junior to amateur and semipro.

Most of the members are coaches, umpires, and former teammates and managers. Any one of them can regale you for half an hour with the details of how he "first saw big league promise in the kid when he was pitchin' on the sandlots and tipped off the Cleveland club." One of them was a candidate for public office in Des Moines last year. The electioneering cards he handed out bore the legend "the man who found Bob Feller," which, of course, brought heated protests from other members of the club.

This office-seeker, who, incidentally, was defeated, is John J. McMahon. He asserts with considerable pride that the Indians paid him a "very satisfactory amount" for his part in luring Cyril G. Slapnicka, a Cleveland official, out to Van Meter to view a demonstration of Feller's prowess in the summer of 1935.

Another claimant of that honor was not content with the reward given by the Tribe. Pat Donahue, a former Western League strike caller who worked with McMahon in several of Feller's amateur games, is said to have protested when the Indians sent him a check for only $100 for his efforts in heading Bob toward Cleveland.

But, as one of Feller's closest Iowa friends said the other day, after hearing a couple of club members argue the point: "The only guy who *found* Feller was his dad." Most citizens will agree. From the time young Bobby was old enough to clutch a baseball, Father Bill Feller was pointing him toward a major league career.

He didn't know then that this dimple-chinned son was blessed with the greatest natural throwing ability of any boy since the days when Walter Johnson was growing up, back in the gay nineties. But Bill did everything possible to improve that native talent.

Bill himself was thwarted in his ambition to be a professional player. "Had to stay home and work on the farm," he explains. But when, on that November day in 1918, the doctor announced, "It's a boy," Bill vowed that this son was "to the diamond born."

Bill kept his vow just as faithfully as his now-lionized son has kept a 1941 New Year's resolution to answer every fan letter he receives. Bob has had to enlist the services of a typist to maintain his promise. The letters are myriad and some of them ask for enough money and gifts to reduce his princely salary to a pauper's cigarette funds.

One of the biggest stories of the early summer of 1941 concerned the possibility that Bob would be drafted into Uncle Sam's new army in August. The fact that this would have about the same effect on Cleveland's pennant chances as a bomb dropped into the tribal dressing room at clothes-changing time was not the main thing that worried Feller's Iowa admirers.

No, sir. What they were fretting about was the likelihood that there would be no Feller Homecoming at Van Meter early in October.

Every autumn since 1936, the year this Iowa high school boy exploded into the American League with his fearsome strikeout weapon, the governor and ten to twelve thousand other Iowans have swooped down upon the cornfield-surrounded village of Van Meter to welcome their Bobby home. The Feller Homecoming has become one of the big holidays of the state. It's a gala occasion when the business section of the town, designed to accommodate the buying needs of the community's four hundred population, is roped off for the day.

There is a carnival in the streets, bands play, the governor, Cy Slapnicka, and other notables speak. There is a ball game between two of the best teams of the area and Feller pitches a little for each. That's the main thing these people — some of them from out of the state — come to see. And they yell their lungs out at every strike Bob throws.

Among the crowds that gather, the name of Feller is the thing that somehow gives sense and meaning to the Mardi Gras atmosphere. Many of the welcomers knew Bob as a boy, and they are eager to recount the early exploits that foreshadowed the things to come.

Some of these stories are true. Some may be tinged with the elaboration of storytellers who have a good theme and want to make the most of it.

But the truth is spectacular enough to uphold the myth: how Feller began throwing through a wire hoop when he was eight; how, when he was in the sixth grade, he pitched for a grade-school team he had organized and beat the high school varsity seven out of eight times; how as a thirteen-year-old freshman he shut out Minden High School; how he played third base on the Booneville town team when he was only eleven . . . and on through the gamut of legends that always surround a conquering hero.

Although he is only twenty-two, Feller is already more a myth than a man to many small boys in his native Dallas County. He is a modern Paul Bunyan; a wizard who took a scuffed baseball out behind his father's big red barn and wrought magic that carried him to gold and glory. Except perhaps for his lust for speed on the highways, Bob is a paragon to be pointed out by the parents of all growing boys.

There's only one time that can be recalled when he "let down" his youthful admirers. Late in 1938, Feller was arrested for speeding eighty to eighty-five miles an hour en route to Des Moines. Twenty-three Boy Scouts, being shown through the police station by a patrolman, encountered Bob as he was brought in for booking.

"Gee, that's Bob Feller," said one of the boys.

"Naw," said the patrolman. "What would a guy like that be doing here?" The whole troop turned.

"It's Bob Feller, all right," said one, crestfallen. "I've seen his picture a hundred times." The rest were silent.

Bob has more than made up for that with the hundreds of talks and demonstrations he has given to Boy Scout troops, high school and other youth groups. When he speaks to the boys, he scorns softball as a sport "all right if you're over forty."

The adults like to hear him, too. No other Iowa speaker is so much in demand at luncheon clubs, fraternal organizations, and public meetings in general. Last fall he gave a widely advertised pitching demonstration between halves of a Morningside College football game, and the Sioux City, Iowa, school drew its biggest crowd of the year.

It was at Morningside, incidentally, that Jim Steck, another Iowa small-town boy, received his education the past year by way of the first of the scholarships upon which Feller will spend $1,000 a year.

Mostly, though, Bob likes to sit obscurely—which is seldom possible—and absorb full pleasure from the sports events he watches. There was that time, for example, at a night football game at Drake University, when Bob, unaccompanied, sat high in the stands, sat there shivering until a friend of mine sitting next to him offered America's most famous young man a portion of a welcome blanket.

Bob bought hot dogs to repay the favor, chatted about the game—about every subject but himself. Everything simple and natural. A few rows down, one of the college's minor heroes, who gets his name in the local paper when the track season rolls around, talked loudly and strutted about pompously at halftime. It was a refreshing contrast, my friend says.

Except when he's away on hunting trips (his expeditions last year ranged from Ohio, where he went by plane for some duck shooting, to the Dakotas), Bob attends most of Iowa's major sports events and a host of minor ones, including the basketball games played by both the boys' and girls' teams of Van Meter High.

Bob was a center on the Van Meter quintet which was one of sixteen, from a starting field of about 900, to reach the state's final tournament in 1936. Van Meter lost its first start in this Iowa classic, Bob fouling out after sinking a pair of field goals. Feller will admit, however, that he "wasn't much of a basketball player — I just filled out a good team."

It's something of a paradox that young Robert was never able to pitch Van Meter into the state prep baseball finals, which includes teams winnowed out from an original array of about 500. Van Meter lost in the 1936 district eliminations when its hurling bulwark was shelved by a sore arm.

Bob has witnessed almost every University of Iowa football game, at home or away, the past two seasons. Last winter he flew to New York to see his friend Lee Savold, a Des Moines heavyweight, lose to Billy Conn.

Feller's latent interest in boxing was revealed at that time. He had a punching bag installed in the basement of the $25,000 home he built for his parents and his twelve-year-old sister, Marguerite. And he announced he would take a few lessons in boxing from Savold. Not that he thought he would need this protection in fisticuffs on the diamond. He isn't the type of chap who becomes so deeply involved in arguments that he has to fight his way out. He simply thinks it would be fun to know how to box.

Bill Feller came up with the information that Bob, when he was younger and smaller, used to fool around with boxing gloves quite a bit and seemed to like it. Bill chuckled when he told how a boy at school, much larger than Bob, insisted that young Feller put the gloves on with him. "Bob didn't want to box, but the big boy forced him into it," Bill explains. "Bob ducked the first swing that came his way and let loose with a punch that caught the big boy on the chin and knocked him down. That was the last time any of the boys wanted to fool around with him with boxing gloves."

There is no record that Bob has socked anybody since then, although there was the time a couple of years ago when he might have felt like punching a certain fellow who was responsible for the romantic linking of Feller's name with that of Betty Jensen, daughter of

Congressman Ben Jensen of Exira, Iowa.

This chap, who Feller had believed to be a friend, wrote that Feller was seen nightclubbing on a certain night in Washington with Miss Jensen. "The truth of the matter is," says Bob, "I had to pass up my dessert to catch a train at about 6:30 that evening."

Earlier that day, the alleged friend had snapped a picture in which he posed the pitcher with Miss Jensen. Later Bob discovered the photo had been sold to a news service and published throughout the country over suggestive captions.

"I thought it would be a picture for himself like so many fans take," Feller explains. "I suppose it doesn't make much difference, but I think it gave a lot of people the wrong impression about me when it was published."

Feller has shown no concentrated interest in any one girl, although there's no denying he's been the most eligible young bachelor in the majors. Indications of his growing interest in girls — in general — developed in 1938 when he learned to dance.

When Bob ignited his major league rocket in 1936, he was a bashful, rather awkward farm boy who was shy on confidence when he spoke in public. Often he ducked at the approach of a pretty girl — a tendency he has neatly overcome.

Every year on his return home, Iowans have noted the subtle cultural changes that have come over their Bobby. Living in metropolitan circles during the season has given him poise and polish. Now he wears suits that cost $100 — and wears them well — drives an expensive car, lives in one of Iowa's finest rural mansions. Still, his Iowa neighbors have been unable to detect any change in the Feller attitude or character. Deftly he has maintained his quiet modesty.

"I've cut his hair for a good many years and his head is exactly the same size it was before he got into the big leagues," comments J. F. Fritz, the Van Meter barber. "They don't make 'em any better than Bob." And that about sums up the respect and admiration his fellow Hawkeye Staters have for the No. 1 native son.

Bob has no illusions about his abilities outside baseball. He has turned down a couple of movie offers, one of which had him scheduled to star in a series of six westerns. "I know I can't act," he admits. His histrionic efforts have been limited to a pair of brief appearances in the minstrel shows staged by a Des Moines fraternal organization. Bob isn't a member; he just did it to help out. He realizes that offers for his services in other professions are only the result of the spectacular publicity he has received.

*   *   *

Most youths would be happy to derive, in a lifetime, the publicity Feller earned as a sixteen-year-old amateur hurler in 1935. Even then his fame was so slight that several newspaper accounts spelled his name "Fellers." The high spot of Bob's career in Iowa came on August 25, 1935. Here's the way one Des Moines writer described it for a newspaper with statewide circulation:

> Hurling for the second successive day, Bob Feller, brilliant sixteen-year-old speedball thrower, pitched the Farmers Union of Des Moines into the Iowa amateur championship Sunday at the Iowa State Fair. The champions beat the Cascade Reds, 4 to 2.
>
> With the count tied 2-all in the seventh, Feller broke up a hurling duel between himself and Dale Meredith of the Reds with a single scoring Paul Brownell. In addition, Feller hit singles in the second and ninth innings.
>
> He held the opposition to six hits, only two of which were bunched. They came in the second inning behind a pair of errors and provided Cascade with its only runs. Feller's wildness provided the Reds with scoring opportunities but they couldn't hit in the pinches, thirteen of them walking back to the bench after waving at third strikes. Feller walked only four, but twice gave two in succession.

It was Feller who put Farmers Union into the final tournament. In the central Iowa joust, Bob was called to the mound with two out in the fifth of the seven-inning championship game. Only seven men faced him and he struck out every one. He also sparked a winning four-run rally in the seventh frame. A month later in the national amateur championships at Dayton, Ohio, Bob struck out eighteen, including six in succession in the first two innings, but dropped a 1–0 decision to a Battle Creek, Michigan, team. The prep pitcher walked only two, although he plunked a pair of batters. He didn't allow an opponent to reach second base until the ninth, when, with one out, he surrendered a double and a single for that heartbreaking tally.

It was then that the horde of major league scouts besieged this boy who took a baseball in his long fingers and turned it into a smoking projectile. They didn't know that wily Cy Slapnicka already had the signatures of young Feller and his father on a Cleveland contract (rather, a Fargo-Moorhead contract). Bob didn't report to the minor league team because of a sore arm.

But in June he was in the Cleveland ball park, lobbing pitches to teammates and undergoing treatment by the trainer. Bob's first appearance against major league competition was in an exhibition with the St. Louis Cards on July 6, 1936. The seventeen-year-old pitched three innings and struck out eight.

He made a few relief appearances, then benched fifteen St. Louis Browns on strikes. Later in the season, he struck out seventeen Philadelphia Athletics to tie the then league record.

After that, he returned home and finished high school!

*   *   *

Ironically, before joining the Indians, Feller had failed to impress a committee of baseball experts as a prospect who would soon be ready for competition in the Class A Western League, let alone the majors.

It was the custom to select the "outstanding prospect" in the Iowa Open Tournament and give him a trial with the Des Moines club. Two players, instead of one as was customary, were chosen as the competitors who appeared to have the best future in organized ball. Their names were George Hutchinson and Walter Menke. Ever hear of 'em? Nor was Feller one of the three pitchers selected for the all-tournament first team, although he was listed on the second squad.

It should be explained, however, that there were some forty teams in the tournament, and all-star preference was given those players whose teams played the most games. Feller and his Farmers Union mates were ousted in the second round. Here's part of a newspaper account of Bob's first start in that tourney, the state's blue-ribbon semipro event:

> The Farmers Union of Des Moines moved into the second round of the state semipro tournament Sunday night by defeating the Ames Merchants, 7 to 4, behind the three-hit pitching of Bob Feller, highly touted youngster from Van Meter.
>
> All three of the hits off Feller were more or less flukey, but he had two bad innings in which he was wild and in which Ames scored all its runs. Feller struck out nine in the seven-inning game. Two successive walks at the start of the sixth inning were his only free tickets, but he hit one batter.

Four days later Farmers Union was eliminated despite Bob's relief stint in which he gave up only two hits and struck out nine hitters in four-and-two-thirds innings.

Bob did more pitching as an amateur in 1935 than he did in either one of his first two seasons with the Indians. Working for Van Meter

High and the Farmers Union, he won twenty-five and lost four. As a high school junior in 1936, he chucked five no-hit, no-run games.

*   *   *

It appears that Mrs. Bill Feller is generally overlooked when it comes to passing out kudos for her son's baseball success. Not that she fed him a special breakfast cereal to produce those Herculean biceps and deltoid muscles. Not that she showed him how to grip the horsehide for a curve. But she tolerated all that early ball playing, didn't she? All those almost interminable games of catch that forced her to keep supper waiting until, proverbially speaking, "the cows come home."

And the cows must have come home mighty late on the Feller farm, for the twilight had to be a deep purple before the Fellers, senior and junior, reluctantly came in with mitt and glove. Also, Mrs. Feller never put her foot down and ordered the men folk to stick around home a little more instead of galavanting about the countryside to play ball games.

It seems she never protested when Bill Feller sometimes neglected his agricultural labors to put his personally organized Oak View team through a practice session on the diamond he and Bob had scraped out in one of the meadows. Through it all she showed remarkable restraint. Furthermore, she probably contributed to young Robert's innate ability, because her own father was a better than average semi-pro player.

Of course, Mrs. Feller isn't at all sorry now that she never interfered with her husband's ambitions. As a result of her son's ability to puncture the strike area with violence and telling effect, she now has as beautiful and modern a home as any farm woman in Iowa. It's an imposing brick structure of English architecture, with twelve spacious rooms and all the latest electrical and automatic devices.

Were it not for the magic and mastery that the gods infiltrated into the sinews of Bob's right arm, the Fellers probably would still be living in the old, two-story frame home where he was born and where he grew up. The old home had its own electric plant. Aside from that it had no modern improvements.

Bob's favorite part of the new home is the game room in the west wing of the second floor. There he displays his fine collection of rifles and shotguns. There, too, he shows more than a modicum of skill at table tennis. He is less proficient at the billiard table, which was installed in the basement at his father's behest. Nor does he show much skill at tennis, which is one of the favorite sports of his twelve-year-old sister, Marguerite. It is unlikely that in all the nation there is a prouder sister than Marguerite, who in 1936 began a scrapbook of Bob's clippings. On the cover of the book she had written, "The Title of This Book — From Sandlots to the Majors."

Marguerite's sense of humor is reflected in the name she selected for the family pet, a weird, leonine mongrel of unidentified parentage. She calls him Rollie, in honor of Catcher Hemsley, Bob's battery-mate who is a frequent visitor at the farm home three miles east of Van Meter. Hemsley, in retaliation, has named one of his bird dogs Bob.

*   *   *

Bob doesn't talk much about his throwing techniques. "What I know about pitching I'm keeping to myself," he explains. "If other pitchers on the club want to ask me something, that's all right, but I'm not volunteering any information. They may be traded to another club someday." It is unlikely, though, that Bob could, even if he wanted to, impart the secret of his sizzling speed. He could throw as fast as most men when, at the age of fourteen and packing only 135 pounds on his five-foot, seven-inch frame, he struck out fifty-eight players of three heavily "spiked" opposing town teams on successive weekends.

Although he can look forward to many more great seasons in the majors, Bob says that he wants to settle down on a modern farm of his own when the steel spring in his right arm has rusted. "I've always been called an Iowa farm boy and I'm proud of that title," he says.

EDITOR'S NOTE: Two months after this story was written came Pearl Harbor, and two days later Feller joined the navy. Nearly four years passed before Bob was back on the mound for Cleveland in April 1946 — and he blazed his pitches past the New York Yankees for a no-hit game. He finished the season with twenty-six victories, including his eighth one-hitter, and broke the strikeout record of Rube Waddell by fanning 348 in 371 innings.

Although the war robbed him of nearly four of his best young years as a major league pitcher, when he retired after the 1956 season at age thirty-seven he had posted a total of 266 triumphs and 2,581 strikeouts. In eighteen seasons with the Indians, he lost only 162 games, pitched three no-hitters and twelve one-hitters, and finished with a 3.25 earned run average. He led the league in wins five times, tied one other time and led in innings pitched five times.

Bob was a natural choice for the Hall of Fame in 1962, and when someone asked who had helped him most in achieving his astonishing major league success, he proudly replied with two simple words: "My father!"

Special Feller Day Was a Near Tragedy

ONE OF THE TRAGIC IRONIES of Feller's career occurred during a special Mother's Day and Feller Day celebration in Chicago in May of 1939. Bob's mother went to Chicago with her family and a delegation of Van Meter fans to see her son pitch against the White Sox. The occasion was "Feller Day," and 28,000 persons went to Comisky Park to pay tribute to the young fireballer.

To Bob, however, this was Mother's Day and he promised Mrs. Feller he would win this one for her. Going into the last half of the third inning, Cleveland was leading, 6–0, and young Feller was well on his way to fulfilling his promise. Mrs. Feller sat beaming in a front row grandstand seat to the right of home plate with her husband and their daughter, Marguerite.

Marv Owen, Chicago third baseman, was the batter. Feller wound up and threw a fast one. Owen swung and tipped a foul into the stands.

The ball struck Mrs. Feller above the left eye and shattered one of the lenses in her glasses. Blood streamed from her eyelid and forehead. Lefty Weisman, Cleveland trainer, rushed to the stands, assisted Mrs. Feller to an automobile and sped her to a hospital.

For a moment, Bob stood stark still on the mound. He knew it was his mother who had been struck. Before he could regain his composure, Chicago had scored three runs, but Bob continued to pitch.

At the hospital, Mrs. Feller was found to be suffering from cuts around the eye and a possible mild concussion. Six stitches were required to close the wound around her eye. Doctors said there were no symptoms of a fracture, but Mrs. Feller was hospitalized overnight for observation.

Immediately after the game, which Cleveland won, 9–4, with Feller pitching all the way, the young hurling ace sped to the hospital to find his mother sitting up in bed, her head swathed in bandages. "Everything is all right," she assured Bob as he embraced her. "I just didn't see that ball coming."

Contract Allowed Felle
To Play Basketball, Visit Folk

IN ADDITION TO BASEBALL, Bob Feller was fond of basketball—so much, in fact, that in his original baseball contract, he insisted on a clause that would allow him to play basketball "at any time." He also was permitted to visit his parents any time he wanted.

Feller's first contract said:

This agreement entered into this day (July 22nd, 1935) by and between the Fargo Baseball Club and Robt. Feller and his legal guardian, W. A. Feller, agreed to as follows:

The Fargo Club agrees to pay Robt. Feller or his legal guardian $500 if he is retained on the roster of the Fargo Baseball Club on Sept. 15, 1936.

The Fargo Club agrees to allow Robt. Feller to visit his folks at any time during the 1936 season, also to invite Robt. Feller's folks to visit him at Fargo during the summer of 1936 at the expense of the Fargo Baseball Club.

The Fargo Club has no objection to Robt. Feller playing basketball at any time.

For a consideration of one dollar paid to Robt. Feller this agreement is declared valid.

Feller Was Faster Than Koufa

WHO WAS FASTER: Flamethrower Sandy Koufax of the Los Angeles Dodgers or Bob Feller?

The man best qualified to answer was Joe Becker, who helped break in both of these hard-throwers when they came to him without benefit of minor league apprenticeship. "Feller," Joe said flatly, "had more velocity than Sandy. And his fast ball was 'livelier'—took off more sharply."

And how about the curve ball?

"There again," said Becker, who also was a former Dodger pitching coach, "Feller had more velocity; Bob was one of the few pitchers who could throw his curve with almost as much speed as his fast ball. Feller's curve was more explosive than Sandy's. But Sandy got a real quick break, too, and he pinpointed his curve better than Bob did."

Becker had left the Des Moines sandlots for modest pro rewards before Feller's hummer began intimidating amateur and semipro hitters in central Iowa. They were thrown together in 1936 when Joe was Cleveland's bullpen catcher and the seventeen-year-old Feller was sacking peanuts in the Indians' concession department while waiting for his sore arm to mend.

"When his arm was O.K.," Joe recalled, "they had him come out and throw batting practice to the pitchers and some of the utility men.

"I was catching Bob to help give him a target. The first batter and I didn't hardly see his first pitch — but I heard it whistle over my head. It hit the back of the batting cage with a big thump. It actually moved the cage back about a foot."

Becker doesn't remember the identity of the batter who was the first big leaguer to sample Feller's firepower. He might have been the creator of the long-lasting gag about the Iowan's speed: "I don't know where the pitch was, but it sounded high."

"Anyway," said Becker, "the guy just walked out of the cage and said he'd wait and hit later.

"A lot of other fellows passed up their turns that day. And the guys who did hit sure weren't digging in. Feller had them ducking and diving all over the place. It wasn't any different when the regulars started hitting against Bob a few days later."

The Indians didn't relax until Manager Steve O'Neill turned Feller loose on enemies instead of friends. That was in a midseason exhibition against the St. Louis Cardinals. Bob fanned eight in his three innings.

Cap Anson: The Honest Man Who Saved the National League

MARSHALLTOWN, IOWA, has never produced the athletic equal of its very first native son. For that matter, what Iowa city, town, or rural retreat has come up with an athlete to match Adrian Constantine Anson?

"Cap" they called him, or "Pop" in the gloaming of his twenty-two-year career with the Chicago White Stockings (1876–97). Nineteen of those seasons he also was the manager, though captain was the preferred title in the years when the National League was a rough, rowdy, and roistering pup.

Cap Anson

Never a hint of scandal touched the name of Anson, though the National's growing pains were complicated by gambling, bribery, and brawling; by players who were roughnecks, game "throwers," or drunkards. True, Cap himself was a betting man. Even when his White Stockings, ancestors to the Cubs, were finishing tenth in a twelve-club league, he was always willing to bet $1,000 a game on his club. But never on anybody else.

And Cap was a loud and boisterous competitor who spared neither the opposition, his own players, nor the umpires. Contemporaries have written that Anson would roar like a goaded bull when he thought an umpire's decision went unjustly against him. They said, too, that Cap was the first to use his position on the coaching lines as a stage from which to deliver lusty comments on the abilities and personalities of rival players.

Yet, it also was Anson, a stubborn, rugged man of many sides, who brought to baseball an aura of respectability and who once saved the National League.

His rescue came at the time of the brotherhood strike, a revolt of a majority of National League players to form their own league, in 1890. The Players League offered him $25,000 a year to manage one of its clubs. Fiercely loyal, Cap stayed with Chicago for a $3,000 salary and led the successful counterattack against the rebels.

"Had Anson jumped," said John B. Sheridan, a sportswriter of that era, "it is probable that the National League would have died."

Such was the influence of the robust Iowan that many players, on the verge of joining the brotherhood, stayed with the National. The old league rode out the storm; the Players League gave up after one season.

When Anson died on April 14, 1922, *The Sporting News* called him "one of the greatest figures and most admired characters in baseball."

Sheridan wrote:

> Rough at times, free-spoken, the butt of many jokes, but always beloved and respected by everyone – that was Anson.
>
> He was one of the men who, when baseball was rotten to its very core, was straight and honest; one of the men who . . . carried the game through the dread era of the gambler, elevated it from the saloon to the college and halls of state and enshrined it in the hearts of the people.
>
> When players were quartered at cheap boarding houses, the White Stockings always stayed at the best hotel. When players rode in smoking cars, the White Stockings rode in Pullmans. When players rode from

hotels to parks in cheap buses (horse-drawn, of course), the White Stockings rode majestically in carriages.

Old Anse did it all. There was not much money in baseball then, but Anson always insisted that his players should sleep and dine with the best, travel with the best, act like the best. . . .

Anson also was the first to take a club south for spring training. That was in 1886. But the main purpose of the jaunt to Hot Springs, Arkansas, he explained, was to "boil the winter beer out of 'em."

*　　*　　*

Ironically, it also was Anson, perhaps more than any other man, who was responsible for keeping blacks out of the major leagues in the 1890s.

John Montgomery Ward, captain of the New York Giants, had completed a deal for George Stovey, a black who won thirty-five games in one season for Newark. Anson roared so loud that league authorities put a stop to the transaction. From that stemmed the unwritten law against blacks in the major leagues, a hush-hush edict that wasn't flouted until Jackie Robinson began playing for the Brooklyn Dodgers in 1947.

There was no such ban in the minor leagues in the 1880s and '90s and, once at an exhibition game in Toledo, Anson withdrew his White Stockings, at a sacrifice of $1,500, rather than play against Moses Walker, a black right fielder. The same situation came up later in Newark, but that time the game went on because Stovey, who had been selected to pitch, agreed to stay off the field.

*　　*　　*

Anson was an outstanding football and baseball player at Notre Dame in 1869–70 as well as the university's champion fancy skater on ice. Cap was at Notre Dame only because, as he recalled years later, the State University of Iowa "finally became too small to hold me. I was as wild as a mustang and as tough as a pine knot, and the scraps I managed to get into were too numerous to mention.

"The University of Notre Dame in Indiana, then noted as being one of the strictest schools in the country, was selected as being the proper place for 'breaking me into harness.' "

The Notre Dame interlude marked Anson's first extended sojourn away from Marshalltown, where he was born on April 17, 1852, in a log cabin built the year before by his father.

Henry C. Anson had defied the flooded Cedar River and the threat of an Indian uprising to found the town of Marshall, named for his former place of residence in Michigan. The *town* was added in 1854 to avoid conflict with an Iowa post office of similar title.

Cap's sports reputation was first built upon his ability in billiards. Many a traveling salesman paid in embarrassment, as well as in bets with witnesses, for beatings from a gawky country lad at the pool table in his father's hotel. Years later, Anson defeated several professional and high-ranking amateur billiard players.

*   *   *

Baseball, in its new and refined state, was unknown in most of Iowa when Anson was a sprout. A more primitive form called "soak ball" was his favorite schoolday sport. It was no game for sissies. A base runner was out when soaked by a thrown ball.

When baseball began to take hold, Adrian (the "Cap" and "Pop" nicknames were still far in the future) decided the village square, donated by his father, would be the ideal spot for a ball field. There was one drawback: the number of trees growing there. Undaunted, Adrian sharpened up the family ax and chopped them down.

When the square later became the site of the Marshall County Courthouse, the citizens had to set out a new array of elms.

Marshalltown, whose semipro and professional teams were long known as the "Ansons" in honor of old Cap, had its first club in 1866. The name Anson was prominent on the club, but it was Adrian's father, at third base, and his older brother, Sturgis, in center field, who were leaders of the team that beat all comers in 1866 and '67. Adrian was merely a substitute until late in the second season, when his dad insisted upon his promotion.

The Marshalltown athletes were so formidable that, at a tournament in Belle Plaine in 1867, other teams refused to play them unless they were allowed six outs each inning to three for Anson and Co.

Marshalltown beat them all anyway and carried off what was perhaps the first pennant in baseball. The women of Belle Plaine presented a silk flag to the winners.

While young Adrian was away at college, catastrophe struck Marshalltown. Des Moines came up and, before a stunned and horrified crowd, seized the championship. The townspeople could hardly wait for Adrian to come home and win it back. He did, as the leader of a reorganized club.

What was a semicolon in Anson's college career became a period because of a visit by the famous Rockford Forest City club. Rockford, with the great Al Spalding pitching, won two exhibitions from Marshalltown, 18–3 and 35–5, but signed up Adrian Anson and two of his mates to play for the Forest Citys in 1871. Anson's salary was to be sixty-six dollars a month. Sam Sager and a fellow named Haskins were to accompany him.

"All that winter," he wrote in his autobiography, *A Ball Player's Career,* in 1900, "Sager and I practiced as best we could in the loft of my father's barn, and I worked as hard as I knew how in order to become proficient in the ball-playing art." Anson became so proficient that, as a nineteen-year-old third baseman, he was Rockford's leading hitter in the National Association in 1871.

Compared with some clubs, the Forest Citys lived in luxury. "We traveled in sleeping cars and not in ordinary day coaches as did many of the players," said Anson. There was one handicap, especially for a young giant like Cap, who was six feet, two inches and weighed 180; the players had to sleep two in a berth.

Thus began a twenty-seven-year professional career in which Anson only twice dipped under .300 as a batter. This muscle work was combined with the brain work of managing as Cap goaded his strapping, scrapping White Stockings to National League championships in 1880, '81, '82, '85, and '86.

* * *

There was no doubt who was boss when Anson was captain and manager of the boisterous Chicago White Stockings from 1879 until 1898. To make sure his players turned in early at the start of a road trip, Anson kept the railroad and Pullman tickets and each man had to report to him.

One night "Bad Bill" Dahlen stayed out late and just barely made the train. He tumbled into a berth and when the conductor came along, Dahlen told him to go to Anson for the ticket. "I won't give you his ticket," Cap roared. "Put him off the train!"

The conductor did—at a water tank in Indiana in the middle of the night. It took Dahlen two days to catch up with the ball club.

Bill Lange missed a train once, and showed up in Washington after the game was under way. Cap socked him with a $200 fine — important money in those days — and sent him out to center field. This was one time Cap relented — but not until the 230-pound Lange had hurtled through the wooden fence in a shattering blast for a catch that saved the White Stockings in the eleventh inning.

* * *

Big, blustering Anson probably never tried harder to behave with dignity and decorum than he did once in London. Two all-star major league teams were on a world tour in 1889, and British royalty and society were well represented for the exhibition.

Cap was introduced to several lords and ladies, who were curious about America's "professional class" of athletes. Anson and the suave John K. Tener, Chicago pitcher who was to become governor of Pennsylvania, assured them that baseball players came from colleges and genteel society — much like English cricketers.

Cap cautioned the players to guard against rough language and uncouth gestures. Their behavior was exemplary until the pitcher of Anson's team began walking batters one after another.

The catcher came storming out to Cap at first base. "Get that blankety-blank-blank wild man out of there!" he demanded loudly. This was more than Anson could stand. "Get back in there and catch, you blankety-blank-blank!" he bellowed. "I'll tell you when the time comes to take any blankety-blank pitcher out of this blankety-blank-blank ball game!"

* * *

Cap's Chicago career of twenty-two seasons, nineteen as manager, ended in a bitter dispute over policy and stock ownership. He complained that club leaders reneged on an offer to let him and his backers purchase controlling interest. Anson left in a huff, became manager of the New York Giants for 1898, but quit within a few weeks after an argument with the owner.

Chicago fans planned a testimonial fund for Anson and it was expected to approach $50,000. Cap indignantly refused to accept any financial tokens of esteem. "Since when," he demanded, "has Anson fallen so low that they seek charity for him in his name?"

Cap's overzealous loyalty as a bettor had a lot to do with his failure to save much of his baseball earnings—that plus a number of ill-advised business ventures.

He would wager $1,000 on his White Stockings for any game and once bet that sum on the condition he wouldn't call on Clark Griffith, his stalwart relief pitcher, before the eighth inning.

But Bill Hutchinson, the starting pitcher, was on the brink of blowing a lead in the seventh. Cap kissed the $1,000 goodbye and called in Griffith.

Griff figured in another incident that revealed Anson's inherent honesty. Only one umpire worked major league games in those days, and the lone official didn't show up. Each team selected a player to combine on the umpiring, and Anson picked Griffith.

There was a close play at first and Griff called it against the rival club. The reaction was immediate and noisy. Griffith, who later owned the Washington Senators, stuck by his guns until, as he recalled later: "To my surprise, I heard Cap say: 'Come on, quit kicking and start the game. The man was safe. I know it, because my foot was off the bag.' "

Anson put up a goodly sum one time to stimulate a rival club. Near the close of the furious 1886 pennant race, Cap offered a trunkful of clothes to each Philadelphia player if the Phils won a doubleheader from Detroit. The Phillies did it and it kept Detroit from overtaking Chicago. It cost Anson $1,600 for the bonuses—which were legal then.

*   *   *

After his retirement from professional baseball, Anson operated a billiard and bowling establishment in Chicago for a time, managed a semipro team that toured the country, was city clerk of Chicago for one term, and appeared in vaudeville several years with two of his four daughters.

He suffered another bitter blow from baseball when he was spurned in his candidacy for the position of commissioner. Anson was given slight consideration when club owners selected Judge K. M. Landis. Just before his death in 1922, Anson had landed his first good job in years: manager of a new golf club in Chicago.

Cap made only occasional vists to his native Marshalltown once he departed to play professionally, first with Rockford for one year, Philadelphia for four, then Chicago.

One Marshalltown native who remembered Cap was Maury Kent, probably the second-best athlete the city produced. Kent, who was freshman baseball coach at the State University of Iowa, recalled that he and another high school youth were playing catch near the old Anson home when Cap suddenly appeared. "Work on your change of pace, young man," the portly Anson told Maury. "Use it on the best of hitters."

Kent did and became a successful pitcher at Iowa and in the minor leagues.

The Storm Lake Frost Bowl

4

Iowa Had the Great-Granddaddy of All Bowl Games

THE ROSE BOWL calls itself the "granddaddy of all bowl games." In that case, then, Iowa had the great-granddaddy of all bowl games.

The first Rose Bowl game wasn't played until 1902 and the second wasn't contested until 1916 (after Michigan whomped Stanford, 49–0, in '02, the Tournament of Roses had chariot races as the New Year's Day entertainment for thirteen years).

Iowa had its second annual January 1 football game in 1896. The third is yet to be played.

Storm Lake was the scene of the games in 1895 and 1896. The city didn't have a bowl, but it called them bowl games nonetheless.

Storm Lake's imitators have called their bowls after a bountiful product of the nation in the particular area of each: Rose, Sugar, Cotton, Orange, etc. Storm Lake's name was just as appropriate; the title was the "Frost Bowl."

There were collegians playing in the Frost Bowl, but not college teams as such. Denison got up a town team to play Storm Lake on January 1, 1895. The next New Year's Day, the bowl bid went to Fort Dodge.

"The teams were made up at each place, mostly from football players home from college for Christmas vacation," according to the late W. C. (Billy) Edson of Storm Lake, a pioneer player at both Iowa and Iowa State. He said several of the players were from Iowa and Iowa State.

But, there also were a "few farmers, blacksmiths, and ex-prize-fighters, which made all of these teams tough and rugged." And frost-proof?

Storm Lake made it a happy New Year's for the hometown fans each time. Denison lost, 36–0, and Fort Dodge fell, 48–0.

Drake Played First Night Football Game in 1900

ANY FOOTBALL PATRON who might happen to browse through the ancient files of the *Des Moines Register and Leader* is bound to do a double-take if chancing upon a headline in the sports section of October 3, 1901.

It says: "HARD PRACTICE YESTERDAY PROMISES BETTER RESULTS IN GRINNELL GAME TOMORROW NIGHT."

Night? Surely the editor meant late afternoon, the way kids do when they say, "We'll do it tonight after school," but meaning the time right after they are freed from the classroom. Or possibly it was to be a twilight game.

But, by golly, the editor said night and he meant night – after dark. There were several notes preceding the body of the story and one said: "Drake plays Grinnell Saturday night at 8 o'clock."

And then you discover that this was not to be the pioneering effort in regularly scheduled college football games under outdoor lights. "This year," it said later in the story, "the management will provide better light for the evening game than heretofore."

So a little more researching discloses that Drake played its first night game on October 5, 1900, when the Bulldogs defeated Grinnell, 6–0, and another a week later, a 50–0 rout of Iowa State Normal (now Northern Iowa University).

This evidence knocks out the claims that the first scheduled football game under outdoor lights was played at either Los Angeles or Wichita.

Frank G. Menke, in his *All-Sports Record Book,* reported that "The first regularly scheduled and executed outdoor night football game was between University of Arizona and St. Vincent College (now known as Loyola University of Los Angeles) on November 25,

1905, in Los Angeles, St. Vincent's defeating Arizona, 55–0."

Even after that was published, there were boasts from Wichita that the Kansas city had presented the first night game, but the year given was 1906.

Menke and other historians reported an indoor experiment with night football as early as 1891, when Amos Alonzo Stagg's Springfield, Massachusetts, YMCA Training School played a make-shift Yale team in old Madison Square Garden in New York. The historians say the game began at midnight but didn't explain the late start.

After the two games in 1900 and the one in 1901, Drake gave up after-dark football until 1927, when the university became one of the first to play frequently under modern floodlights.

Incidentally, it was the success of Drake's football illumination that gave Lee Keyser the idea for night baseball. Keyser, owner of the Des Moines Western League club, startled the minor league convention in December 1929 with his announcement that he was going to install lights and play most of his home games at night.

The first outdoor night football game was played in what was then Des Moines's Western League baseball park, at a downtown location.

Before the 1901 game with Grinnell, Drake officials admitted that the lighting arrangements the year before hadn't been ideal, but that they had come up with a solution.

"Last season," the newspaper reported, "the arc lamps were used exclusively and were arranged along the side fences, leaving the center of the field in shadow. This year, however, both incandescent and arcs will be in use. A pole has been erected in the center of the park, and lights are arranged along wires reaching from the top of the pole to the fences, making the whole field evenly lighted."

The game story in the Sunday sports section made no mention of the lights, except for this explanation by the committee in charge, tacked on under the heading, "The Lights":

"We desire to say to the football patrons that the insufficiency of lights at the baseball park was not due to the failure on the part of the management of either team. But a small per cent of the contract lights materialized. This, together with the clouds of dust, made it hard to distinguish plays and players."

Don Evans, a Des Moines attorney who played for Grinnell in the 1901 game, once recalled that there was one big post inside the playing field near the sideline and from it wires were strung across the field. This post was padded with about two feet of burlap. Carbon lights were strung above the wires.

"I would go back to help the safety when a punt was expected and I remember that we could see quite well and that the ball almost never hit any of the wires on kicks."

Evans also recalled how a rash suggestion by William L. Bliss, later an Iowa Supreme Court justice for many years, provoked a slugging incident late in the game.

The way it was described in the newspaper in 1901 was: "Grinnell fumbled just as time was called and Bacon got on the ball and raced down the field, but was called back by Referee Lane. Just then some cowardly ruffian struck Lane from behind, and a riot seemed imminent, but prompt action by the police prevented further trouble."

Evans said Justice Bliss told him years later, "I don't know why I did it, but I was the one who told George Graeser to sock the referee. In the excitement, I shouted, 'Hit him!' and George did, apparently acting spontaneously with the suggestion."

Justice Bliss was known as "Pinky" in those days, when he was a Drake halfback. The newspaper account said Bliss's end runs were a feature of the game, but his dashes couldn't keep Grinnell from winning, 6–5.

Iowa Coach Was First To Be Hung in Effigy

AN IOWA FOOTBALL COACH probably had the dubious distinction of being the first to be hung in effigy.

A dummy bearing the name of the Hawkeye player-coach was found swinging in the autumn of 1891 from a telephone wire that ran across a downtown Iowa City street to the post office.

Iowa, like most colleges then, had no hired head coach. The captain or an alumnus handled the job, and the Hawkeyes' double-duty leader that year was quarterback Frank Pierce.

Pierce and his cohorts opened with a 64–6 victory over Cornell College in Iowa's third intercollegiate season, no doubt inflaming the hopes of followers.

Disenchantment set in when the Hawks played Minnesota for the first time and lost, 42–4. Next they fell to Grinnell (then Iowa College), 6–4.

Perhaps the hanging stimulated the Hawkeyes. Anyway, they

finished by beating Nebraska and Kansas.

Although the hanging was a college first, the 1891 Hawkeye malcontents didn't succeed in establishing a cultural custom.

Inspiration for the wave of dummy-dangling by young intellectuals over the years could have come from more ancient history.

Virgil wrote of effigies in *The Aeneid,* though the old Greeks didn't merely hang dummies of villians and enemies. They also burned 'em.

Effigy hanging and burning has been a popular sport and a holiday rite in England ever since 1606. The guy they still string up was the quarterback of the London Bombers. Guy Fawkes was the ruddy bloke who was supposed to light the fuse for his team, thereby blowing up King James I and the whole darned Parliament.

The Royal defense trapped Fawkes on his bootleg play, November 5, 1605, and the next year that date became a holiday marking the defeat of the Gunpowder plot.

The cases of Fawkes and football coaches aren't exactly parallel. Guy was hanged for real before they began making a dummy out of him.

And here's a cultural bonus: our word *guy* comes from the grotesque Fawkes effigies and originally was a bloody insult.

Football coaches, or unreasonable facsimiles thereof, have taken over where once criminals, traitors (Benedict Arnold was an early American favorite), and politicians swung.

Dummies used to provide an out for the French *flics* ("policemen") when they were too dumb to catch a guy charged with a capital crime.

Up to the time of the first revolution in France, execution by effigy was a solemn legal institution. The criminal might be reveling on the Riviera, but his dummy was choked on the gallows and, sacrebleu! he was officially dead.

So there is the background on the hanging of football coaches.

Davenport Team Routed, 119–7
in First Baseball Gam

THE CIVIL WAR had been over only one year when the Davenport Union club in 1866 became the first Iowa team ever to play in a baseball game.

The game was with the Wapellos of Rock Island, Illinois, and "defeat" was the charitable verb used by a Davenport newspaper over its story, which said:

"The match game between the Union club of this city and the Wapello club of Rock Island came off last Sunday at the appointed place and resulted in a victory for the Wapellos.

"A large number of spectators attended, the greatest portion being ladies. The following is an official report of the game. We wish the Union boys better luck next time."

There followed a rudimentary box score, listing the runs scored by each player, and it gave the first clue to the result: Rock Island 119, Davenport 7.

There were at least a half-dozen Iowa teams active the next year, when Cedar Rapids made its baseball debut with a 31–14 success against the Oatka club of Vinton.

A newspaper account said it was a "very pleasant affair, all parties conducting themselves in a most gentlemanly manner."

It was further reported that E. A. Allen of Marion "received the thanks, expressed in three rousing cheers, of both clubs for the able, efficient and impartial manner in which he discharged the duties of umpire of the occasion."

The state's first baseball tournament was played at Burlington in the fall of that year. The Hawkeyes of Mount Pleasant left no lingering doubt of their right to the championship. They bashed the Burlington Westerns, 115–42, in the final and carried off first prize of $200 in folding money and a $75 rosewood bat.

Professional Baseball Made Its Debut in Iowa in 1875

PROFESSIONAL BASEBALL was born in Iowa in 1875 when ambitious Keokuk entered a team in the National Association, forerunner of the National League.

Keokuk probably owns the distinction, too, of presenting the first black player in organized baseball. That was in 1885, when the city was in the Western League.

He was a second baseman named Fowler, who transferred to Topeka, Kansas, and batted around .400 when Keokuk dropped out of the league the next year.

Keokuk's first experience with commercial athletes was not a stupendous success. The Gate City won once, lost thirteen times in the haphazard schedule of the pioneer pro league.

Natives were mighty proud of their hirelings, however, when they held Boston's eventual champions to a 6–4 decision before a crowd of 1,000 at Keokuk on June 11. Pitching for Boston was A. G. Spalding, the leading hurler of his era and the founder of the sporting goods empire.

Later Iowa pro teams made up for Keokuk's lack of success against athletes from big cities. The Chicago White Stockings, for example, twice had cause to regret excursions into Iowa.

In 1879, Dubuque and Davenport, Iowa, combined with Rockford, Illinois, and Omaha, Nebraska, to form the Northwestern League, the first minor circuit west of the Atlantic seaboard.

Chicago's proud National Leaguers came out to Dubuque for an exhibition game on August 4 of that year and had their ears pinned back, 1–0.

"Old Hoss" Radbourne, who became one of the greatest major league pitchers of all times, plastered the shutout on the White Stockings.

One of his teammates was Charley Comiskey, who piloted the St. Louis Browns to four straight pennants in the next decade and later founded the Chicago White Sox dynasty.

Dubuque won the 1879 pennant with seventeen victories, seven defeats. Rockford was two games back, while Davenport won five, lost thirteen to share third with Omaha.

The White Stockings suffered another blow to their prestige when they visited Sioux City in 1894 for a three-game postseason series with the team then known as the Cornhuskers.

Chicago was no better than eighth that year in the twelve-club National League. Still, any major loop club could be expected to clean up a Western League outfit.

But the Cornhuskers didn't merely win the series—they swept it: 9–6, 8–3, 14–11.

Greatest Sports Car Was Built in Iowa

THE DUESENBERG automobile, considered the "greatest American sports car ever built," was designed and built in Iowa by two brothers—Fred and Augie Duesenberg.

Originally brought to Iowa from Germany as children by farming parents, Fred and Augie came to Des Moines in 1900 after operating a bicycle shop in Rockford, Iowa, for a few years.

They had a bike shop in Des Moines, too, then built motorcycles and switched to automobiles when they built the two-cylinder engines for the Mason car in 1904.

They went to Waterloo to build Mason-Maytag cars, but returned to Des Moines when the company decided to concentrate on washing machines.

Out of their downtown machine shop came the first of what *Sports Illustrated*, in 1955, called "the greatest American sports car and our greatest luxury car."

It also became so popular as a racing car that, by 1922, seven of the first ten places in the Indianapolis 500-mile race went to Duesenbergs.

A "Duesy" was the only American car to win a European Grand Prix—the road race at LeMans, France, in 1921. The same speedster won the Indianapolis 500 in 1922. Three years later, another Duesenberg broke the 100-mile-per-hour barrier at Indianapolis. Pete De-Paolo averaged 101.13 in winning.

Fred Duesenberg died, ironically, in an automobile accident in 1932. Augie, an engineering genius, died in 1955.

Woman Umpired Games in Iowa in Early 1900s

AMANDA CLEMENT of Hudson, South Dakota, was looking for other sports fields to conquer after she starred in basketball at Yankton College and won her state's tennis championship along about 1905.

Amanda made an impressive sight on the diamond, but not impressive enough to overcome the prejudices of the men who operated professional baseball. They wouldn't even give her a chance to umpire in the lower minor leagues.

Amanda began umpiring "more or less as a joke" in games between lodges.

She did so well and earned so much respect for her decisions that she soon became in demand for several years as an umpire of semipro games in northwest Iowa, southern Minnesota, and the Dakotas.

The Boo Is New

Booing Replaced the "Razzberry"

THE BOO is a comparatively recent development in sports, best known to basketball referees and the New York Yankees. The partisan sound of displeasure used to be the jeer, the catcall or the raspberry (usually spelled "razzberry"). While the sound has changed, the attitude is the same as it was almost a hundred years ago.

After Harvard's baseball team played a game in Philadelphia in 1867, a newspaper of that city reported: "The behavior of some of the friends of the Harvard nine was not calculated to exalt them in the estimation of disinterested spectators. . . . The umpire's decisions were opposed and hooted at, and cries of 'no, no, no' would greet the ear when he would declare a Harvard man out."

If Harvard were to encourage or permit such conduct, the writer warned, it would surely "let loose upon the world . . . narrow-minded, selfish, and ungentlemanly specimens of unfinished human-ity."

Most basketball officials steel themselves to ignore their hecklers. The late Ernie Quigley was an exception. Quigley, a National League baseball umpire from 1913 through '37, officiated basketball in the winter with a cockiness and flamboyance seldom equaled.

Quigley once worked a noisy game in one of those small gyms with a balcony. Suddenly he stopped the action with a whistle blast, thrust up a hand to command attention and proclaimed: "There's entirely too much officiating from the balcony."

The sudden silence of the crowd was broken by a lone, shrill voice: "Yes, and too little on the floor!"

College Cheers Developed from Ancient Aristophanes Play

THE ONLY organized college basketball cheers that come through clearly these days seem to demonstrate the ability of the assembled students to spell the name of their school. This gives Iowa's Big Ten teams one of the shortest spelling lessons: "I-O-W-A."

What has happened to all the imaginative and elaborate, even rhyming, cheers we used to hear? What has happened to the earliest of all American sports cheers, which Princeton built around "Sis-sis-sis . . . Boom-boom-boom . . . Aaaaaaaaaaaaaah!"

Does any school still perpetuate a college cheer of even earlier vintage? This one was taken from the Greek by Italian university students. The way it goes is: "Pheu, pheu; baru!" The interpretation makes it sound like just the thing to stimulate a team: "Alas, alas; way down in the dumps!"

Yale, as you might expect, is an American university that went back to the Greeks for one of its yells. Princeton and Harvard affiliates might hint that Yale made an error in translation, thinking Aristophanes was talking about bulldogs — which Yale teams are called — rather than bullfrogs. However, Yale historians explain it thus: members of the Thirteen Club, an eating group of the class of 1886, derived it from Aristophanes's play, *The Frogs,* in order to serenade Frank Bigelow Tarvell, their Greek professor. It was later adopted as a cheer at sports events.

Yale can blame Aristophanes for the first two lines which go: "Brek-ki-kex, koax, koax! Brek-ki-kex, koax, koax!" But somebody else has to answer for the rest of the yell:

> "O-op, O-op, parabaloo,
> "Yale! Yale! Yale!
> "Rah, rah, rah, rah, rah,
> "Rah, rah, rah, rah,
> "Yale! Yale! Yale!"

Yale went farther back than Princeton for its yell, but the Tigers had theirs sooner, and it was all-American. Some historians say it was adopted during the Civil War when the New York 7th Regiment passed through Princeton, New Jersey, home of the university, and gave out with its skyrocket cheer, which ended "Sis, boom, aaaaaaaah!" Princeton took this for its very own by tossing in "Rah, rah, rah!" then "Tiger, tiger, tiger!" and, at the end, "Princeton, Princeton, Princeton!"

The University of Iowa didn't have its first official cheer until 1894, Dick Lamb discovered in doing research for *75 Years With the Fighting Hawkeyes*. It wasn't one that could very well be carried over to basketball, for this is the way it went:

> "Come right this way,
> "Iowa.
> "Football we play,
> "Rush lines we break,
> "Touchdowns we make,
> "We take the cake,
> "Rah! Rah! Rah!"

Coaches Are Meant To Be Ridden,
Not Carried off the Field

WHEN FANS CARRY their coach off the field or court after a victory, they're getting the cart before the horses; rather, on top of them, figuratively speaking, that is. Also figuratively, athletic coaches are meant to be ridden, just like stagecoaches. Hardly anyone rides them, though, when they are winning.

Coaches, who give the word on play, got their name from a play on words. The Hungarians had the word for it.

Coaches are sometimes confused, but no more so than the persons who first called them names. Their title comes not from the thing they represent, but from the place it originated. Literally, a coach would be a *szeker,* or whatever the Anglicized form is.

This explanation won't sound so ridiculous if you ever "rode a pony" through a Latin course. You call a sports boss a coach because the first *szeker* ("cart") designed for the comfort of passengers was made in Kocs, Hungary, a few centuries back. When the idea got to

England, translators gave up on *szeker,* and "Kocs" became "coach."

"He must have been a brave man who first announced that coach is from Kocs, a village in Hungary; surely no one believed him. But now no one doubts," said word authority Alfred H. Holt.

In his *Phrase and Word Origins,* Holt explained: "The tutoring coach preceded the athletic coach by about forty years. In 1848, Clough used the word, the notion back of it being that a tutor, like a stagecoach, aided your progress. By 1885 the word had been transferred to athletics, but the baseball and football mentors of those early days . . . were called 'coachers.' Before 1900, the *r* was dropped."

But not in pro baseball. They were "coachers" in the official rules until 1955, though nobody had called them that for forty years or more.

If you are one of those who helped ride the coach out of the scene of joyous bedlam, maybe you object to being called a fanatic. "Fan" would have been all right, though, wouldn't it? But fan is only a shortening of fanatic—and has been ever since 1682, says the *Oxford English Dictionary.*

Pity the poor immigrant who becomes an American sports fanatic and has to try to sort out our titles of leadership.

A fuzz-cheeked youngster trails the basketball team into the arena, carrying towels and the trainer's kit. "He is," you tell our newcomer, "the manager."

"Ah, yes," says the immigrant in whatever broken English you care to imagine. "Like the great baseball leader, Casey Strangle."

"No, no," you have to say. "He's sort of the errand boy for the coach."

"Ah, yes, the coach—a flunky who takes orders from the manager and stands near the bases and wig-wags strange signals."

Now you have to explain that, while a coach in pro baseball is quite inferior to the manager, in college and other amateur sports, the coach is always the big boss. Even in baseball.

"Ah, yes," says the alien. "It is the professionalism that makes the difference. Your Vince Lombardi was such a great football general at Green Bay that he was called the general manager, no?"

"No. He was the general manager only when he ran the business affairs of the Packers. When he actually directed them on the field of play, he was the coach."

See how easily you can manage to coach a novice in our simple sports idioms?

How Football Teams Got "Spotters in the Press Bo

BECAUSE GREASY NEALE got kicked out of a big league baseball game, football coaches began taking a different look at their own sport. Neale, whose Washington and Jefferson football team had tied mighty California in the Rose Bowl game the previous January 1, was in his seventh season as a big league outfielder in 1922. Greasy, playing for the Cincinnati Reds, exchanged blue-smoke language with an umpire early in a game and was evicted. He changed to street clothes and went up to the press box.

"It was a revelation to me to watch a game from that elevation," said Neale, whose coaching spanned five decades in college and pro football.

"Up there, I saw all the players and all the plays. Down below, you don't command the field—you see only two or three men at a time. It occurred to me that same thing is true in football," added Greasy, who made it a point to watch his athletes occasionally from high in the stands the next fall, and found it "a great help in my coaching."

Later, of course, the system was refined. Telephones were installed so the head coach could give his stalwarts his personal inspiration while one or two assistants served as his eyes from on high.

Vince DiFrancesca, a former Iowa State University coach, was one head coach who gave a try to the idea of leaving the assistants on the field while taking the upper perch to dictate plays. In his haste to get down for a stimulating message to his charges between halves, Vince fell and skinned both knees on the concrete steps. He grounded himself thereafter!

It Took Seventy-five Years for Battin Helmets to Catch O

BATTING HELMETS are commonplace now, but it took more than seventy-five years to convince most batters that they should protect their noggins against missiles traveling up to 100 miles an hour. The attitude of the hitter was that they wouldn't be caught dead in anything as conspicuous as a helmet. A number of them were caught dead in cloth caps after stopping pitches with their heads.

Only one big league batter has been killed by a pitch: Ray Chapman, a shortstop for the Cleveland Indians, in 1920. But many others—notably Mickey Cochrane, Joe Medwick, and Hank Leiber—had their skulls and careers broken by bean balls. And before the era of helmets, there were a number of deaths in the minor leagues and on the sandlots.

Batters have been offered the protection of some kind of head gear ever since 1875, when a hat made of strips of iron, with iron "ear muffs" was patented. After that, lead was tried, then impregnated wood, even paper. All were abandoned as either too conspicuous or too cumbersome.

One manufacturer came out in 1905 with a canvas headgear, to be pumped full of air. Its advertising declared "the pneumatic head protector will . . . inspire confidence in the timid batter who is afraid to hug the plate, which is the secret of all successful batters." It was endorsed by Roger Bresnahan, a great catcher who had narrowly escaped death when conked by a pitch, but it never caught on.

Helmets of the light, sturdy type used today were introduced in 1941. Most big league players wouldn't wear these sissy things, though, until they were ordered to do so.

The Pirates were the first major league club to wear the fiberglass and polyester hats, lined with airfoam. Branch Rickey, their general manager, said they had to. There were innuendoes that Rickey's order was influenced by his presidency of the American Cap Company, one of the first to manufacture baseball helmets. Whatever Rickey's reason, he started a trend toward safety. It wasn't long before all other clubs were following the Pirates' example.

It's Apropos To Call Kentucky Derby
Mecca of Horse-lovers

THE FIRST SATURDAY in May is a time when people who don't know the difference between a charley horse and a thoroughbred show their once-a-year interest in a "hoss race."

There are richer races than the Kentucky Derby. There are many with older and faster horses than these comparative novices, three-year-olds in their second year of competition. Yet this is the one horse race that enchants the general public. Men who think a form chart is a movie queen's measurements will challenge the professional odd-makers with their annual wagers.

No other race spawns the widespread office pools that the Derby does. None has a television audience anywhere near the size of the one that will watch the hoof race at Churchill Downs—and then, in most cases, ignore the thoroughbreds for another year.

*   *   *

It would be trite to call Louisville the mecca of horse lovers, but it would also be apropos.

Sports historian Frank Menke wrote that it was Mohammed who popularized horseback riding, along about the year 600 A.D.: "Having founded a new religion, he was eager that his disciples carry the fundamentals to the far places, in the fastest possible time. Therefore he mounted them on horses.

"The sight of the riders astride the horses created astonishment. The combination was held in awe and superstitious reverence, and the missionaries were given most eager audience, thus aiding the ambitions of Mohammed for converts."

It was from Mecca, in Arabia, that Mohammed sent his horse-men. The Arabian influence on horse racing is still alive in the Kentucky Derby—or anywhere else that thoroughbreds run.

*   *   *

Horse racing has been called "the sport of kings." Royalty figured largely in the early breeding of racers. King Henry I was the first to import Arabian horses into England, in 1110 A.D. But it remained for a queen to establish the rules of standardizing the breeding of thoroughbreds. Queen Anne (1702–1714) ruled that a certain number of stallions and brood mares be selected as founders of a family of "thoroughbred horses," meaning horses whose blood lines could be traced back directly to Arabia. Queen Anne also thought of an extra incentive for owners and jockeys that hadn't occurred to kings. She had the idea of cash prizes to go with the usual trophies.

Eventually, British racing authorities determined that, in order to qualify as a thoroughbred, a horse had to be descended from just three founding sires. Talk about exclusive families—all the thoroughbreds in the world today can be traced in their male lineage to those three stallions of more than 300 years ago.

*   *   *

The Kentucky Derby had its first running in 1875, 210 years after the first competition at a public racecourse on American soil. That was at Hempstead on Long Island, New York. Until the year before, the Dutch had controlled the colony and the only horses they cared about were the kind strong enough to do rough farm work. They plodded, but that didn't matter. Hardly anybody bet on plowing races.

Then along came Colonel Richard Nicolls, the first English governor of New York, and one of his first acts was to call for faster horses and a place for them to race. His request has been paraphrased into a popular saying by bettors who proclaim that they are "contributing to the improvement of the breed."

The races called for by Colonel Nicolls would not, he said, "be so much for the divertissement of youth as for encouraging the bettering of the breed of horses which, through neglect, has been impaired."

Sparistike, Anyone? Or Perhaps *Battledore?*

SPARISTIKE, ANYONE? Or would you rather go to court for a little battledore and shuttlecock — the old poona, you know? All right, if you want it simple: Do you want to play tennis or do you prefer badminton?

Sparistike is the name a British army major tried to inflict upon lawn tennis when, in 1873, he refined and altered the ancient court game to create our present sport. Major Walter C. Wingfield wanted everything new and different in his form of the pastime, including the name. So he came up with the Greek word *sparistike. Sparistike,* said the inventive major, meant an order to take or be ready (for the serve), same as in the old French *tenetz* or *ten-ez.* Players pronounced the major's new game excellent. But, maybe because they couldn't pronounce the new name, they stuck to tennis.

Now the latest Webster's dictionary gives evidence that Major Wingfield was barking up the wrong source. The name, say the lexicographers, is due to the fact that the early balls were made of a light cloth produced at Tinnis, a medieval town in lower Egypt that was famous for its cloth. British army officers apparently had a lot of time for fun and games in the 1870s.

Like modern tennis, badminton was perfected in England, also in 1873, and by military men on leave from duty in India. Some sources say the officers derived it from an Indian game called poona. Others say they only improved a children's game, long known in England and on the continent, called *battledore* (racket) and *shuttlecock* (the bird, then a cork with feathers stuck in it).

Anyway, it's called badminton because the new form of the pastime was launched at a party given in 1873 by the Duke of Beaufort at his country place, Badminton. Badminton players can give thanks that it was not introduced at Wales, say at the village of Llanfairpwllgwyngyllgogerychwyrndrobwllllantysiliogogogoch. (You wanna bet there isn't such a place?)

The American Badminton Association now claims to have more players than tennis. Most of these, no doubt, play the informal backyard variety. And probably with a little less violence than the experts, who can drive the shuttlecock off the racket at a speed of ninety miles per hour.

Badminton is more popular than tennis as a home pastime because not many people have a yard big enough for a tennis court (thirty-six feet by seventy-eight feet for doubles). A badminton court is twenty feet by forty-four feet. Aside from real estate, badminton is a lot cheaper than tennis. Twenty bucks will buy all the backyard equipment needed.

A Lovely Tennis Question

DON'T ASK ME, as some people already have, how the tennis fathers ever hit upon that 15–30–40 scoring system. All I know is that there have been arguments for years to ditch it in favor of plain old 1–2–3 to simplify things for new players and spectators.

Some of the more violent wallopers of tennis balls, eager to remove the last vestiges of gentility in what was once a "sissy sport," also would like to get rid of love. Love in tennis, as sometimes in romance, means zero. Grandfathers will remember when a young man walking down the street with a tennis racket was likely to be greeted with a limp-wristed wave and a "Thirty-love, dearie!" from youths whose tastes ran to the rough-and-tumble muscle matches.

Today's hard-hitting tennis players, of course, have long since demonstrated theirs is a rugged, demanding sport. It took a long time, though, to overcome the circumstances of its introduction to America.

Mary Outerbridge of Staten Island, New York, saw the game played by British army officers in Bermuda (but not in shorts) in 1874, came home with equipment and taught the pastime to her female friends. "For several years," says the *Jarman Journal Of Sports,* "it was considered strictly a girls' game." For one thing, "men didn't cotton to 'love' as one of the scoring terms." Nor were they fond of one of the rules, imported from England, that "gentlemen are not to play in shirtsleeves in the presence of ladies." That didn't mean they could strip down to whatever the T-shirt of their day was. It meant they had to wear coats.

The scornful males eventually overcame their prejudices — against everything except possibly "love" — until now tennis leaders claim to have at least 1.5 million more players than golf has.

It might be as hard to get rid of love in tennis as it would be to banish it from popular songs. The term goes back to 1742. Love in tennis is not the same as in amour. When you get it in tennis, you don't score. Or, if you like the French derivation, you lay an egg.

In *Phrase and Word Origins,* Alfred H. Holt says there is "an ingenious conjecture that it might come from French 'l'oeuf' (egg-hence, zero)." (A scoreless inning in baseball is sometimes called a "goose egg.") But this, Holt comments, "is not supported by dictionaries. The credit is usually given to such a phrase as 'play for money or play for love,' that is, for nothing."

First Football Game Was Actually a Soccer Match

WHAT HAS GONE DOWN in history as the first intercollegiate football game, between Rutgers and Princeton in 1869, was actually soccer, with no ball carrying. The most popular touch to the game, the touchdown, wasn't generally accepted until 1877 — after Harvard borrowed the idea from the Canadians.

The Harvards of the 1870s allowed their men to run with the ball, though not for scores. Kicking was the only way to get points. Consequently, the Harvards couldn't get the non-running Princetons or the Yales and the few other football schools to play them. So they scheduled McGill University of Montreal, Canada, in 1874. The Canadians, influenced by rugby with its ball carrying, had adopted rules that permitted players to run for touchdowns. Harvard gave this revolutionary system a try and liked it.

The Yales finally agreed to a game under Harvard rules in 1875. Though they lost, four kicked goals and three touchdowns to nothing, the Yales made history by admitting that something good had actually come out of Harvard. By 1877, all college football teams were on the run.

Monument Marks First Time a Ball Was Carried in a Game

THE IDEA of carrying a ball in a game was introduced at Rugby College in England by a maverick to whom a monument was erected on campus.

"This stone commemorates the exploit of William Webb Ellis, who with a fine disregard for the rules of football, as played in his time, first took the ball in his arms and ran with it, thus originating the distinctive feature of the rugby game, A.D. 1823."

And, of course, eventually American football.

Profanity Led to the Invention of Basketball

AN OUTBURST of profanity was indirectly responsible for Dr. James Naismith's creation of the game of basketball. The lusty maledictions were uttered by a teammate of Naismith's in football practice — and thus was begun an intricate process which ended in the new sport.

It started back in the 1880s. Naismith was a seminary student at McGill University in Canada. His football mates therefore were cautious about their conduct in the presence of this embryo minister of the gospel.

But this time, one of the linemen — who probably had just been kicked in the teeth — couldn't restrain himself. He swore long and loudly. Suddenly he stopped. Embarrassed, he turned to Naismith. "Oh, I beg your pardon, Jim," he said. "I forgot you were there."

"I hadn't paid particular attention," Dr. Naismith recalled years later, "for I had heard more fluent swearing than that in the lumber camps of Canada. But it set me thinking about this matter of personal influence and I talked about it with the YMCA secretary. He told me of the YMCA college at Springfield, Massachusetts.

"I was all for stopping my ministerial career right then, and going to that college. However, I was dissuaded and received my ministerial degree. But I never held a pastorate."

At Springfield, necessity became the mother of invention, so Naismith became the father of basketball. It happened because, after he was graduated and became an instructor there, his gym class clamored for a new and exciting indoor game.

Incidentally, if the janitor of the college had been able to find a couple of eighteen-inch boxes instead of a pair of peach baskets that eventful winter day in 1892, the sport probably would have been boxball instead of basketball. Boxes were in Naismith's original plans, but the janitor could offer nothing but baskets for the goals.

* * *

Naismith previously had demonstrated his inventive skill with a device for protecting his ears in football at McGill. It was of flannel, but it was a forerunner of and similar in pattern to the leather headgear which followed several years later.

At Springfield, Naismith was a classmate of Alonzo A. Stagg, who went on to football laurels at Yale and a coaching career that bridged more than fifty years. It was Stagg who recommended Naismith for the Kansas University physical education position the doctor held the last forty-two years of his life.

Naismith personally thought wrestling and fencing better exercise than basketball. In his later years, he was much more likely to be found watching athletes in those sports.

Ironically, Naismith had only modest success when he gave a try at coaching the sport he invented.

First Packer Players Earned $1.52 per Game

THERE ARE PROBABLY some old gaffers up in Green Bay, men in their eighties, who have a better right than most to sift their memories at the fireside and wish they had come along late enough for the good new days of professional football. Most of them, like their coach, Curly Lambeau, have passed on, spared the envy for the hundreds of thousands of dollars the stars of the Green Bay Packers earn these days.

The old gaffers had no idea what a gold mine was opening for future football generations when the Star Packing Co. moved from Providence, Rhode Island, to Green Bay and was persuaded by Lambeau to back a pro team in 1919. The company's total investment was $500 for uniforms and equipment. The only proviso was that the new jerseys carry the name "Star Packing Company" across the front.

Those Packer pioneers were pros—but just barely. The twenty-one members of the team divided the profits at the end of the 1919 season. Each man received $16.75, or $1.52 for each of the club's eleven games. That included their playoff shares. The playoff that year didn't have quite the significance of today's Super Bowl.

The Packers' career in the NFL was still two years from its inception. Their 1919 climax was for the championship of Wisconsin. (Green Bay had won ten games in the regular season, outscoring the opposition 565 to 6.)

The Packers lost their first title game. They could have been excused for being misled by the nickname of their rival from Beloit. The Beloit team was well known as the Fairies. For some reason, the name has never been adopted by other athletic teams. Actually, it was short for Fairbanks-Morse.

Lambeau never came right out and said that the referee, Baldy Zabel, was prejudiced against the Packers in that 1919 playoff. Curly, who led Green Bay for its first twenty-nine years in the NFL, recalled once the circumstances that led him to suspect the referee's impartiality.

"We were behind, 6–0," said Lambeau, "and we got to the Fairies' three-yard line with time running out. On the first play, I went off tackle for a touchdown. But the referee said we were offside. So we had to run the next play from the eight. I went around left end and into the end zone. Once again ol' Baldy said we were offside.

"I called time and told the boys: 'On this play, just stand still till after the snap. Don't even charge.' So there was hardly any blocking, but I got around right end and across the goal for the third time. Baldy didn't call us for offside that time—but he blew his whistle and said we had illegal motion on the play. It put us back on the eighteen. We couldn't get across on the play or two we had time for."

The $16.75 salary, obtained by passing the hat at home games, wasn't clear profit. The players had agreed to pay their own medical expenses. At least three of them required treatment for broken bones, thereby making the Packers the pioneers in liberal use of the forward pass.

"We played a tough team from the iron country at Stambaugh, Michigan," Lambeau recalled. "On each of our first three running plays, we had a player suffer a broken bone. For safety's sake, every play from then on was a pass. We won."

The Woman Who Got a Hit
in a Regulation Major League Game

KITTY BURKE made baseball history when she hit a pitch thrown by the St. Louis Cardinals' Paul Dean. It was the first—and only—time a woman has batted in a regulation major league game. This little-known incident happened on the night of July 31, 1935, when baseball under the lights was new in the majors and the Cincinnati Reds sold standing room just about everywhere except on second base.

Larry MacPhail, the madcap promoter who was Cincinnati's general manager, had sold thousands of tickets to clients who were coming on special trains from cities in Ohio and Kentucky.

The trains were late. Meantime, MacPhail let the box offices keep selling tickets. When the rail travelers arrived, all seats were filled. An estimated ten thousand out-of-towners were herded onto the field. They lined the foul lines all the way to the fences and hundreds crowded between the plate umpire and the grandstand. It was a night to remember even before Miss Burke high-heeled her way to the batter's box in the eighth inning.

When outfielders caught fly balls near the foul lines, standees wrested the baseball away from them. Overworked policemen had to keep shoving customers off fair territory. One overzealous fan of Paul Derringer dashed out to the mound to get the Cincinnati pitcher's autograph while Paul was waiting for the catcher's signal. When Paul tried to chase him away, his admirer pulled a knife on him. More work for the police.

Hitters had to have firm grips on caps and bats to keep them from being stolen as they fought through the crowd from dugout to plate. Babe Herman was a little loose with his grasp when he struggled out to bat for the Reds in the eighth. Miss Burke grabbed his bat and ran to the plate. The fans yelled for Paul Dean to let her hit. Paul lobbed one up — and Kitty hit it. The pitcher fielded her tap and, ungallantly, tagged the only woman ever to bat in a major league game. The out didn't count against the Reds.

*　　*　　*

Women have been playing baseball, though usually against each other, since 1883. An 1884 baseball guide reported, among its highlights of the previous season: "Philadelphia and Chester, Pennsylvania, enjoyed the distinction of possessing artistically dressed nines of ladies.

"The Chester nine's uniforms consisted of red and white calico dresses of remarkable shortness."

At the turn of the century, there were touring female teams playing the game for money against men's semipro clubs. Skirts were out of fashion then, as the names of the teams indicated. They were called "Bloomer Girls."

One of the best pitchers the American League ever had, as well as several other players in the pro leagues, bloomed in the ranks of the Bloomer Girls. Some of the spectators at the Bloomer Girl games must have marveled that a woman pitcher could throw that hard. A woman pitcher couldn't.

Close shaves and wigs were required of pitchers for the women's clubs. They were men. So, often, were the catchers and players at another position or two. (Babe Didrikson reversed the procedure. The former Olympic champion and eventual golf queen pitched one summer for the otherwise male and bewhiskered House of David team.) One of these female impersonators, he admitted years later, was Joe Wood. Known as "Smoky Joe," he once pitched the Boston Red Sox to the pennant with a 34–5 record.

Two women actually have been signed to playing contracts in men's professional leagues. Neither ever played in a league game, but one of them struck out Babe Ruth and Lou Gehrig in succession in a 1932 exhibition game for Chattanooga of the Southern Association against the New York Yankees. This feat owed more to Ruth's and Gehrig's gallantry of the era, however, than to the pitching prowess of Jackie Mitchell.

Harrisburg, Pennsylvania, of the International League signed

Eleanor Engle as a shortstop in 1952. Those spoilsports who ran the show later cancelled the contract, however.

Baseball's Plural Problems

BASEBALL has had a plural problem for more than 100 years.

Why are the Philadelphia-Kansas City-Oakland Athletics called that instead of Athletes? Athletics are (is?) what they engage in. The participants are the athletes. Philadelphians, for reasons that have gone with them to the grave, chose to add an *s* to the last part of their baseball club's name.

As early as 1864, five years before baseball had its first out-and-out pro club at Cincinnati, Philadelphia was represented by its Athletic Club. It's the oldest continuing nickname in United States athletics.

When the team moved to California from Kansas City, a lot of Oaklanders didn't appreciate the idea of being Athletic supporters. Some wanted to revive the nickname the city used in its Pacific Coast League days—the Oaks. But no one voiced a desire to go back to the nickname of the city's first pro club in the 1890s—the sponsors got to name the team, so it was called the Greenhood and Morans.

Nor was there much call to restore the nickname of Oakland's first club in the California League of the early 1900s—the Greeks. (Among their opponents were the Los Angeles Loo-Loos.)

*   *   *

Cincinnati's first pro team was known as the Red Stockings. It wasn't long until this was shortened to Reds, a nickname that has endured except for one short spell. In deference to Communist-haters, the club officially readopted the Redlegs label in 1955–1958. It didn't have a leg to stand on in efforts to popularize the nickname.

They've been plain old Reds again ever since, except in the Spanish language newspapers of Latin America, where they are referred to as *Communistos*.

THE MOBILE MONUMENT to Abe Saperstein—the Harlem Globetrotters basketball team—is still going strong.

Saperstein was the undersized Chicagoan who created the team fifty years ago from talent that had never seen Harlem. Abe and his entire squad traveled in one Model-T Ford then and the farthest they trotted about the globe was to a few rustic gymnasiums in Iowa and other midwestern states. Long before he died in 1966, however, Abe had authenticated that originally deceitful nickname by taking his Trotters to every continent and every nation that is even faintly civilized.

"More than anyone else," the late Bill Veeck once wrote in a memorial tribute to Saperstein, "he gave to Mr. Naismith's little game an international impetus and provided blithe and cheery entertainment to the topsy-turvy world. He overcame the barrier of race and language to illustrate that fun and games need never recognize the limitations of nationalism."

Veeck pointed out the lesser known fact that Saperstein also had a role of some importance in baseball. It was a part especially important to Veeck, among others, who were struggling to keep an American Association franchise alive in Milwaukee in 1941.

"It was Abe Saperstein who volunteered his services and those of the Trotters to help keep the boat afloat," said Veeck. "Suddenly we were basketball promoters. And that winter it was basketball that kept the wolf sitting on the porch instead of joining us in the parlor."

The success of the Milwaukee baseball venture, with basketball's aid, made it possible for Veeck to take over the Cleveland Indian franchise and introduce black players into the American League. Saperstein was a big help there, too. "It was Abe," said Veeck, "who recommended Larry Doby, Minnie Minoso, Luke Easter, and countless others. It was Abe who wandered into Cleveland to suggest that the time was ripe to unveil the incomparable Satchel Paige and who handled the negotiations with Tom Baird for his purchase."

Baird was the owner of the Kansas City Monarchs, for whom Paige pitched in the Negro American League. As such, Baird was a rival of Saperstein. For Abe, meantime, also had become a franchise owner. He purchased and operated the Chicago American Giants of the Negro League.

Larry Doby had, late in the 1947 season, become the first black player in the American League. Jackie Robinson beat him to the majors, under the aegis of Branch Rickey at Brooklyn in the National League. Veeck, not Rickey, would have been the pioneer of baseball integration though, except for Ford Frick. Saperstein was his scheduled helper in that operation, too.

The Philadelphia Phillies' franchise was headed for bankruptcy in 1944 and Veeck offered to buy it from Gerry Nugent, the sinking owner. Bill planned to stock the club liberally with black players, to be assembled by Saperstein and Doc Young, sports editor of a Chicago black newspaper. While negotiations were in progress, Veeck said, the Phils' franchise was turned over to the league. Bill had to deal with Frick, then the National League president. Frick sold it to William Cox for, said Veeck, "about half what I was willing to pay."

The Phils were not integrated for years.

Blacks Were Suddenly "Banned" from Pro Football

IN 1946, baseball abrogated its unwritten rule and allowed black players to compete. It was the year Jackie Robinson signed with the Dodgers and played for their Montreal farm club. There was far less ado when another racial barrier crashed the same year—in professional football.

There were several black players in the National Football League's pioneer years of the 1920s. Among them was Iowa's Duke Slater, the first black voted into the collegiate football Hall of Fame. But from 1934 until 1946, not one was offered an NFL contract.

A. S. (Doc) Young, who deeply researched the NFL's "lily-white" era, said there never has been a satisfactory explanation of just what happened to cause pro football to exclude blacks after the Chicago Cardinals' Joe Lillard, the NFL's only black in 1933, retired that year. This was a switch by a sport whose 1920 world champions were an integrated team—coached by a black.

Fritz Pollard, a bouncy 155-pounder, wasn't the first black all-American. He missed that distinction by twenty-four years. William H. Lewis, a Harvard center, was chosen on Walter Camp's all-American teams in both 1892 and '93. After graduation, Lewis became Harvard's line coach. But Pollard was the first black to play in the

Rose Bowl, for Brown University in 1916. He also was the first black to play in organized pro football, with the Akron, Ohio, Indians in 1919. And in 1920 he coached the team.

Not only that, his Indians were acclaimed world champs after they whipped George Halas's Decatur, Illinois, Staleys, forerunners of the Chicago Bears, in Chicago's Wrigley Field. That was considered pro football's first *big* game, with a crowd estimated at forty-five thousand.

As Akron's coach for four years, Pollard was in charge of a predominantly white team, including one or two southerners who resented his presence. "There was one player in particular who resented the idea of being coached" by a black, Young quoted Pollard. "But I solved that problem by letting him carry the ball for touchdowns and catch most of the passes in a big game. After that, he was my greatest admirer!"

It was an interesting coincidence that the person who broke the racial barrier in pro football was Jackie Robinson's running mate at halfback for UCLA in the late 1930s — Kenny Washington. Washington became the first black since 1933 offered an NFL contract when the Los Angeles Rams signed him in April 1946. A few days later, they added Woody Strode, an end who had played with Robinson and Washington at UCLA.

In August, the Cleveland Browns of the new All America Conference signed Bill Willis and Marion Motley.

*   *   *

Basketball was much slower to permit integration. The National Basketball Association didn't permit blacks until 1950 and, surprisingly, it wasn't until 1963 that Minnesota became the last of the major midwestern universities to present an integrated basketball team. The Gophers had had blacks on their squad before, but only as little-used, token reserves — until three black sophomores made the starting team in '63.

Basketball was the last major college sport to open its doors to blacks on integrated teams. *Re-open* would be more accurate, for there were a few black players in the early years of the game, beginning with Fenwich Williams, who captained Vermont in 1908. Nebraska, which had a black football fullback — George Flippen — as early as 1892, pioneered in midwestern basketball integration with Wilbur S. Woods, a letterman in 1908, '09, and '10. Cleve Abbott, another black, played for South Dakota before World War I. But for the most part, basketball was off limits to blacks at white-dominated colleges until the post World War II years.

The Big Ten apparently had no black basketball player until one became a regular for the University of Chicago in 1943–1944. Iowa was next with Dick Culberson, an Iowa City youth who played enough as a reserve to win a letter with the Hawkeyes' conference champions of 1945.

The Wild Horse of the Osage

Pepper Martin: The Rough and Ribald Jokester

"THE WILD HORSE OF THE OSAGE" was rather tame, alas, by the time he reached Des Moines as a baseball manager in midseason of 1955. Pepper Martin, the one-time "Wild Horse," had, as he described it, "got religion." With it came a measure of decorum that made Pepper reluctant to talk about the rough and ribald days of his youth.

He didn't like to be reminded of the story that, having cashed in the rail ticket sent by the Cardinals, he rode the rods of a freight train from Oklahoma to spring training at St. Petersburg, Florida. And that, arriving at the Cards' plush hotel, he was due for the bum's rush until General Manager Branch Rickey recognized his prize rookie under the grime and the barbed wire beard.

Martin, who died in 1965 at the age of sixty-one, likewise shunned conversation about some of the other times he had made Rickey shudder.

Once was when Branch learned that Pepper, in those days of sunlight baseball, was spending his nights driving a midget auto at various tracks. Another time, Rickey and several Cardinal players were special guests at a rodeo in St. Louis. Branch watched with calm contentment until he saw Martin go down out of the stands and, in his street clothes, bulldog a calf.

Again, Rickey quailed when word got to him that Martin and

Pepper Martin, 1955

pitcher Dizzy Dean were hurling each other to the concrete floor or banging each other into lockers in clubhouse wrestling matches every day. "They were just friendly scuffles," said Martin. "We never hurt each other much."

The Cardinals of Martin's flamboyant days in the 1930s were known as the "Gas House Gang." They got the name from a New York writer because they appeared in uniforms that were wrinkled and caked with mud. There hadn't been time for a cleaning job after a game played in the rain at Boston the day before.

Playing in a soiled uniform was nothing new to Pepper. He never had a clean one for more than five minutes. That's how long it took him to get it dusty from cap to socks. Martin was a reckless headfirst slider, and he picked up more dirt than a steam shovel.

The only time Pepper, when he was managing Des Moines, talked about the jokes, practical and impractical, pulled off by the Gas House Gang was when a magazine story about one of their pranks was pointed out to him. "They got it all wrong," Martin bridled. "They call Leo Durocher one of the Gas House Gang. He was on the team — but he wasn't one of our gang.

"Also, that episode in the hotel in Philadelphia wasn't planned in advance. It was spur-of-the-moment. I went out one morning to buy me a pair of coveralls and a cap to wear on the ranch. Dizzy and Rip Collins and a couple of other boys went with me. They decided that they'd buy some, too, and, just for fun, we put 'em on over our regular clothes and wore 'em back to the hotel."

It was just by chance, Pepper insisted, that when the players got back, they discovered the brushes, ladders, and tools of a crew of painters and carpenters who had gone to lunch.

"Ol' Diz led the way," said Pepper. "We went into one dining room and started moving tables away from people and setting up ladders. Then we went to the ballroom, where there were speeches going on at a luncheon of some kind. We started moving furniture and banging away with hammers. They were pretty mad, and they called the manager. Then the chairman recognized Dizzy and me and he invited all of us to stay as guests of honor — had 'em bring us lunch, too."

Blades Once Drew Eighty Dollars a Month from Webster City Team

RAY BLADES, a former St. Louis Cardinal outfielder and manager, once drew $80 a month for his second base play in semipro competition at Webster City, Iowa, and at Stratford, Iowa, in 1916.

"The Webster City team was managed by my cousin, George Wheeler. He was responsible for getting me up there from my home in McLeansboro, Illinois," said Blades, who was baseball's miracle man of 1939 when he hoisted the Cards, sixth-place finishers the year before, to a close second.

"The (Webster City) team broke up in midseason, and Stratford hired me and a couple of other fellows for an important game with another small town—I can't remember the name of it. Us 'ringers' helped them win, so they hired us for the rest of the season. In between games, we helped out the farmers. First time I ever saw barley, I helped shock it."

It was six years later that Ray made the grade with the Cardinals. In between came eleven months' duty in France during World War I, more semipro competition, and two pro seasons at Memphis and Houston. Thus began the fulfillment of an ambition that caught fire when Blades saw his first professional game in 1910 at the age of fourteen.

"My folks had moved to St. Louis and ran a rooming house there for five years. That spring of 1910, I saw the Cards play St. Paul in an exhibition game. It was quite a coincidence, I think, that I later managed both clubs—the Cards in '39 and '40 and St. Paul from '44 through '46."

Two years later, Blades met the man who was to be his boss through a large share of his professional life, Branch Rickey. "Mr. Rickey umpired the game when I pitched our high school team to the city championship in Sportsman's Park."

Rickey signed Blades for the Cards after Ray helped a Mount Vernon, Illinois, semipro team beat the big leaguers in an exhibition in 1919.

Ray was a second baseman at Memphis and Houston. "The Cards had Rogers Hornsby at second, you know," said Blades, "so I had to look for a new job.

"Mr. Rickey was the Card manager in '22, but Barney Shotton had charge of the club on Sundays. Mr. Rickey wouldn't go near the park on Sundays.

"One day, Barney told me, 'Ray, you're playing either third base or left field today.'

" 'Well, it won't make any difference,' I said, 'since I've never played either one.'

"He tried me first at third. He hit me seven or eight grounders and I only stopped one — then threw the ball up in about the tenth row of the stands. 'Kid,' he said, 'you're playing left field.' "

Blades, equipped with speed and a good arm, practiced every morning until he had mastered the knack of catching fly balls. He was a regular then, until he crashed into a wall and injured his knee in 1926. That caused him to miss the Cards' first World Series appearance, but he was in the big title shows of 1928, '30, and '31.

In thirteen years as a manager — at St. Louis, St. Paul, New Orleans, and Rochester — Ray was never out of the first division. Between his two seasons at New Orleans, he was a coach for Cincinnati and served the Dodgers in the same capacity in 1947 and '48. He later became a troubleshooter in the Brooklyn Dodgers' farm system and visited Iowa many times before his death in 1979.

Babe Adams: Baseball's Most Accurate Pitch

BENJAMIN (BABE) ADAMS, who probably learned his most valuable pitching lesson from a "spiked" team representing Lamoni, Iowa, was without a doubt the supreme pitching sharpshooter since the first baseball was stitched together. Babe gave up an average of only 1.30 walks per game, and that puts him in first place in baseball's record books with room to spare. Even as a semipro novice, he could throw a baseball with bomb-sight precision — this darkly handsome young man who was to become the first and only rookie to win three games in one World Series.

Yes, Babe could throw straight and he could throw hard. But he had no curve ball for deception when he pitched for the village of Mount Moriah against Lamoni in a special match at Blytheville, Missouri, in 1903. The Iowa team, loaded with imported sluggers, belabored Adams's fast ball for a thumping victory.

"I decided then," said Babe, "that I had to have a curve. There was a fellow named Adams in Mount Moriah — no relation — and he knew how to hold a curve, but he couldn't throw one.

"He showed me the grip and I practiced till I could break off a good one—right where I wanted it, too," once recalled Babe, who in retirement operated the old family farm ten miles south of the Iowa border until his death in 1968.

Later, Babe's arsenal included the fadeaway, a pitch that became famous again as a screwball when Carl Hubbell threw it. Only the famed Christy Mathewson knew the secret of the fadeaway until Adams, by studying Christy's reverse forearm twist, was able to copy it. And so successfully that he won seven of his eleven duels against the illustrious Giant pitcher.

Surprisingly, Adams's professional career didn't begin until he was twenty-three years old. "I never played a game of ball till I was twenty-one," said Babe. "Wasn't anybody to play with till Fred Coffman started a team. He was the town barber."

Coffman may have regretted launching a team with Adams as the pitcher. Old-timers recalled that Coffman was a fairly small man, and every one of Babe's pitches would literally lift him right off his feet.

Coffman's uniforms were memorable, too. "Brightest red you ever saw," Babe explained. "Red velvet. Fred had a dressmaker in town make 'em." Old-time southwest Iowa fans probably recall the red uniforms, for Babe and Fred wore them in games at Lamoni and Kellerton. The gaudy suit was worn by Adams in his professional tryout with Parsons, Kansas, of the Missouri Valley League in 1904. Not for long, though. He was persuaded to lend it to a first baseman named Brown because the club was short of uniforms for a spring exhibition trip.

The red suit got into competition before Babe did. He was left behind by manager Hamilton, a former Pacific Coast League umpire, who had signed Adams after seeing him pitch for Mount Moriah.

Babe's first professional baseball job was painting the new ball park at Parsons—fence, grandstand and all—for $3 a day. "I worked from sunup till dark every day for two weeks," Adams recalled. "Finally I got to wondering why Hamilton hadn't taken me on the barnstorming trip.

"When they got back, I told him, 'I'm going home. I came down here to play ball, not to paint.'

"Well, Hamilton reassured me right away. He said he already knew what I could do and that he was using the exhibition trip to try out our other pitchers."

Hamilton's confidence was justified when the St. Louis Cardinals bought Adams in the middle of the 1906 season. The Cards gave up on him too quickly, though. They released him to Denver of the Western League after a four-inning test. The Grizzlies soon sold him to Pittsburgh for $5,000 — then a breathtaking price.

The Pirates farmed him to Louisville for one season, but kept him for 1909, when he won twelve, lost three. He didn't attract much attention though, until he turned back Ty Cobb, Sam Crawford, and other fearsome Detroit Tigers three times in the World Series, 4–2, 8–4, 8–0.

The Pirates, like the Cards before them, also gave up too soon on Adams. Babe had averaged sixteen victories in seven seasons, but was released as a worn-out veteran after winning only two and losing nine in 1916.

The big right-hander decided to retire permanently to his farm. That he didn't was due to the persuasiveness of Jack Holland, who talked Babe into pitching for his St. Joseph Western League club in 1917. He went on to Kansas City and the Pirates brought him back late in 1918. He was still with them in 1926, at the age of forty-four.

Babe's 1917 Western League pitching control record was phenomenal: one walk a game, on the average, in 308 innings.

The bushy-browed farmer was even more precise when he got back to the Pirates. Through the entire season of 1920, he never allowed more than two bases on balls a game. In twenty-six of his thirty-five games, not one opposing batter got a free trip to first. His total generosity amounted to eighteen walks in 263 innings for the season, the second straight in which he won seventeen games for a team that had branded him as "finished" in 1916.

Young pitchers were always asking Babe how they could improve their control. "There's nothing I can tell them," he once said. "I never had any special practice — never threw at a target on a barn or flung stones at squirrels. It just came natural."

Tim McCarver: The Super Hustl

IF A BIG LEAGUE ball club "had twenty-five guys like Tim McCarver," Red Schoendienst once said, "the manager wouldn't even have to come to the field. All he'd have to do," the former St. Louis Cardinal skipper added, "would be to put up a notice about what to do that day, then sit in the clubhouse and relax. As it is, Mac leads by example, because he bears down as hard in practice as he does playing a game—and nobody bears down harder than that."

Tim always had a zest for baseball, and he once explained that, "Everything in baseball has seemed easy, after what I went through in my first twenty-four hours as a pro up in Iowa."

McCarver expected a rather leisurely approach to his professional career at Keokuk in the Midwest League: Arrive a day early, get a good night's sleep, then watch from the bench for a few games to study the veteran catcher.

McCarver was seventeen years old in June 1959, freshly graduated from Christian Brothers High School in Memphis, Tennessee. "I'd just agreed to terms with Buddy Lewis, a Cardinal scout," said Tim, who was thereupon richer by some $80,000 in bonus and guaranteed salary for three years.

"Buddy drove me in to St. Louis to sign the contract, then he drove me on to Keokuk. The club was playing in Waterloo and I expected to join them when they came back home the next day. But Frank Calo, the manager, had left a message that if I arrived that day, I was to come to Waterloo right away."

So Tim and Lewis got back into the car and drove on to Waterloo. "I didn't get there much before the game," said McCarver, "but Calo put me right into the line-up. Galon Cisco was pitching for Waterloo and he was about the best in the league. I went 0 for 4.

"I rode back on the bus with the rest of the players, and I think that was one of the first buses ever made. We didn't get back to Keokuk till about 3 A.M. and then Calo announces we're going to have morning practice—at ten o'clock. So nothing in baseball seemed hard to me after that.

"I enjoyed playing in Keokuk, though. I've never met friendlier people anywhere. I even got so I didn't mind the bus trips."

The Cardinals' bountiful bonus, trumping one almost as large offered by the Yankees, lured McCarver away from the college football scholarships he could have had. One possibly would have come from Notre Dame. "Possibly" is the word Tim used.

"I've seen it written," he said "that I turned down an offer from Notre Dame. But I can't really say that I did. They had me up to visit the campus while I was still in high school. They seemed to show interest in me as a football player, but it never got to the point of actually offering me a scholarship."

McCarver had what is known in baseball as "the good hands," and, with his quickness, they made him a skillful catcher. "But I had bad hands in football," said Tim. "I played end in high school, but I was 'ol' steel-fingers' and I wasn't much at catching passes. I never could have made it as an end in college. Tackling was the best part of my game, so I probably would have been a defensive back."

In addition to the Cardinals, McCarver also served duty with Philadelphia, Montreal, and Boston, posting a lifetime average of .271. He hit an amazing .478 when the Cards beat the New York Yankees in the 1964 World Series.

Generally, catchers are considered slow on the base paths, but in 1966 he had thirteen triples to become the first catcher ever to lead the league in that department.

EDITOR'S NOTE: McCarver became one of TV's better sportscasters and even a best-selling author in 1987 after a superlative career that spanned four decades.

An Iowa Snooze Helped Mal Reggie Smith a Hitting St:

REGGIE SMITH traces his rise as a super hitter to his failure to rise on time from a snooze in Waterloo, Iowa, in 1964. It took a twenty-five-dollar fine to wake Smith up to the necessity of concentrating more on the pitches and stopping his wild swinging.

These defects already had cost Reggie a demotion from Reading, Pennsylvania, of the Eastern League, where he had hit only .154 earlier that season. "I wasn't hitting much more than that my first month or so at Waterloo," once recalled Smith, whose batting and centerfielding as a rookie in 1967 had a lot to do with the Boston Red Sox' championship.

"I didn't really start bearing down at the plate and waiting for the good pitches till I had a chance to get my fine back with my bat. In those days twenty-five dollars was a lot of money to me."

Smith drew the fine for missing the bus on a trip from Waterloo to Cedar Rapids. "We had played in Wisconsin Rapids (Wisconsin) the night before," said Reggie, "and didn't get back to Waterloo until about seven A.M. The landlady where I roomed was supposed to call me at one P.M., but I guess she forgot. Anyway, by the time I woke up, it was too late for me to get to Cedar Rapids in time for the game.

"When I did join the club, the manager — Matt Sczeny — fined me the twenty-five dollars. But he said he'd give me a chance to earn it back. He said he would refund five dollars to me for every game in which I had two hits."

With this financial stimulus, Smith said he became more choosy about the pitches he swung at. "Before then, too," he said, "I'd been trying to knock them all out of the park. Now I was satisfied to go for singles. But I still got as many home runs — maybe more."

Did he get all his fine back? Smith smiled. "Yes," he said, "I got that back fast. In fact, within the next month, I had four hits or more in nine different games. In one of them I hit for the cycle (single, double, triple, home run). I hit pretty close to .400 the last month of the season and got my final average up to .318."

Sczeny, besides providing Smith a batting incentive, was the first manager to recognize the advantages of Reggie's speed and strong arm in the outfield. Smith had started out as an infielder.

In addition to the Red Sox, Smith also played for St. Louis, Los Angeles, and San Francisco in a career that lasted until 1982. He crashed a total of 314 home runs during the seventeen-year career and had a .287 lifetime batting average.

Army Major Orders Willie Mays Yanked from Game

VERN MORGAN was the only manager who ever received orders from higher authority to yank Willie Mays from a ball game for inefficiency. "I had to take Willie out of the first game he ever played for me at Fort Eustis (Virginia) — and in the very first inning," said Vern, who also served a term as the Des Moines Bruins' whistling third baseman in the early 1950s. "Can you imagine anybody ordering me to bench the greatest player who ever lived? But when it's a military order, all you can do is say, 'Yes sir.'"

Morgan was named manager of the Fort Eustis team in 1952. "Willie was assigned to us after playing for a month or so with the Giants," said Vern. I soon found out about Willie's great sense of humor. But I didn't see anything funny about it right off, because the first thing Willie did was put on this serious expression and say, 'I'm sorry, but I didn't come down here to play ball.' Then Willie grinned and began to unpack his luggage—and I started breathing again. He had three gloves, seven pairs of spikes (baseball shoes) and a dozen of his own bats."

So Mays was ready to play the night of his arrival. "We'd been drawing a few hundred for our games," said Morgan, "but that night there must have been ten thousand soldiers and civilians on hand just to see Willie. "Willie came up in the first inning with two out and hit a single. I batted next and singled him to third. I took a long lead off first and the pitcher tried to pick me off. As soon as he turned to throw, there was Willie breaking for the plate. If the first baseman hadn't been real alert, Willie would have made it. They just nipped him by an eyelash . . . and that's when the major gave me the big shock."

The major, whose name Morgan always declined to mention, was in charge of all athletics at the fort, and sat on the bench in uniform—military uniform—during games.

"The major called me over right away," said Vern, "and demanded, 'Private Morgan, did you order that man to steal home?' I said, 'No,' and I started to explain how you let a great player run on his own, and how it was a fine move and so on.

"But the major cut right in on that explanation and said: 'It was very foolish and inefficient. Take that man out of the game immediately and send him to the dressing room.' It looked like there was nothing else I could do without being court-martialed, so out Willie went. The crowd sent up an awful uproar. Luckily, they blamed the major instead of me."

Luckily for Vern also, Mays just laughed it off. "That was the last order we ever had from that major," said Morgan. "I guess he must have heard from his own superior officers."

Mays endeared himself to his fellow soldiers not only with his .400-plus hitting, but also with his unfailing good nature and his generosity. "Our army team didn't play on Sundays," said Vern, "so I helped Willie organize the Willie Mays All Stars. He'd give up big shares of the receipts when we played around at towns in Virginia and North Carolina.

"And when we'd go away for a game, Willie would leave the keys to his big white convertible and let his buddies use it."

The Homer That Bounced off the Outfielder's Head

CHARLIE TEAGUE, who played for Des Moines's Western League team during the 1950s, always liked to recall the time Bill Pinckard got a home run when the ball bounced over the fence off an outfielder's head.

Honest to goodness, it's true. It happened in Denver on August 9, 1952. Dick Cordell, a lanky redhead, raced back to the left field fence and set himself to haul in a high fly hoisted by Pinckard. Cordell reached confidently, but all he clutched was a bunch of Denver's rarefied atmosphere. The ball hit the ten-foot high wall above Dick's head, caromed off his noggin and bounced right up and over the fence. To make the humiliation even worse for Cordell, that was the only run of the game.

Teague also recalled a couple of other carom shots that involved him in his 1950–1953 Des Moines career—but not with laughter. Well, he managed a chuckle over what shortstop Ed Plank thought was a consoling remark after the weird play in Pueblo that ended second baseman Teague's hopes of a big league opportunity.

Charlie's spikes caught in the adobe clay of the Pueblo infield and he lurched into the path of a savage bouncer. The ball smacked him squarely in the mouth and down he went. "But the ball ricocheted right into Plank's hands," Charlie recalled, "and he threw to first for the out.

"There I was sprawled on the ground, half my teeth knocked loose and blood all over my face. Plank bent over me and said: 'Well, anyway, Charlie, you got an assist on the play.' "

Teague's only worry then was his teeth, four of which eventually had to be pulled and replaced. Charlie didn't know he had a broken ankle that would force him to retire the next season. The ankle hurt some. But, after all, he was able to walk on it—even part of the way to the ambulance.

"I also walked to the bathroom at the hospital that night and again early the next morning," said Charlie. "The doctor had the ankle X-rayed, but I thought it was just a sprain. I wouldn't believe it when the doctor said it was broken and was going to put a cast on it. I wasn't convinced till he got the X-rays and showed me the fracture."

The other carom shot injured only Charlie's emotions. "It was our last game in the 1950 playoffs against Sioux City," Teague said. "Last inning, two outs, runners on second and third for us, and me up. All I needed was a single and we would have won the playoff. Boy, I sure thought I had it when I ripped one back up the middle. I can't remember who the Sioux City pitcher was. But I'll never forget how that shot hit him on the toe—and caromed right into the hands of the first baseman for the last out."

Other Teague Western League memories were more pleasant. One was the time that Mike Blyzka, a Wichita pitcher, tried to give Charlie an intentional walk. Southpaw Charlie reached out and slashed the way-wide pitch past third for the winning run in the ninth.

Des Moines never had a more consistently pesky hitter (.274, .272, .277, .270), and certainly never had a more fiery competitor.

A Pipe-smoking Ballplayer Will Never Make

JIM BROSNAN, the Cincinnati pitcher who later became a best-selling author, was a member of Des Moines's minor league team in 1950 and again in 1953—and he was never considered "one of the fellows." Jim's scholarly appearance and vocabulary set him apart from the run-of-the-field ball player. In the clubhouse or the dugout, Jim would usually have his nose stuck in a book or a magazine, ignoring the customary crude bantering and horseplay.

"He'll never make a ball player," said salty Charlie Root, Brosnan's 1950 manager at Des Moines. "You know how he spends his afternoons? Reading and listening to classical music on that portable record player of his. Not only that, he smokes a pipe. You never see a good ball player smoke a pipe." And Charlie lit up another cigar.

Brosnan did, however, prove to be major league material, and his best-selling books included many earthy, racy stories and some painful digs at some of the people he didn't like in baseball.

Satchel Paige: The Man of Many Age

EDITOR'S NOTE: Satchel Paige spent most of the summer of 1962 with semipro teams "barnstorming" around scores of Iowa towns and cities. Bryson caught up with Paige one night in Des Moines and wrote the following column in July of that year.

GAME TIME was only a half-hour away when Satchel Paige shambled into the clubhouse, looking like a mailman at the end of a long hilly route. Satch appeared plumb exhausted after the ten-yard walk from his pink Cadillac. One observer felt tempted to help the doddering old man over to the bench.

Paige, a uniform satchel hanging from baseball's most enduring arm, slow-motioned his way to the rubbing table in the middle of the room and deposited himself loosely. It didn't seem possible he'd ever be able to get up again, let alone throw baseballs for three innings against the Kansas City Monarchs that night. "You get my time of life, you don't jangle around so much — just enough to keep the blood circulating good," said the man who was marking his fifty-sixth birthday (or maybe his fifty-eighth).

The rubbing table is designed for the trainer's convenience in administering to muscle strains and pains, mostly in pitching arms. To Paige, the rubbing table was only a good place to sit because it was high enough to allow his long, skinny legs to dangle.

The name of Doc Ritter, the Demons' trainer from 1959 through '61, was brought up. Had Doc rubbed out the kinks for Satch when both were with Miami of the International League for a couple of years? Paige snorted. "No disrespect to Doc," he said, "but there ain't nobody ever rubbed this arm." Satch proudly flexed the weapon that has pumped baseballs in more than six thousand games since the early 1920s.

"If I'd paid attention to trainers and managers, I'd been through long ago," he said. "Kept after me to have my arm rubbed. Kept after me to run, run, run. In the big leagues, too. What do those sharecroppers know about keepin' me and my arm in shape? They'd have plumb wore me out years ago."

A suspicion that Paige's right arm is made of India rubber, rather than flesh and bone, was dispelled when Satchel said, "Sure, I had a sore arm — once. I was down in the winter league in Venezuela in 1933. Went swimmin' and got a cold in it. Manager he say, 'You can pitch it out.' Sure sometimes you can pitch out the soreness, but sometimes you can make it worse, too. I knew what I needed — rest. I went home. By spring, I was as good as new."

When Satchel finally reached the big leagues in 1948 at the age of forty (or maybe forty-two), he and manager Lou Boudreau failed to see eye-to-eye on the subject of running.

"Told me to get out there and run after fly balls with the other pitchers," said Paige. "What for? I don't catch no fly balls in the

game. But I went out to make him happy. Fly ball come my way, I'd sort of saunter over and take it on the second bounce. Boudreau was mad, but he let me alone 'cause I kept winning."

By now Satch had stripped down without once touching his feet to the floor. He had merely shifted from one haunch to the other in skinning off his sharply creased slacks. Out of the gaudy cocoon of street clothes emerged a trim body that would be a pride to most men of thirty-five. There are no gray hairs on head or chest. Only the wrinkled solemn face betrays Paige's advance beyond the prime years.

Satch pulled a wrinkled uniform and a pair of size thirteen-and-a half shoes from his satchel. It was worth watching him getting into his working clothes without abandoning his sitting position. Then, a dragging walk to the field, a five-minute warmup, and the old fellow was ready for his sixteenth three-inning job in seventeen days. Three shutout innings, too.

*   *   *

They always called Paige ageless. That isn't true. Nobody had more ages than Satchel, nor more different birthday anniversaries.

Paige was at least forty years old when he threw his first pitch in the big leagues, for Cleveland in 1948. The age was Satchel's own reckoning. He said he was born in Mobile, Alabama, on September 22, 1908. Cleveland's roster the next spring went along with the 1908, but listed his birth date as September 11.

Later, the editors of the *Official Encyclopedia of Baseball* accepted the evidence of a birth certificate, unearthed in Mobile, that "Leroy Page" was born July 7, 1906. "That ain't me," Satchel scoffed. "The name ain't even spelled the same."

But Bill Veeck, who introduced Paige to the majors in midseason of 1948, said that he "could prove that Satch was a minimum of forty-eight years old" when he joined the club.

Veeck, the Indians' president, found a skeptic in his official family after he brought in Paige — Manager Lou Boudreau, no less. Boudreau couldn't see how a man that old and that skinny could throw a baseball hard enough and accurately enough to cope with sharp-eyed young big-leaguers.

Veeck knew Satch would have to rely on the precision of his fastball, along with an artful change-up. "His curve was only a wrinkle then," said Veeck. "He didn't develop a really good curve until he was fifty-four!"

121

Satchel Paige, 1939

Bill wasn't worried too much about Satch's control. He had often seen Paige's demonstration before games on barnstorming tours. Satch would have a one-by-two board set up behind home plate, then take a hammer and tap in four tenpenny nails, just far enough so they'd stay. Then he'd go to the mound and drive the nails in with fastballs.

Boudreau insisted upon a tryout for Paige before he was willing to approve a place for Satchel on the roster. The man he chose to test Paige with was a batter leading both majors at the time with an average close to .400 — Lou himself.

Satch allowed he'd better limber up a little before his trial, and "run around the park a few times." He jogged out to about middle distance in the outfield, thought better of it, and jogged back. Manager Boudreau's skepticism wasn't diminished when he saw that Paige was puffing a little from even this exertion.

They used to say of Paige that all he needed for a warmup was to shake hands with the catcher. He'd often go into a game after only three or four practice throws. Satch tossed a few more than that, Veeck recalled, to get ready for Boudreau.

Then Paige cut loose with twenty pitches to the manager. "Nineteen of them were in the strike zone," said Veeck, "and a lot of them were cleanly missed. Lou had nothing that looked like a base hit.

"After a final pop fly, Lou dropped his bat, came over to me and said, 'Don't let him get away. We can use him.' "

They could, indeed. Satchel, forty going on forty-eight, had a 6–1 record — just enough to clinch the pennant.

The Cob Job Led the Waners to the Hall of Fame

LONG BEFORE SCIENTISTS found a place for it in industry, in the making of charcoal and solvents and stuff, the rough and ruddy corncob served many a humble but useful function. Many senior citizens will recall those functions: everything from kindling for the kitchen range to homemade pipes to plugs for gasoline and kerosene cans with lost lids; even as a paper substitute in an unmentionable function.

The role of the unglamorous corncob in sports was limited and not well known. But it helped put two men into baseball's Hall of Fame — the only brothers who have gained that distinction.

The late Paul Waner, when he was a minor league batting coach for Philadelphia, made occasional trips to Des Moines to instruct the Phillies' farmhands. Once he remarked that "if those kids think a curving baseball is hard to hit with a big bat, they ought to try hitting a corncob with a hoe handle."

"That's the way Lloyd and I practiced batting when we were kids down on the farm in Oklahoma," Paul explained. There wasn't much money for balls and bats. Once in a while we'd get a cheap ball, but it wasn't long before we'd lose it or knock the stuffing out of it. Then we'd go back to breaking off chunks of cobs and taking turns pitching to each other.

"Those cobs would dart and dance and jump so much, they made the curves look simple when we started playing baseball. It was the best eye-sharpening practice I ever had."

The most striking record Lloyd Waner carried into the Hall of Fame is one for avoiding strikes, especially third ones. No National Leaguer was harder to fan, over a long career, than Lloyd. It probably won't grab you to read a bunch of figures such as 173 strikeouts in 7,772 times at bat through eighteen seasons. Toss in a couple of comparisons, though, and Lloyd's resistance to whiffs takes on a meaningful glitter.

"Little Poison," voted into the Hall seventeen years after brother "Big Poison" made it, averaged just one strikeout for every 449 official times at bat. In eighteen years, Lloyd didn't whiff as many times as Dave Nicholson did in *one* season. That was the year, 1963, when Dave reached a humiliating big league high of 175 strikeouts.

The Spit That Split Iowa and Iowa State

Saliva War Breaks Up Baseball Series

THERE HAVE BEEN various reasons for splits in Iowa-Iowa State athletic relationships through the years but only once, apparently, was there a breach because of the application of saliva.

Hawkeye officials didn't mind if Cyclone pitchers spit on the sidewalk. Their only request was that they refrain from spitting on the baseball.

The moisture argument came to light in the meticulously handwritten card index of results Merle Ross kept when he was one of the ISU Athletic Department's most valuable and most durable members. A footnote on the 1920 baseball record was: "Second game with Iowa, scheduled at Iowa City, not played because of dispute over spitball." The Cyclones held out for the legal spitting rights granted them in their conference, then the Missouri Valley.

When professional baseball outlawed the spitball, along with other adulterated deliveries, in 1919, the Big Ten went along with the pros, Ross explained. The Valley didn't.

Iowa refused to condone saliva for the return game, even though the Hawkeyes had won the first meeting at Ames that season.

The first football break between Iowa and Iowa State since 1900 came the next year and endured, except for a 1933–1934 resumption, until the 1970s. Spitting on the football had nothing to do with it.

Iowa Quarterback Yelled Out the Plays

FOOTBALL TEAMS have code words for the quarterback to shout out at the line of scrimmage to indicate when his "audible" or "automatic" is to replace the play that was called in the huddle.

"I thought a secret audible code was necessary," said Forest Evashevski, "until Kenny Ploen came right out and yelled what he was going to do—and got away with it."

Evy, the former Iowa coach and athletic director, had Ploen as his do-everything quarterback in the 1954–1956 seasons of his Hawkeye coaching era. Iowa had a code in living color for its audibles, Evy explained. "Ploen would insert colors among the numbers when he called signals at the line," said Evy. "We'd have a different 'live' color for each quarter."

The other colors, no matter what, were red herrings, designed to confuse the enemy. "Pink, say, would be the code word in the first quarter," Evy said. "That meant the next number Ploen yelled out would be the new play. Then maybe blue would be the live color in the second quarter, lavender in the third, and yellow or something else in the fourth."

If this confused the enemy, it also, alas, confused some of Ploen's confederates. "We had a couple of linemen who kept forgetting what the live color was," said Evy. "They'd miss the audible and throw the wrong blocks.

"One time when we were playing Indiana, Kenny called a play to the right in the huddle. Then he saw that Indiana's defense was overloaded on that side. Kenny threw out the color code. He just yelled out, 'Bootleg left.' Then he simply rolled left and threw a 30-yard pass for a touchdown."

From then on, said Evy, Ploen made no attempt to camouflage the signal for the new play. "He would just give the standard number of the play on his audibles without any code word," Evy recalled. "You're not supposed to do that, for fear that repetition of the number would let the opposition catch on to what's coming. But Kenny would defy the defense even more than that. He'd switch to a pass play and yell: '127—left end hook.' Then he'd make it work."

The Day Woody Hayes Backe
Down from Evashevsl

VOLATILE WOODY HAYES once backed down after threatening Forest Evashevski during a meeting of Big Ten coaches and athletic officials at Iowa City. The flare-up occurred after Hayes criticized Iowa coaches for their behavior during a 1964 game at Minnesota. Evashevski mentioned something to the effect that Woody was a fine one to talk about the behavior of football coaches in view of some of Hayes's sideline outbursts.

Witnesses said Hayes, who was fired at Ohio State a decade later after punching an enemy player during a bowl game, charged around the conference table at the Iowa athletic director. But Evy sat firmly with arms folded. Woody's temper blew out and he desisted short of assault.

The Strangest Home Run Ever Hi

THERE WAS ONCE a "home run" in a Des Moines ball game that was untouched by a bat, with the ball winding up on the roof of the Des Moines grandstand—behind home plate. This strange incident, undoubtedly the only one of its kind in the history of professional baseball, occurred on July 5, 1901, and an Omahog named Frank Genins was the beneficiary of the peculiar ruling.

Omaha players may have been known by a more elegant nickname in their home city, already noted for its stockyards and packing plants, but according to the story about the game in the Des Moines newspaper, they were the "Omahogs."

The Des Moines club had two nicknames: "Prohibitionists" and "Midgets."

There's no way of telling whether Genins's clean miss went into the official records as a homer. But home run it was called in the *Register*'s story of the game: "It remained for Omaha to show Des Moines something about baseball they never saw before. A home run was made without the ball being hit, and all through the batter striking at a wild pitch."

With two out in the ninth, Genins swung and missed for an apparent third strike, but the pitch hit the plate, "bouncing . . . to

Kleinow's shoulder and passing upward until it found a resting place on top of the grandstand. Umpire McDermott treated it as a ball 'out of bounds' and allowed Genins to circle the bases."

Catcher John (Red) Kleinow entered the argument along with Captain Hines and all his teammates, but McDermott was not to be swayed. "Hines served notice," said the story, "that a protest would be entered in the event of the home run proving to be the deciding run." It wasn't. It merely padded the Omahogs' margin to 6–4, and that was the final score.

Cedar Rapids Basketball Team Won, 128–0

YOU'VE HEARD of shutouts in football and baseball, of course, but in basketball?

What is probably the record was set in 1912 when Cedar Rapids' only high school of that era walloped the daylights out of Tipton, 128–0. James Yuill led the rout with twenty-four field goals. Four years later, Cedar Rapids chose a district tournament game for another "zeroic feat," this one against Williamsburg. The score was 86–0 and Ralph Yuill, brother of James, whipped in sixteen baskets in his twenty-four minutes of action.

These were the only shutouts unearthed in a dusty excursion into old newspaper files, but several teams missed such ignominy by the barest possible margin. District results in 1917 alone included these: Sioux Center 33, Kingsley 1; Algona 33, Somers 1; West Side 37, Irwin 1; and Linn Grove 6, Spirit Lake 1.

Just three years later, Spirit Lake had improved so much that it went to the final round of the state meet at Ames, losing to Boone, 25–20. Jefferson, the eventual winner, had trimmed Nevada, 8–1, in the Ames invitational tournament in 1913, but the real massacre there was West Waterloo's 67–3 victory over Webster City. All the losers' points came on free throws.

Whatever pride Webster City salvaged from that trouncing was wiped out when its conqueror lost to Jefferson, 17–12, and Jefferson was then whacked, 30–11, by Davenport in the first round of the state meet in Iowa City.

Team Made a Profit because Player Shunned Haircut

THE LATE W. C. (BILLY) EDSON of Storm Lake once kept a complete financial report on the first team he played for, and helped organize, at Buena Vista's Preparatory School in 1893. The prep's first season netted a profit of $1.53. A major reason for this was that the players credited themselves for the haircuts they went without for three months.

"For headgear," said Edson, "we let our hair grow." The treasurer's report included: "Credit thirty-three haircuts in three months at twenty-five cents each — $8.25."

The field equipment came to the whopping total of $1.94 for six two-by-fours, each twenty feet long (the goalposts), eight spikes, and half a sack of lime. Under team equipment was: "eleven prs. white painter's pants — $8.45." (These, Edson said, were turned up at the knees. Cotton was used to pad the knees and hips.)

Wool socks cost eighty cents a pair. Players furnished their own "old sweaters." Cotton "for all purposes" came to one dollar. Shoes? "Our cobbler nailed leather cleats on our old shoes," said Edson, "at fifty cents per pair."

The final expenses entry was "one football — $5.00," bringing the total outlay to $30.69. A mass meeting of the student body raised $23.97. Credit the amount saved on the haircuts and there you have it — a treasury balance of $1.53.

Looking on the Bright Side of a 73–0 Defea

SPORTSWRITERS who visit the losers' dressing rooms in search of quotable comments after football games are familiar with the saddest words of tongue or pen. Nowhere else will you so often hear "what might have been."

When the Washington Redskins lost to the Chicago Bears by the improbable score of 73–0 in the 1940 National Football League playoff, a partisan sportswriter wanted to help the victims contrive an alibi.

Early in the calamity, the Redskins' Charlie Malone dropped a sure touchdown pass from Sammy Baugh. "Until Malone dropped the pass, it was still anybody's ball game," the reporter prodded Baugh in the dressing room. "Now if he had caught the ball and we had scored that early, how do you think the game would have turned out, Sammy?"

"Seventy-three to seven," Baugh softly replied, knotting his tie.

The Syntax Champions

CASEY STENGEL and Yogi Berra were always far ahead of all challengers for baseball's scrambled syntax championship. Berra possibly reached his malapropian peak one time when he was honored by admirers in his native St. Louis. The former Yankee catcher said he wanted to "thank everybody who made this occasion necessary."

One time Stengel was expressing his gratitude to the incorrigible fans of his doormat New York Mets who, despite losing 120 games, drew more than nine hundred thousand customers during the 1962 season. "The way I figure it, it was like this," Stengel said by way of clarification. "We got great support from the New York fans and they are the ones we have to thank for the whole problem."

The Year of the Painful Experiment

IF YOUR SYMPATHY is stirred when you see a batter struck by an erratic pitch today, then you'll want to shed a retroactive tear for the National League hitters of 1901. For the first and only time, the National that year didn't even let a wounded batter have first base for his pains. If a batter was hit, it was merely called a ball. (The American League didn't go along with the rule change.)

In the Hole, Literally

DAVE SISAM said he was going to hit one "in the hole" for his Grand View second baseman, Ike Bidstrup. The phrase turned out to be more literal than the coach intended.

"The hole" in baseball is a gap between infielders. Sisam, hitting practice grounders before a game, meant the hole between Bidstrup and the shortstop.

Dave gestured with the bat to show Ike he was going to bounce one down the middle. Bidstrup glided to his right, braked to a stop behind second — and disappeared up to his waist.

Grand View was playing on a new diamond, and some of the recent fill over a water main had given way to a depth of three feet. The startled Bidstrup, who was unhurt, got only halfway to the record for fielding in depth.

A couple of pro outfielders had total subterranean experiences — one by accident, one by design.

Red Worthington, a former big leaguer, was swallowed up by the earth once when he chased a fly ball while playing for Portland in the Pacific Coast League. It turned out that the boards covering a forgotten cistern, topped by dirt and sod, had given way. Onlookers were shaken up emotionally, Red only a little physically by his six-foot drop.

The outfielder who vanished intentionally was Casey Stengel. Who else?

When Casey was a young pixie playing center field for the Giants in an exhibition, startled witnesses saw him emerge from nowhere to pursue a fly. "There was this manhole with a lid on it out in center," said Casey. "I guess so the groundskeeper could get down and check the drainage system. I sneaked into the hole real quick and pulled the lid back over. I could tilt the lid a little and see the batter. The fans were yelling that we didn't have any center fielder just before the batter hit one. Then they saw me appear by magic and go after the ball.

"I coulda caught it, too, but the left fielder beat me to it."

Team Was Aweigh Off Targe

THERE'S PROBABLY NOTHING to rival the embarrassment of the young man who was navigator of a U.S. Coast Guard Academy craft bearing the school's basketball team.

In keeping with the academy training program, athletic teams were transported by sea whenever possible from the home base at New London, Connecticut. This time the scheduled port was Boston, where the academy had a game with Tufts. After landing, the Coast Guardsmen discovered they were in Nashua, New Hampshire—a navigation error of thirty-five miles.

The basketball team didn't arrive in the Boston gym until more than half an hour after the scheduled starting time. Before the sailors began to recover their composure, they were behind by 20–3. They lost, 94–69.

Will Overhead's 500 Victory: The Classic Blunder

ONE OF THE MOST delightful blunders in American newspaper history took place on Memorial Day of 1933, when readers of the Walsenberg (Colorado) *World-Independent* were uniquely informed, in a blaring headline on page one, that Will Overhead won the Indianapolis 500. Every other newspaper in the land proclaimed Lou Meyer the winner of the celebrated automobile race.

If ever a story sounded like a fabrication of a supercharged imagination, it was this Walsenberg tale told to me by a couple of Pueblo newspapermen when I was out there with the Des Moines ball club in the late 1940s. But doggoned if one of them didn't go home to get his prized copy of that edition of the *World-Independent*. Sure enough on the first page was a big, black five-column banner: "Overhead Wins Indianapolis Classic." The story below told how the victory went to driver Will Overhead.

The newspaper did correct its error—but ironically not until sixteen-and-a-half years later.

The monstrous misunderstanding happened in the first place because the Walsenberg paper had a new editor whose inexperience was equalled only by his eagerness and ambition. He wanted to give his readers the result of this great race. Not having on-the-spot radio and television coverage to rely on, he wired the Associated Press bureau in Denver to get him the name of the winner—and pronto. The AP, wanting to assure the editor that it would comply, wired back: "Will overhead winner."

What the novice editor didn't know was that, translated from press association jargon, this meant the winner's name would be "overheaded"—sent by collect telegram—as soon as possible.

The editor accepted the preliminary wire as the conclusive answer to his request for the result. So the good people of Walsenberg read that Will Overhead was the new Indy champion.

The editor had long since been replaced when humorist H. Allen Smith resurrected the boner in 1949. The Walsenberg editor of that time became indignant because Smith had added error to blunder by putting the incident in an Indiana setting. The editor was quick to demand, with justifiable choler, a correction from Smith for this slight to his people and to Walsenberg.

Smith cheerfully corrected his error. But he also pointed out to the editor that the first error was still on the books, so to speak, because the Walsenberg paper had never printed a retraction. It had continued to let its readers believe that Will Overhead had won the race.

The editor studied Smith's message and agreed that his paper had, indeed, been remiss. A new chapter to American newspaper lore was thus added when, in December 1949, the Walsenberg newspaper greeted its readers with a five-column headline in big bold letters: "Lou Meyer wins Indianapolis Classic." There was no explanatory story; just that startling banner on Page 1.

If this sixteen-and-a-half-year-old bit of news left readers somewhat confused, at least the record was set straight. The Walsenberg *World-Independent* had done its duty.

Baseball's Disciples of Dece

THE DELICATE ART of deception is what makes baseball fun. Take the case of Joe King, an old Western Leaguer who pretended to catch a fly ball which actually sailed over his head for a home run. King would have gotten away with his skullduggery. His fakery fooled everybody in the park — except a couple of fans, who screamed for justice. Only then was a confession wrung from Joe.

Awaiting construction of its own municipal stadium, Omaha played its 1947 Western League games in the American Legion Park across the Missouri River in Council Bluffs. On this particular night, Denver was the opponent and the visitors' left fielder was King.

Ed Lewinski, Omaha first baseman, smashed one over the high screen in left field — or so he thought. First thing Ed knew, there was the ball coming toward the infield. He held up at second base.

Everybody was all set to resume play with a new batter up. Everybody, that is, except two sharp-eyed fans who jumped out of the stands, screaming and pointing. Finally, the umpires called time and began an investigation. They listened to the fans and called King in for a few questions.

King finally confessed that he had concealed a baseball inside his shirt when he took his position in the field. As Lewinski's drive cleared the fence, Joe cleverly spirited his personal baseball from its hiding place, threw it against the wall, and caught it on the rebound.

The upshot was that Lewinski's homer was allowed, and eventually Joe was fined fifty dollars by the league president. "It was fun," Joe said later, "but not worth fifty dollars."

*   *   *

Many of Des Moines's Western Leaguers used to come to Iowa's capital city by way of Asheville, North Carolina, a lower farm club in the Chicago Cub organization. They couldn't practice the same deception in Des Moines that they did there.

The Asheville ball field was in a city ball park, and to preserve its landscaped beauty, the city would allow no fences of any kind. Bushes marked the outfield boundaries.

"But," Fred Richards, who played a season there, once related, "the ball was still in play if it went into the bushes and not over them. Our outfielders used to hide balls at different spots in the bushes so they could 'find' them in a hurry. This worked fine till one night a ball went into the bushes in right-center. Two outfielders got there at the same time—and all at once two baseballs came flying in."

*   *   *

Des Moines fans of a much earlier era once saw the Demons beat Omaha, 8–7, in thirteen innings when outfielder Pug Griffin used a con game on the pitcher.

Pug was at bat with two out and Petey Brausen on third base in the thirteenth. Griffin was loudly accusing Paul Rasmussen, the Omaha pitcher, of throwing the illegal spitball. Pug stepped out of the batter's box and asked Rasmussen to let him examine the ball. The naive pitcher tossed the ball to Griffin. Pug stepped aside, the ball rolled to the grandstand and Brausen frolicked home with the winning run.

Stan Musial, 1948

Griffin's trick is said to have been worked a few times on raw recruits in the big leagues. That was in the days before umpires were so quick to call time.

*   *   *

One of the old-time capers, at least on the sandlots, involved a potato. The pitcher, in an apparent pickoff attempt, would throw the potato over the baseman's head. The runner would be fooled into taking off, then the pitcher would throw the baseball and nail him.

Timm Won Two Letters — before He Got to High School

CAP TIMM, the long-time former Iowa State University baseball coach, won two high school baseball letters before he ever got to high school.

There was no four-year varsity limit when Cap was in school at Arlington, Minnesota. As a seventh-grader, Timm beat out all the older boys for the regular prep catching job. He also won a dozen other letters in football, basketball, and track.

"You Don't Have To Play in Front of Him"

JOE GARAGIOLA liked to recall the time he was catching for Pittsburgh and Stan Musial stepped to the plate. Garagiola said his young pitcher kept shaking off his signs and fidgeting around on the mound. Garagiola said he went out to sooth and encourage the kid with: "Don't be afraid of Musial. Do you think I am?"

"No," said the pitcher, "but you don't have to play in front of him."

Player Hits the Ceiling — and Loses the Game

THERE WAS ONCE a player from McAuley High School of Joplin, Missouri, who, in his exuberance over the prospect of a rare victory, hit the ceiling and lost the basketball game.

McAuley was ahead by two points and had the ball out of bounds with only one second left. There was no way to lose. But the Joplin kid found one. Giddy with success, he threw the ball as high as he could. It struck a rafter. The officials ordered the clock reset and gave the ball to the other team, St. Agnes of Springfield, Missouri, ruling the ball out of bounds.

St. Agnes beat the clock with a pass and a shot, tied the score— and won in overtime.

Fidel Castro: The Little League Plagiaris

FIDEL CASTRO, the Cuban dictator, once sent Mickey McConnell a copy, in Spanish, of a book, *How to Play Little League Baseball.* McConnell, for years a Little League director, had the book checked over by a friend who speaks Spanish. They discovered that it was, word for word, a translation of Mickey's own volume on the subject.

"Oh, there was one exception," said McConnell, "my name wasn't in it anywhere. Under the title it said, 'By Dr. Fidel Castro.' "

It Was Hard Keeping the Basketball Roun

BASKETBALL is referred to now and then as "round-ball." As labels go, this is about as distinctive as "made in Japan." Aside from football, what ball game can you name that isn't played with a round ball?

The label is especially significant to basketball people because they had such a hard time finding a ball that was really round—and would stay that way.

People well past middle age can remember starting a game with a ball that seemed to be a perfect sphere, only to have it develop a slight bulge here or there. Sometimes a game ball became so lopsided by intermission that it had to be replaced for the second half.

It wasn't until 1949, fifty-eight years after Dr. James Naismith invented the game, that basketball had a missile that would hold its shape. It gave legal acceptance that year to a ball with the leather molded and sealed to a fabric girdle.

Players of an earlier era also had the distraction of lacing, which sometimes unbalanced the ball or made a dead spot when it came to dribbling. The laceless ball wasn't officially adopted until 1937.

The old-time ball was bigger as well as more cumbersome. Since 1930, the circumference has gradually been reduced from thirty-two to twenty-nine-and-a-half inches.

The Film Star

THERE WAS ONCE a high school graduate down in Missouri who wouldn't get Jack Wallace's endorsement as a college football prospect. The former Drake coach would have been happy to have recommended him, however, to a Hollywood film studio.

"The boy—a center—wanted a football scholarship," said Jack. "He sent us a movie of his high school competition. But, instead of sending a film of a complete game, or several games, he sent us a highlight film."

"He had taken copies of movies of the whole season and edited them himself, winding up with a bunch of plays in which he was the central character. And, boy, did he look great! Here'd be a scene of the boy opening a hole for a touchdown run. Next there'd be one of him crashing in for a sensational tackle, and so on."

Wallace's first reaction was, "Give this boy a scholarship right now before somebody else sees this movie." But Wallace had some second thoughts and wrote to the school requesting a movie of the kid for an entire game.

"It showed that, overall, the boy was awfully slow. It showed defensive linemen knocking him over, and it showed him missing tackles.

"But, oh boy," he added, "what a film editor that kid was!"

Forget the Pitcher, Sign the Hitter

WHEN CHARLIE GRIMM was serving one of his terms as manager of the Chicago Cubs, a scout phoned him to report excitedly on the pitching phenom he had just seen in a Wisconsin sandlot game.

" 'The greatest young pitcher I ever saw,' " Grimm quoted the scout. " 'He struck out all twenty-seven men and only one of them could get as much as a foul tip.'

"I told him," said Charlie, " 'Forget the pitcher. Hitters are what we need. Sign the batter that got the foul tip.' "

Player Was Traded — for Himself

LES MOSS had the unusual distinction of being traded for himself.

The Boston Red Sox, needing a catcher in 1950, swung a complicated deal with the old St. Louis Browns for the promising Moss. Several other players were involved, plus a one hundred thousand dollar payment by Boston and the promise of another "player to be named later."

Moss didn't live up to his billing. At the end of the season, the Red Sox still owed the Browns a player.

They gave them one — Les Moss.

First Team To Get Sixty-five Runs Wins

WHEN AMHERST AND WILLIAMS got together for the first college game on July 1, 1895, they agreed that victory would go to the first team scoring sixty-five runs.

Amherst reached that total in the top of the twenty-sixth inning and won, 66–32.

Up, Up, and Away Go Pro Football Profits

IF PRO FOOTBALL pioneers had started one of those financial wall charts to show the increase in franchise costs, the line would be through the ceiling and headed for the outer planets by now.

The 1920 membership fee in the original American Professional

Football Association (changed to the National Football League in 1922) was $100. The franchise fee went to $500 in 1925 (for admission of the New York Giants and Detroit), and on to $10,000 in 1933 for the entry costs of Philadelphia and Pittsburgh.

Now, of course, a franchise costs millions.

Yankees Had a Fine Time off the Field

IN ADDITION to unparalleled success on the field, the New York Yankees had a fine time off the field. In fact, the New Yorkers for years were record holders in monetary assessments dished out for delinquent behavior.

The record for the Yankees, and all professional baseball at that time, in freestyle fining on a mass scale was set in 1957, when Billy Martin's birthday party at the Copa Cobana night club turned into a thousand-dollar-a-plate dinner for Billy and four teammates. Rookie pitcher Johnny Kucks was let off with a five-hundred-dollar plaster, while thousand-dollar fines were levied upon Whitey Ford, Mickey Mantle, Hank Bauer, and Yogi Berra.

The birthday festivities included a brawl that resulted in a suit brought against Bauer for socking a patron. The charges were later dropped.

The birthday boy suffered more grievously than his exuberant mates. Within two weeks, Martin was exiled to the Kansas City Athletics.

The Yankees also set what was then the record for an individual fine when Manager Miller Huggins had five thousand dollars deducted from Babe Ruth's paycheck in 1925 for insubordination.

Ted Williams was fined a similar amount in 1956 because he chose the wrong place to spit. Spitting on the sidewalk would have cost him only five dollars. But Ted cut loose on the ball field as a gesture of contempt for the Boston clients who had been jeering him. Owner Tom Yawkey of the Red Sox levied the record-tying fine.

Manager's Trick Nabbed Curfew Breaker

IN THE OLD DAYS, most managers had to stay up late to catch players who might be violating the team curfew. When Ben Chapman managed the Phillies in the 1940s, he could retire early and still be sure of knowing which players were out past the deadline during spring training.

Chapman found that the night elevator operator at the club's hotel came on duty at midnight. Ben gave him a new baseball and suggested he have the players autograph it when they came aboard. The night owls couldn't very well deny the evidence of their own signatures when Chapman examined the liberally autographed ball and assessed fines the next day.

Heisman's Teams Literally Stunk

JOHN HEISMAN, for whom college football's prize individual trophy is named, had a long and distinguished career as a coach.

But he had stinking teams.

Heisman had a theory that hot water and soap were debilitating for football players, and he permitted his athletes only cold, soapless showers.

The Coach Also Was the Referee

REAVES PETERS, a former Big Eight Conference commissioner, began his salaried sports career as a coach and referee—in the same game.

Peters recalled his double-duty start in his first job at a Missouri high school in 1913. "I took my first football team over to Jefferson City," he said, "for our opening game. It was starting time, but I didn't see any officials. I called the Jeff City coach out and asked about it. 'Oh,' he said, 'they're already right on the field.' I took another look around. 'You and me,' he said. 'You'll referee and I'll umpire. Nobody else around here knows the rules.'

"So I officiated the first game I ever coached. Later I also had to referee several basketball games played by my team. There just weren't many qualified officials in those days."

Volleyball Cost Red Sox Williams as a Coach

TED WILLIAMS was against the idea of volleyball as a spring training game for baseball players — and it cost the Red Sox Ted's service as a batting coach.

Williams left the Boston camp in a huff early in 1967 training. He came out of the spring clubhouse in Winter Haven one morning and was greeted by the sight of two groups of Red Sox players playing volleyball. Ted wanted to know, in effect: "What kind of blankety-blank way is that to get a ball club ready for the season?"

Manager Dick Williams said he thought it was a pretty good way. The suggestion was made that, if Ted didn't care for the way the Red Sox were being trained, he didn't have to stay around watching it.

That was the last the Boston varsity saw of Ted.

Pitcher Intentionally Walked In Run

BASEBALL has records for almost everything, up to "most times resin bag squeezed by a left-handed pitcher on a Friday night" — but pre-meditated walks with runners on first and second are not among them. However, there was one case of caution that was even more extreme. The Giants once intentionally walked Bill Nicholson of the Cubs with the bases full.

It was in the eighth inning of the second game of a doubleheader in New York on July 23, 1944. Nicholson already had crashed four homers in the two games, giving him six in the last four contests.

The Giants purposely passed Nick even though the gift run cut their lead to 10–8. Manager Mel Ott left himself open to criticism when the Cubs followed with two more runs. Ott had his vindication, though, when the Giants came up with two in their next turn and won, 12–10.

When a Winner Wasn't Needed

HOLLIS (SLOPPY) THURSTON pitched twenty victories for the Chicago White Sox in 1924, even though his team finished in the cellar. This monument of success amid the ruins merited a raise, Sloppy figured. He wrote the management a long letter to that effect.

The White Sox replied with a telegram that didn't even use up the allotted ten words: "No raise. We would have finished last without you."

Referee Said Booing Helped Him Do a Better Job

THERE ARE basketball officials who insist that their concentration on the job at hand is so intense they are barely aware of the boos from the multitude.

Ben Bidwell confessed that he not only heard the booing, but welcomed it—if the outbursts didn't exceed three a game. "The booing was just about right tonight," said Bidwell, a veteran Big Eight official, after one whistle concert at Iowa State. "The fans had three good roars at me. I wouldn't want them booing me every few minutes, but I figure it's good for me to get it every now and then.

"Officials are only human. They need stimulation, just like the players. A good round of boos starts the adrenalin pumping—speeds you up and makes you more alert."

Same School, Three Different Names

DUANE JOSEPHSON, who was a catcher with the White Sox and Red Sox from 1965 to 1972, listed three names under "colleges and universities attended"—but they're all the same institution.

The New Hampton, Iowa, native began at Iowa State Teachers College and was an underclassman when the title was changed to State College of Iowa. He signed with the White Sox in 1964 and baseball, both summer and winter, delayed completion of work on his degree until the school was renamed Northern Iowa University.

How To Handle Alibi Ike

ROOKIES who haven't made the grade usually protest, alibi, or complain they weren't given enough of a chance when they become victims of cutdown time in the big leagues.

When Branch Rickey was general manager, first of the Cardinals, later of the Dodgers and Pirates, he liked the rookie who took the demotion hard, then blinked back a tear, gritted his teeth, and vowed to return. So it was that Rickey never forgave Gus Bell his indifference.

142

Rickey told Gus one spring the Pirates were farming him out to Hollywood. Bell shrugged. "Aren't you going to complain?" Rickey demanded. Gus shrugged again. "Would it help?" he asked softly. "You're the boss."

The next winter, Rickey traded Bell to Cincinnati for such ciphers as Joe Rossie, Cal Abrams, and Gail Henley. Gus became one of the strongest hitters in the majors.

*   *   *

Managers know how to handle the Alibi Ikes — and have known how for at least one hundred years.

Lee Allen, who was curator of the Baseball Hall of Fame at Cooperstown, once sent me a story that he had copied from the *Cincinnati Enquirer* of August 10, 1884.

A number of years before, the story said, Manager Frank Bancroft of Worcester had given a trial one afternoon to a player named Barrett. Later, Barrett accosted the manager with: "I was a little off this afternoon, Mr. Bancroft."

"Yes, and you'll be a damned sight further off tomorrow," said Bancroft, handing Barrett his release.

*   *   *

When Andy Cohen managed Denver of the Western League, he used to tell of his first spring tryout with the New York Giants of John McGraw. "I was having an awful time at second base in one of the early games," said Andy. "I lost a couple of pop flies and almost got hit by another one. "Finally I went over to Mr. McGraw and said: 'That's a terrible air current out there today, sir. Those whirlwinds make the ball do funny things.'

"Mr. McGraw said: 'Those aren't whirlwinds young man — those are trade winds. And you're going to Waco tomorrow.' "

*   *   *

Mike Kelley, a retired manager, was visiting the Cardinals' camp one spring when coach Tony Kaufmann was trying to show a smart alec rookie pitcher how to stand on the mound. The rookie was scornful of all advice. Exasperated, Kaufmann turned to Kelley and asked: "Isn't his right foot in the wrong place, Mike?"

"I'll say it is," said Kelley. "And so is his left. They both ought to be in Terre Haute."

*   *   *

Casey Stengel's worst season in baseball, until he met up with the Mets, came when he managed Toledo of the American Association in 1929. That was the summer before the market crash, and Casey couldn't get his last-place players to concentrate on baseball. All they could talk about was the killing they would make in stocks.

Stengel came into the clubhouse one day to find most of his players absorbed in the market pages.

"Buy Pennsylvania Railroad stock boys," Casey told them. "It ought to go up 'cause I'm going to be sending so many of you guys out of here on the Pennsy."

"Four Errors, and I'm Out of the Game

IN THE WANING DAYS of his brilliant career, Mickey Mantle was allowed to remove himself from exhibition games whenever he wanted to.

Before a spring training game one day, a reporter asked Mantle how long he intended to play. "Two at-bats," said Mickey, "or four errors, whichever comes first."

Righty Becomes a Left

THE ONLY major league pitcher to operate both as a right-hander and a left-hander was Anthony (Count) Mullane. He became a southpaw after his right arm conked out when he was with Detroit, then of the National League, in 1881.

Mullane had a 1–4 record that year on his way to a thirteen-year career mark of 287–214. He returned to his normal style when his right arm recovered in 1882. But, wearing no glove, he threw with either hand to pick off baserunners.

Book's Listing Goes Awry

ONE OF THE LARGEST dealers in sports publications, new and used, was Adco of Los Angeles. It once issued a catalog listing "fiction—all sports." One entry, among the baseball books, was *Catcher in the Rye* by J. D. Salinger.

Baseball's Temper Tantrum Champions

BASEBALL'S temper-tantrum-throwing championship should probably be shared equally by Lefty Grove, Wes Ferrell, Russ (Mad Monk) Meyer, Ted Williams, and Jim Gentile.

Grove, a Hall of Fame pitcher, used to rip his uniform to shreds and hurl benches about the clubhouse after a tough defeat.

Ferrell would rend not only his uniform, but also his glove. One day he came to the bench after being hit hard by the opposing team and started to tear apart his glove. The seams were tougher than usual and Wes couldn't rip them. So he sent the batboy to the clubhouse for a pair of scissors and cut the glove to bits.

Lefty Gomez, a pitching contemporary of Ferrell, was once asked if he considered Wes temperamental. "Yes," said Lefty, "he's temperamental all right—ninety-nine percent temper and one percent mental."

Grove and Ferrell escaped personal injury in their tantrums. So did Meyer as long as he stuck to his specialty of kicking clubhouse benches, a practice that earned him his "Mad Monk" nickname from Cub teammates. Once in 1949, though, Meyer couldn't wait until he reached the clubhouse to start kicking. After a home run flew off his delivery, Russ took a vicious kick at the rubber—and broke his ankle.

Williams used to throw his bat occasionally in disgust. Ted was never hurt in the process, but one time his bat skipped into the stands and struck a woman spectator in the head. The woman's injury was not serious, but the contrite Williams never threw his bat again.

Gentile hurled himself out of the big leagues in 1966. Jim first showed his displeasure over a called strike by raising his bat high over his head and smashing it down on the plate. Then, after walking away a few steps, he flipped the bat back at umpire Ed Vargo, barely missing him.

Until then, Gentile had been the Houston Astros' regular first baseman. Within an hour, Manager Grady Hatton had assigned Jim to Oklahoma City of the Pacific Coast League.

Rookie Stages One of the Longest Holdou

ONE OF THE LONGEST holdouts was by a player who never appeared in a big league game.

Frank Saucier was named "minor league player of the year" in 1950 after his .343 average led Texas League hitters. The year before, Saucier had hit .446 in a Class B league. Such credentials earned Saucier a tryout with the old St. Louis Browns. Frank didn't want it — unless the Browns were going to pay him what he thought he was worth. They weren't.

Saucier kept turning down contracts and the Browns finally suspended him on May 3. Finally, on July 20, he'd missed enough paydays. He modified his demands and signed up.

It was Saucier's first and last big league contract. The Browns used Frank in eighteen games. His batting average was .071. Saucier went back to the minors, never to rise again.

Gentry's Holdout Turned Out To Be a Lifetime O

A LOT OF PLAYERS have staged holdouts through spring training and early season games in salary disputes, but Rufe Gentry held out for an entire season. Gentry didn't think the Detroit Tigers showed enough financial appreciation for his rookie pitching record of twelve victories and fourteen defeats in 1944.

Rufe sat out the entire 1945 season, thus missing not only his salary, but also a winning World Series share. So Gentry signed the first contract the Tigers sent him for 1946. Thereupon, Rufe shot himself in both hands while cleaning his hunting rifle.

The wounds weren't serious, but they set him back so much in training that the Tigers sent him back to the minor leagues. Detroit brought him up for three more trials, but Rufe never won another big league game.

Duffy's Pants Problems

COACHES AND MANAGERS, who aim to show their charges that feared rivals are only human, have been quoted as saying: "They put their pants on one leg at a time, same as we do."

The late Duffy Daugherty, who was as much a comedian as he was a coach when he bossed Michigan State, once told reporters before a game with Minnesota: "We're going to do something different. We're going to pull on our pants two legs at a time." Duffy was reminded of this when the Spartans lost.

"We did it," he said. "Only some of the boys stuck both feet down the same pant leg."

Softball Ace Was a Bomb When He Tried Baseball

ONE OF THE MOST remarkable pitchers to face major league batters was Eddie Feigner. Who else ever whipped his arm around his back, letting a pitch go from the opposite side for a strike to Willie McCovey? Who else ever fanned Willie Mays on a pitch delivered between the pitcher's legs?

Other formidable big leaguers also were victims of futility against the man who made many Iowa tours during the summers of the 1960s and 1970s.

There was a catch to Feigner's pitching success. He was using his favorite weapon, the softball, and hurling it from the sport's shorter pitching distance — forty-six feet.

Feigner never publicly tried his softball-pitching style with the normal-sized hardball from the sixty-and-one-half foot distance. But one uncommonly good softball pitcher did. What's more, he did it in actual professional competition, in the Pacific Coast League. He was a horrible flop.

The distance adjustment might be easier for the strong-armed Feigner. Iowa witnesses saw Eddie serve strikes from near second base as part of his trickery in exhibition appearances around the state.

Feigner toured as The King and His Court. There were only three men in his court — a catcher, a first baseman and one fielder. That's all the support Eddie needed to win practically all his games.

When the late Fred Hutchinson was managing Seattle of the

Pacific Coast League in 1955, the city had a softball pitcher who had spun fifty-five no-hitters in ten years and was one of the nation's best. His name was Bob Fesler. In an exhibition before a Seattle-Sacramento game, Fesler pitched to eleven batters from the two clubs and struck out every one of them. He was throwing a softball from forty-six feet, and the hitters used softball bats. Even so, Hutchinson was so impressed that he signed Fesler to a contract to pitch for his Seattle club that was headed for the pennant.

Baseball's pitching delivery in the early years of the game was the same as softball's now. The ball had to be served underhanded with the arm closely parallel to the body. Fesler was the first to throw in that fashion in a pro game since baseball removed all restrictions from the serve.

There have been underhanded pitchers in the majors, but they didn't pitch with the straightforward action required in softball. They would reach farther out to the side and down.

Distance isn't the only adjustment a softball pitcher has to make in a switch to baseball. The rising effect in softball is aided by the delivery from flat ground. The launching pad in baseball was a mound then fifteen inches high. Fesler couldn't adjust. Control was his big problem. Bob made his first start against San Francisco. In two-thirds of an inning, he allowed five hits, five walks, made two wild pitches and a balk and was tagged for five runs. Fesler didn't improve in three subsequent efforts. He departed from pro baseball with a record of no victories and two defeats.

The Foibles and Chumps Departme

IN THE FOIBLES and chumps department of sports, there have been two classic accidents. Both happened in major league baseball and both were self-inflicted.

First of the involuntary masochists was Dick Williams, a Baltimore outfielder. Dick was loosening up for his turn at bat. He held the bat behind his back, one hand at each end as he flexed and twisted. All of a sudden — pop! — something pulled loose in one shoulder and Williams was out of action several weeks.

Then there was Earl Battey, the Minnesota catcher. In his haste to fling off his mask to pursue a foul, Earl missed the crossbar and jabbed a finger into his eye. He had to leave the game.

Newsom's Problems Were the Breaks of the Game

BOBO NEWSOM, the boisterous old pitcher, literally knew all about some of the breaks of the game. He once got in the way of a blind throw by Ossie Bluege after the Washington third baseman fielded a bunt in the third inning of the 1936 season opener against the Yankees.

Bobo refused to leave because, he said, "President Roosevelt came out to see ol' Bobo pitch." He finished up with a 1–0 victory, then had X-rays that showed his jaw was fractured.

When Newsom slipped back to the minors in 1949, he dashed to cover first base, saw he wasn't needed and veered off. An infielder's wild throw hit Bobo in the foot—two broken toes.

All told, Bobo shrugged off eleven fractures to pitch nineteen years in the majors.

Newsom, the contemporary who came closest to Dizzy Dean in loud confidence, was to have been a Cub rookie in 1932. During the winter, he wrote long, chummy letters to William Wrigley, owner of the Cubs, congratulating him on his perspicacity in buying Bobo, who would win the pennant for the Cubs, of course. Bobo didn't mention that many of the letters were written from a hospital where he was recovering from a broken leg suffered in an auto accident. A few days after his discharge from the hospital, Bobo went to a livestock auction. A mule kicked him in the leg and broke it again.

Bobo never made it with the Cubs, but seven other clubs got 211 victories from him.

Bobo admitted he had only himself to blame for the third fracture of his right leg, this time of the kneecap, in 1935. "I told Earl Averill," he recalled later, "that I was gonna strike him out on an outside pitch. He told me if I threw him an outside pitch, he'd hit it right back at me.

"He sure enough did—busted my kneecap and laid me up for five weeks."

Football's Skin Game

ONLY THE MORE mature football buffs can remember when the moleskins and the pigskins were tucked away after Thanksgiving Day, except by the two college teams that were going to extend the season clear up to January 1 in the Rose Bowl.

Moleskins? Pigskins? Maybe even the newcomers to old age can recall when these were still familiar words in the sports section; when football teams were still elevens, just as basketball clubs were fives or quintets. "Moleskin" was a twilled fabric long used for football pants. It had become the generic term for the entire uniform as in: "Well, it's time to put the ol' moleskins in the mothballs till next September."

Yeah, September. Even the pros of the 1920s didn't think of getting out the pigskin to start training until the end of August.

The pigskin was the football. And that was a slander to the bovine population, which had been sacrificing its hides for years to provide autumn toys for the youth of America. Even in the 1890s, sporting goods companies were advertising that their footballs were made of "genuine cowhide"—and they have been ever since.

Nobody seems to know how the pigs managed to hog the football publicity.

Basketball Has Become a Mighty Different Gar

THERE OUGHT TO BE a special section in the tournament records for preps who had to operate under the restraint of the old basketball rules. It has become a different game in the last eighty-five years. Scoring has more than doubled since the era of the center jump (after each basket) and the standard two-hand shot. And the basketball was bigger than the one used now.

The game opened up after the tipoff after goals was done away with. The one-handed jump shot and the use of the fast break opened it even more.

Today's Iowa preps are better shooters, better trained, faster and more skillful all around. Still, there ought to be permanent recognition for old-timers such as a youngster named Kline (early sportswriters never bothered with first names), who scored thirty points for Clinton in a 46–28 state tournament victory over Fort Dodge in 1915; Dick Davis of Ottumwa, who whipped in twenty-three points in the 38–20 championship triumph over Spirit Lake in 1928; Marcellus (Mike) McMichael, a fourteen-year-old Des Moines Roosevelt freshman when he set a full-tournament record of fifty-eight points in 1931, twenty-eight in one game; Elmer Bratton of Waterloo West with a fifty-seven-point total in 1934. Kline's one-game record stood until

Ray Fontana counted thirty-six for Ankeny in a 1950 game. Davis's high for a title contest also lasted until 1950, when Ed Lindsey hit twenty-five for Davenport.

The one-man shows by McMichael and Bratton add luster when you consider that Mike accounted for 58 of Roosevelt's 119 points, Bratton for 57 of West's 112.

Winning teams in 1941 averaged twenty-six points a game. In 1934, the average was only twenty-eight.

Pitcher Earned His Pay That Day

THE LATE PAT MALONE got far more than he bargained for that day in 1926 when he pitched both games of a doubleheader for the Des Moines Western Leaguers, then known by the euphonious and popular nickname of "Demons."

The first half of Malone's task was a simple one as he shut out St. Joseph in nine innings, 4–0. The last half became comparable to one of the labors of Hercules. Pat, later one of the Chicago Cubs' better pitchers, stuck doggedly to his work through fourteen innings of the second game. Then, with the score tied at 4–4, he decided he had earned his day's pay.

A fellow named McClung took over for the weary Malone, blanked St. Joseph for four innings and became the winner when Fritz Knothe smacked a homer with two out in the last of the eighteenth.

Was It Acting — or Classic Comedy?

WHEN ATHLETES CAPITALIZE on their celebrity as part-time actors nowadays, they have the advantage of hamming it up on television or in the movies. The advantage lies in retakes to correct any flubs before exposure to the public. That may purify the art, but also nullifies the chance of classic comedy presented when athletes played their parts live on the stage.

Cap Anson, Iowa's baseball great of the late nineteenth century, and Jack Dempsey didn't foul up their stage roles. But they suffered embarrassment because supporting actors from the sports world did.

When Dempsey was world prizefighting champion, he married actress Estelle Taylor. She persuaded him to co-star with her in a new play called *The Big Fight*. Novice actor Dempsey was paid one thousand dollars a week, Estelle three hundred dollars.

Jack's opponent in the big fight scene was Ralph Smith, a pro fighter who was almost seven feet tall and weighed 280 pounds. "The script," Dempsey once recalled, "called for Smith to take a dive in the first round. He'd go down for the count shaking the stage and the scenery. He did it so well, the audience thought I had knocked him out for real."

Came a night in New Haven. Dempsey threw the "knockout" punch and stood back to watch another great performance of Ralph going into the tank. Instead, said Jack, "He hit me a right in the chin that made me cockeyed. Somebody had sense enought to ring the bell." Dempsey was able to stagger to his corner.

The scheduled one-round sham battle became two rounds, then three, then four. "I'd keep getting him in a clinch," said Dempsey, "and tell him: 'Hey, you bum, go down. You're ruining the show. If you don't go down, I'm going to flatten you for real.' But he kept hitting back. In the fifth round, I had to do it. I hooked him in the belly. When he doubled over, I hit him on the side of the head with a right. Down he went, just like he used to when he was acting. But this wasn't acting."

Dempsey raged at Smith in the dressing room afterwards. Rubbing his jaw, Smith said: "I'm sorry Jack. You hit me so hard in the first round, I didn't know what I was doing from then on."

The integrity of an umpire was the undoing of Anson when he was the star of a New York production titled *The Runaway Colt*. The climax of the play was a baseball scene with Anson as the batter. The game was tied with two out in the bottom of the ninth.

Cap would swat the ball into the wings. Then he would race off to the wings at the right of the stage, obviously headed for first base. Moments later, he would appear from the wings at the left, thundering for home. A ball would be tossed from offstage to the catcher and he'd take a swipe at the sliding Anson. Then, dramatically, the umpire would bellow: "You're safe!" and the final curtain would descend.

The most colorful National League umpire of the era was Tim Hurst. Anson thought Tim would be just the man for the stage role of the umpire. Hurst agreed to give the part a try for one night. His first performance was also his last, memorable as it was.

Ira L. Smith and H. Allen Smith describe it in their book, *Low and Inside*: "As hero Anson came sliding into the plate on the stage, umpire Hurst bent forward tensely, saw the ball arrive, saw the actor catcher slap it on the runner, and just as the curtain started to come down, he cried: 'YER OUT!' "

He Didn't Have a Prayer with the Umpire

THE SMALL WONDER of college football was Centre of Danville, Kentucky, which had fewer than three hundred students and a team, known as the Praying Colonels, that cut a swath through major opposition in 1919–1922. The coach of these phenoms was Uncle Charlie Moran, who became a baseball umpire in the National League.

Fresco Thompson, later a vice-president of the Dodgers, once recalled the time he brought Moran's football backgound into a debate and lost on religious issues.

As a player for the Phillies, Thompson was called out by Moran on a close play. In the course of a discussion concerning the umpire's eyesight, Fresco suddenly asked Uncle Charlie: "Say, didn't you used to be a football coach?"

Moran gave Thompson the opening he wanted. "Yes, sir," Uncle Charlie said proudly, "I was coach of the famous Praying Colonels."

"What were they praying for?" asked Thompson. "A new coach?"

Fresco says he was "just congratulating myself on the perfect squelch, but I might have known there's no argument with an umpire. Uncle Charlie gave me the piercing eye," Fresco finished, "and then he said: 'Young man, since you've turned this conversation into religious channels, suppose you go to the clubhouse and baptize yourself with an early shower.' "

There's a Gorilla on the Green

The World's Strangest Golf Tournamer

THERE WAS NO golf tournament more noisy, more zany, more nerve-twanging than the "Chinese Open" during the 1950s and '60s at the Clover Hills course in West Des Moines. The same adjectives applied to Frank Donovan, the puckish owner-pro of the course.

Golf is a game of such extreme concentration that, by tradition, tournaments are conducted in cathedral silence. A whisper in the gallery around the green is a sin comparable to firing a gun in church.

Iconoclast Donovan wasn't content merely to fire guns. One year he had two-stage aerial bombs set off every fifteen minutes or so.

Competitors knew from experience they were going to be harrassed by loud band music and such things as a character in a gorilla suit hopping out from behind bushes. They knew they'd be distracted by pretty girls in Chinese costumes or pretty girls in scant garb doing the twist. Yet they filled the entry list to capacity every year.

Half the field was still on the course late in one tournament when Mother Nature did the twist—something close enough to a tornado that nobody cared to argue about any distinction. A huge double willow was uprooted and dozens of tree limbs were blown down against an ominous copper background jagged with lightning.

Golfers hurled themselves full-length on the turf to keep from being blown over. Said one: "If this is part of Donovan's show, I think he's going a little too far."

Donovan, the old mandarin, was once a victim of his own pyro-technics at his carnival shortly after the Chinese Nationalist flag was run up. Frank, who delighted in diabolical devices for disturbing others, had hired a band to play at inappropriate times. The leader was instructed to strike up with quaint old Chinese twist music — or anything shockingly loud. The leader's timing was excellent. He usu-ally selected a moment when a golfer was teeing off, or poised to putt on the nearby third green. Steel nerves turned to spaghetti under the sonic impact.

Donovan, who always competed in his own meet, was among the early starters. He was doing pretty well until he neared the third green. When Frank concentrated on his approach, the musicians blasted out with "The Colonel Bogey March." Donovan overshot the green.

The band played on. Frank overshot the green the other way. There was no surcease until the old mandarin got down in six. He withdrew after nine holes.

The aerial bombs were such a success that neighbors around the nine-hole course were calling the police department all day to find out where the dynamiting was in progress.

"I went over to this place to see about the fireworks," Frank once recalled, with a twinkle in his eye. "The fellow who came to wait on me had only two fingers on one hand, and I said, 'Obviously, you're the man I want to see.' "

The more sadistic spectators always collected around the fifth green. The aerial bombs were set off behind nearby bushes. The bomb man's timing was superb, too. He nearly always managed to get the first boom just as a golfer began his putting stroke. Solid flesh be-came a quivering mass of jelly and jerky putts jumped past the hole.

As for the name of the tournament, Donovan explained: "It was an old golf gag. You'd ask a fellow if he'd ever won a tournament and if he hadn't, he'd say, 'Yeah, the Chinese Open.' That was the most unlikely tournament he could think of." It's still unlikely.

The Man Who Got Golf off the Society Pages

YOU WOULDN'T, of course, think of looking in the society pages for stories about the Iowa Amateur Golf Tournament or about the Masters. But there was a time—a long time ago—in the early history of golf in the United States when the activity was considered merely a social pastime and even the larger tournaments didn't make the sports section.

The man who did most to popularize the sport for the masses was Francis Ouimet who, as a former caddie, won the U.S. Open from Britain's dominating golfers at Boston in 1913. Ouimet soon gained the reputation as "the man who took golf off the society pages."

Si Burick, sports editor of the *Dayton Daily News,* once recalled a visit by Ouimet to Dayton in 1933 for a friendly round with the late James M. Cox, former governor of Ohio.

The sportswriter who covered the event began his story with something like: "Francis Ouimet, who took golf off the society pages and put it in the sports section. . . ."

The reporter, Burick said, turned confidently to the sports pages next morning to look over his story. No sign of it there. He began whisking through the rest of the paper.

"He found it, all right," said Burick. "It appeared on—I'm sure you guessed it—the society page."

Golf in Iowa in the Gay Nineties

Harper's Official Golf Guide for 1901 isn't the type of book most people would select to settle down with for an evening of reading. It's rather on the dull side, but it contains some facts about Iowa golf of 1900 that demonstrate the progress of the sport in this state.

Iowa boasted only twenty golf courses—none over nine holes—in those days, yet ranked twelfth among the forty-seven states that presented facilities for mashie-wielders. (Yep, they had mashies then.)

Idaho was the only state without a course, but Arizona, Arkansas, Delaware, Louisiana, Mississippi, Nevada, New Mexico, Oklahoma, Oregon, South Dakota, Utah, and Wyoming had only one or two each. Sixty-five percent of the clubs were in the East. New York alone had 164 and Massachusetts 158.

The Des Moines Golf and Country Club and the Golf Club at Alton, a village in Plymouth county, were the link pioneers in Iowa. Each was organized in 1897.

Officers of Des Moines's only golf association in 1901 were George F. Henry, president; E. C. Finkbine, vice president; George I.

Gilbert, secretary; Frank P. Flynn, treasurer; and Kirk E. Jewett, captain.

Clubs organized in the state from 1897 to 1900 were at Boone, Burlington, Cedar Rapids, Clinton, Davenport, Dubuque, Emmetsburg, Fort Dodge, Fort Madison, Independence, Iowa City, Keokuk, Le Mars, Marshalltown, Middlesboro (which isn't even listed in the gazetteers now), Muscatine, Primghar, and Sioux City.

Highest entrance fee was the twenty-five dollars elicited by Des Moines G. and C. Club, which also had the peak total of 125 members, while others ranged from one to ten dollars. Annual dues ran from one dollar at Alton and two dollars at Des Moines up to fifteen dollars at Boone and Marshalltown.

Harper's Official Golf Guide for 1901 contains no pictures of Iowa golfers, but we assume they dressed much in the fantastic manner of the champions whose photographs are presented.

Peering down at the ball over the generous foliage of his mustache, Harry Vardon is depicted in the middle of his back swing. Vardon won the 1900 National Open championship with rounds of 79, 78, 76, and 80 at the Chicago Golf Club and received the handsome emoluments of a gold medal and one hundred fifty dollars.

Although Vardon, also the British champ, is pictured against a summer background, he is wearing enough bulky clothes to keep a Fiji islander warm in the Arctic. His woolen socks fit with nary a wrinkle to his knees, but his plus-fours sag like a pair of gunny sacks and his coat looks like a lap robe hastily tucked around his shoulders. His cap resembles a slightly melted phonograph record.

The men didn't seem to put much premium on comfort and freedom of movement in those days. Nor did the women. Miss Frances C. Griscom, 1900 national womens' champion, is shown actually swinging a golf club despite the handicap of some sixteen yards of clothing. The force of her swing has twisted the voluminous skirt around her chassis like bunting around a flag pole, revealing a dainty ankle. Her garment would provide enough material to garb eighteen women golfers of today.

Harper's Official Golf Guide for 1901 "glossary of technical terms employed in the game of golf" would befuddle the modern generation of linksmen. The term *bogey* meant par then and was defined thus: "Usually given to the title of Colonel, a phantom who is credited with a certain score for each hole, against which score each player is competing." This was the first known mention of "the little man who wasn't there."

The glossary also points out, with a hint of sarcasm it would seem, that the course is "that portion of the links on which the game ought to be played, generally bounded on either side by rough ground or other hazard."

Here are some other definitions that mean little — or something else — today:

Baffy — A wooden club to play lofting shots.

Cup — A small hole in the course, usually one made by the stroke of some previous player.

Draw — To drive widely to the left (identical in its results with "hook" and "screw").

Gobble — A rapid, straight putt into the hole such that, had the ball not gone in, it would have gone some distance beyond.

Like-as-we-lie — When both sides have played the same number of strokes.

Made — A player, or his ball, is said to be "made" when his ball is sufficiently near the hole to be played on the putting green next shot.

Play-club — A wooden-headed club, with full-length shaft, more or less supple; with it the ball can be driven to the greatest distance. It should be used when the ball lies well.

Grab a Broom If You Want To Improve Your Golf Swing

ANY OF YOU past-forty golfers want to get in some indoor conditioning? All right, go get a broom.

The broom is recommended as an exercising device before the golfer works up to a garden rake. It is supposed to be swung vigorously to put strength and snap in the ol' wrists.

Neglect of conditioning the hands and wrists is the worst thing that can happen to past-forty golfers, according to Paul Runyun, a former PGA champion. Runyun said the simple exercises with broom and rake "are not strenuous. They do not tax the heart." And they enabled him "to hit the ball harder than I ever did before."

Swing the broom for a few days, Runyun said, then switch to the garden rake: "By using it for no more than two or three minutes a night just before going to bed you can prevent your hands from losing their strength and snap during long periods when you are not playing and you can also add considerably to the flexibility and the quickness of the hands."

Some inconsiderate spouses are bound to object to having a six-foot rake swung in a full and furious arc inside the house. And how's the senior golfer going to explain to the neighbors if seen standing in a half-foot of snow and swinging a rake?

The person more concerned with dignity than par probably will resort to weighted golf clubs, which can be used in the privacy of garage or basement. But these, said Runyun, "are not heavy enough to give your arms and hands the stretching and strengthening produced by a rake. Rakes are also stiffer to swing; with them, the hands and arms must do all the work, because there is no 'give' to the shafts as there is with a weighted club," he said.

There's Too Much Reading in Golf

IF YOU'RE AN AVERAGE GOLFER, your trouble is that you "let the game scare you."

"Too many golfers," said former golfing great Juan (Chi Chi) Rodriguez, "read too many books and try to go out and do exactly what the words say. That is a mistake." Books can be helpful, said Chi Chi, "but only as a general guide." He suggested experimentation with different grips and stances.

The important thing, he said, is to "feel natural. . . . From experience I recommend only what is most comfortable. . . . It took me years—thirteen to be exact—before I came up with the right grip (overlapping rather than interlocking)."

Although the Puerto Rican pixie weighed only 120 pounds in his prime, Chi Chi was able to consistently outdrive such power pros as Arnold Palmer and Jack Nicklaus when he was a fixture on the PGA tours of the 1960s and '70s.

The secret, said Chi Chi, was to do almost everything wrong. "My swing may not be picture-pretty, but it enables me to coil enormous power in my body. . . . It is a swing that confounds the purists because most of the things I do are wrong. But I still get results, my own way."

It is all right to swing and sway with Sammy Kaye, but the sway is the most damaging thing of all to the golf swing, said Chi Chi.

His main secret is to keep the left side of the body perpendicular during the swing, as though pressed against an invisible wall.

You also have to remember, if you're smallish, that you must pigeon-toe your way to birdies. "I admit my left foot is in a very unusual position," said Rodriguez, "because I point it one-half turn to the right. It appears that I am pigeon-toed when I do this. . . . Because of my very hard downswing, my left foot has to serve as a brace. It keeps me from losing my balance and actually falling."

Most Golfers Win by Cheating

REMEMBER THE LAST TIME you played golf and you suspected that all the other members of your foursome were cheating?

Well, they might have been, according to an investigation by *Golf Magazine,* which once set out to discover why golfers cheat. Its editors consulted two psychiatrists, a clinical psychologist, and two psychotherapists in New York. The key words in the head-shrinkers' analysis: status, vanity, security.

That low golf score, said the doctors, is a status symbol, both athletically and socially.

Some golfers, psychologist Milton V. Kline said, have a neurotic need to win, by fair means or foul, because of a feeling of inadequacy and general insecurity.

Then there's the breed of golf phony, said Dr. Fredric Werthman, who actually doesn't realize he's breaking the rules. "He's so intent upon winning that a corner of his mind actually believes he's doing the right thing. When challenged, he will hotly deny any wrongdoing and walk off utterly convinced that it's his opponent, not himself, who is trying to gain an unfair advantage."

So how are you going to better your score if you don't kick your ball out of the underbrush, replace your ball closer to the cup, pull up a tuft of grass, or conveniently forget a score here and there? Here's the way the magazine's editors summed up the doctors' conclusions:

> If you (by cheating) shoot in the low, but undeserved, eighties or thereabouts, you're lulled into believing you're a good deal better than you really are.
> Hence you won't concentrate on any weakness you might have. You simply aren't aware that you have any.

But if you keep an accurate account of your game without mercy or deception, you will see yourself in your true light.

If you're really serious about the game, you'll get mad. Then you'll get to work on the trouble spots.

Pretty soon, you'll be able to save strokes legitimately.

How Would You Like Your Foe To Hit Your Golf Ball Back?

HOW WOULD YOU LIKE to club a screaming drive 330 yards down the middle of the fairway—and have an opponent sock it back toward the tee, possibly into the tallest rough or a bosky dell?

It would be a real Dutch treat for a golfer who is getting whomped to be able to whack a tormentor's ball back away from the hole. Alas, you can't do it without being penalized, criticized, and maybe ostracized.

Yet there was once a legal Dutch treat, a feature of the original game of golf in Holland. That was when golf was just like most of the other popular sports: one ball, or some such missile, with one side trying to advance it in one direction and the other side trying to thrust it in the other direction.

A good way to get in Dutch with a Scotsman is to suggest that his royal and ancient pastime was originated by Hollanders. The Scots and the Dutch for years have been issuing claims and counterclaims over the invention of the game now played by millions throughout the world.

There are holes in the Scots' argument. That's what the whole (or hole) debate comes down to. The authorities of the *Encyclopedia Britannica* and various sports tomes agree that the Scots, while borrowing the tools and the terms of the Dutch, devised the game we know today. They did it by making a hole the goal, rather than a church or some other landmark, then they put in a whole series of holes back around 1500.

Another feature of the early Scottish game was a ball for each player. This no doubt took away some of the danger, but it also removed the excitement of the defense hitting back.

The Dutch soon adopted the holes and the more genteel Scottish rules. But their hit-back form of golf kept going strong for at least a couple of centuries. *Kolven,* they called it, or *kolf,* meaning club, so the Dutch can at least claim the name of the game. They also invented the tee and the name of that exasperating process known as putting.

The mound of sand or snow (hardy golfers, those Dutch) used to set up the ball was called a *tuitje,* (pronounced toytee). And once the Hollanders put holes around the playground, they called them "puts."

The only one who seems to dispute the Dutch origin of the name of golf is a gatherer of the game's tall tales and short trivia, Fred Beck. Beck, in his book *89 Years in a Sandtrap,* says golf has been defined as a "game that entails flogging a ball with a club or a flogger."

And: "At one time the game was called *flog,* until someone noticed that it looked better spelled backward."

The definitive book on the origin of ball games is Robert W. Henderson's *Ball, Bat and Bishop.* Henderson wrote:

> It was not until about 1700, that we have a detailed account of kolven as played in Holland.
>
> It was a cross-country game. . . . Two sides opposed one another, playing with the same ball. The attacking side selected a distant mark a mile or more away, usually the door of a church or a marketplace cross.
>
> The attacking side had to declare that it could drive the ball with its clubs in a certain number of strokes to the selected mark. They started the game with three strokes in succession, after which the defending side took one stroke.
>
> The chosen defender would smack the ball back toward the start, endeavoring to drive it into as difficult a "bunker" as might be within reach.

The Golf Balls Are Red and the Greens Are Black

IF THE HEAT of the golf course gets you down during the warm summer months, think of what it would be like to play golf in Saudi Arabia. American oil workers there have laid out a course near Dhahran — and they must be the grittiest in the world.

The entire course is sand. The "greens" are black (oil is poured on to pack the sand), and the golf balls are red because white ones aren't easily detected in the desert.

The golfers don't have to worry about hitting trees — there aren't any. And temperatures sizzle above 120 degrees in the sun.

Mom Was Upset because Musial Wouldn't Wear His Uniform

Stan Was the Only General Manager Assigned a Uniform

STAN MUSIAL was the only general manager in the big leagues assigned a uniform for spring training. He wore it just once, which was a disappointment to his mother back in Donora, Pennsylvania. "Mother thought I was going to play the whole season," said the man who was the most popular player St. Louis ever had until he took his bushels of records into retirement after the 1963 campaign.

Even then, Musial was far beyond the normal quitting age for active players. "But I guess," said Stan, "that mother didn't realize I retired voluntarily. She must have thought I'd been fired."

When Bob Howsam resigned as the Cardinals' general manager to take a similar job at Cincinnati, Musial was appointed his successor. "I called mother to tell her about the promotion," said Stan. "The first thing she asked was whether that made me the boss over the manager, too. I told her yes, I guessed it did. And she said: 'Oh good. Does that mean you can put yourself back on the active list and play again?' "

The Cubs Turned Down Roger Maris because He Was "Too Small"

OWEN MARTINEZ was quartered in Des Moines as a Chicago Cub scout and was exploring the Dakota frontier one time in the 1950s when he chanced to see a kid named Roger Maris whiplash a couple of line drives in an amateur game in Fargo. Martinez had never heard of Maris and found that not many other scouts had either, except for Cy Slapnicka and Frank Fahey of the Cleveland Indians. They had offered to meet the kid's demand for a bonus — $5,000 for signing, $10,000 more when and if he reached the majors.

Martinez didn't have the authority to dangle bonus bait. He did receive permission to send the youngster into Chicago for a tryout.

Owen said he never knew who examined Roger at Wrigley Field, then turned him down as "too small."

Wid Matthews always swore he didn't know either. Wid was in charge of Cub player personnel then. "I was out of town when Maris came in," said Matthews. "I guess he wasn't impressive enough for anybody to report to me personally. We had several scouts working in the Chicago area then, and it was probably one of them that looked him over."

Maris received no payment from the Cubs, yet the tryout trip wasn't without profit for Rog.

Martinez said Maris didn't want to go to Chicago at first. "He said I either had to top Cleveland's offer right now or he wasn't interested.

"I had to go to Washington to scout some Basin League clubs. Almost as soon as I got there, Maris phoned me. He said he'd go to Chicago if the Cubs would give him round-trip plane tickets for himself, his mother and dad, and his brother. I told him O.K. and I saw that he got the tickets.

"I found out later that they cashed in the plane tickets and rode in and back on his dad's railroad pass."

Maris, of course, eventually signed with Cleveland, was later traded to Kansas City, then to the New York Yankees, where in 1961 he accomplished what no other human in major league baseball has — sixty-one homers in one season.

Maris died of cancer in 1985. He was only fifty-one.

Roger Maris, 1960

Rogers Hornsby

Hornsby Was Convinced He Was the Best Hitter Eve

ROGERS HORNSBY didn't care about turning away wrath, so he never bothered to give a soft answer—or a diplomatic one.

Hornsby had two firm convictions. (1) He was the best hitter who ever lived. "I *hit* for all my averages," he told me once. "Take away all the bunts and leg hits that Cobb got and I was way ahead of him." (Ty's career average was .367 to Hornsby's .358.); and (2) He should say what he felt at all times, regardless of whose feelings were wounded.

"Everybody said my ballplayers didn't like me," said Rog, who managed a dozen clubs in the majors and minors. "Well, that's right. I never asked the players to like me. All I asked of them was to give me a good day's work and play to win.

"I never saw anybody win a pennant with friendship. You don't make ballplayers by pampering them. I wasn't in any popularity contest. I was in there to win ball games," said Hornsby, who died in 1963 at the age of sixty-seven.

Baseball writers liked Hornsby because he neither sidestepped a question nor gave an indirect answer. Oh, there were times when he'd disregard a question if he thought it was trivial or if the answer were obvious. Then he'd fix you with those ice-blue eyes and growl: "That's a stupid blankety-blank question."

Frank Graham, a long-time New York sports columnist, was fond of recalling his first private chat with Hornsby after Rog, manager of the world champion St. Louis Cardinals the year before, was traded to the New York Giants for the 1927 season.

Edd Roush, a strong hitter, had refused to report for spring training. Graham asked Hornsby to tell him "off the record" what he thought of the Giant outfield situation with Roush missing. "I don't talk off the record," said Rog. "Anything I say you can put in the paper. If anybody doesn't like it, they can lump it.

"Now, I'll tell you what I think of the outfield. I think it stinks."

A transfusion of the milk of human kindness would have made Hornsby almost the ideal sports hero. Here was a bear-down competitor who didn't smoke, didn't drink, didn't go to night clubs—unless they served the best steaks in town. Even breakfast was incomplete for Rog if there wasn't a steak.

His dedication to the profession was so zealous that he wouldn't go to movies for fear they would damage his batting eye. For the same reason, he wouldn't read, except for a glance at box scores or averages. "No ballplayer can be at his best," Rog said, "unless he lays off the booze, eats a lot of steaks, and gets eleven hours of sleep a night."

Lefty Gomez: The Team Joker of the Yankees

LEFTY GOMEZ did more than his share to keep life with the New York Yankees from being monotonous in the 1930s, sometimes by sneaking in and nailing Tony Lazzeri's shoes to the clubhouse floor. This pastime didn't pall until Gomez went to his own locker one day and found evidence that Lazzeri had caught on. Lefty's expensive new slacks were shorts—cut off at the knees.

Old teammates of Gomez have said that rookie pitchers could always count on Lefty for help and advice. Lefty was willing to make an exception in the case of Johnny Broaca.

It was late in June of 1934. Gomez, on his way to a 26–5 record, and Red Ruffing, the other stalwart of the staff, were out shagging flies during batting practice with lesser pitchers.

"There was this new pitcher between us," said Lefty, "and I noticed he never threw the ball back to the infield. There were a lot of balls scattered around the outfield and I said, 'Hey, kid, how about helping us throw some of those in?' He tapped his right shoulder and said, 'No, sir. There are only so many pitches in this arm and I'm not going to waste any.' " Little did he know how many he was going to waste before the day was over.

Lefty soon learned that the new pitcher was Broaca, signed with much fanfare after his graduation from Yale. "McCarthy (Manager Joe) sent Broaca out with the bullpen brigade before the game started," said Gomez. "The bullpen was out of sight of the dugout and Joe always phoned out to give orders about warming up relief pitchers.

"Soon as the game started, I whispered to Red: 'Go stand this side of McCarthy so he can't see me.' Then I sneaked over to the phone. I disguised my voice and said: 'Warm up Broaca,' then hung up quick. I forgot who was pitching for us, but he pitched a shutout. Every inning, though, Red would go screen off McCarthy and I'd go to the phone — 'Warm up Broaca.' "

In the clubhouse afterward, McCarthy congratulated the winning pitcher, then turned to Broaca. "Joe said, 'The White Sox are coming in tomorrow, young man, and I'm going to start you against them,' " Lefty recalled. "And Broaca said, 'What! Why you had me warming up the whole darned game today. I'm worn out.'

"Red and I thought we were looking innocent, but McCarthy looked at me and then he looked at Red. 'Why, you so-and-sos,' he said. But he went into his office and we never heard any more about it."

Lefty also was inclined to talk more about the day he pounded four hits than he was about the days (189 of them) that he won big league games, or his six World Series victories without defeat. "It happened in Washington on opening day one year," said Gomez, "and it's a wonder it didn't bring a Senate investigation.

"I was such a miserable hitter that Babe Ruth had bet me $250 to $50 that I wouldn't get five hits all season. Here it was only opening day and I already had four. I was really needling the Babe.

"Well, do you know I was in thirty-some ball games that year. I never got another hit!"

Joe Medwick: The Wrong Man

JUST BEFORE he was inducted into baseball's Hall of Fame, Joe Medwick had the lesser honor of throwing out the first ball for the 1968 All-Star game in Houston. It was a triumphant return to a city where Joe Medwick was unknown, uninvited, and unwanted as a young outfielder in the St. Louis farm system in 1931.

The outfielder Houston wanted for its Texas League club was Mickey King, a nineteen-year-old slasher who had hit .419 for Scottsdale, Pennsylvania, of the Middle Atlantic League the year before. Fred Ankenman, then business manager of the Cards' plantation at Houston, was further enchanted by such King credentials as 22 homers and 100 runs batted in, achieved in just 75 games.

It turned out that Houston got both Medwick and King—in one compact package, five feet, ten inches high and 175 pounds on the hoof.

Ankenman later recalled that in the late winter of 1931, he sorted through his contracts and couldn't find one from Mickey King of Carteret, New Jersey. He did find one signed "Joseph Michael Medwick," a name he had never heard of. It took a call to the Cardinal front office for Ankenman to learn that Medwick and King were one and the same.

Medwick would have been happier if Houstonians hadn't come up with another name for him. They began calling him "Ducky Wucky."

Joe at first thought it was complimentary, if a little nauseating as in "everything is just ducky." But then he asked a young woman fan why she and her friends called him Ducky Wucky. "Why," she said, giving the impression that Joe was belaboring the obvious, "it's because you walk like a duck."

Medwick, who specialized in doubles as a Cardinal (including the one-year National League record of sixty-four), told the reason for his double identity as a fledgling pro.

"Mr. Rickey," said Joe, referring to Branch, then the Cards' general manager, "offered me a contract when I got out of high school. I honestly preferred football back then. I had some scholarship offers and I had just about made up my mind to take one of them. Mr. Rickey talked me into trying baseball that summer. He said I could play under the name of 'Mickey King' so my college eligibility wouldn't be in jeopardy."

That, Medwick hastened to explain, wasn't unusual in those days. "There wasn't an NCAA then," said Joe. "Quite a few college athletes played pro ball under assumed names."

Medwick's rookie .419 average helped influence him to forget college football. Two strong years at Houston qualified Joe for the St. Louis "Gas House Gang."

The Cards, led by such blithe spirits as Dizzy Dean and Pepper Martin, were always ready for a fight or a frolic. Sometimes, Medwick once recalled, the fights were intramural. "They said we were an explosive club," said Joe, "and I guess we were—and not just on the field."

Medwick told of a time in Pittsburgh when Dizzy was pitching and the Cardinals gave him a huge lead. "Typically," said Joe, "Diz began experimenting because he was so far ahead. The only trouble was, the Pirates were slamming his experimental stuff. They were running Terry Moore and me to death in the outfield. I came into the dugout—mad—and squirted a mouthful of water at Dizzy and said: 'Catch that, you big so-and-so.' Dizzy and Paul (the other pitching Dean) started for me. But I picked up my old brown bat and told them, 'O.K., you two keep coming and I'll break up this brother act right now.'

"They didn't keep coming," Joe added.

Dizzy Dean and His Grammatical Curve

DIZZY DEAN was the talkingest man who ever "flug" a fastball or a grammatical curve. His listeners either loved him, or couldn't stand him.

Some buffs, who wanted their baseball unadulterated, would turn off the sound whenever Diz replaced his ol' podnuh, Pee Wee Reese, for a turn on the play-by-play during the 1950s and early '60s. They didn't want to be distracted by Dizzy's spells of ignoring the game to talk about shooting doves, eating (especially them thar catfish and hush puppies), messages from friends, or country music, sometimes exemplified by Dean's own rendition of "The Wabash Cannonball." Yet it was these extracurricular touches that endeared Dizzy to another part of his audience.

English teachers and other purists deplored the colorful inaccurate grammar and pronunciations by Dean, who quit school at the end of the third grade, "because me and Paul (his brother) and Pa had to make a livin' choppin' cotton."

Others, including some of the upper intellectual strata, found Dizzy's carefree style a welcome relief from the careful diction and precise description by other announcers. They expected the unexpected from Dizzy, in the way of phraseology, and they got it in remarks such as:

"They had him th'owed out at third base, folks, but he slood in under the tag."

"Yogi struck out the last time on a disputed strike to the umpire."

"The infielders are going to their respectable positions."

"Look at them life this yere ball club's got."

"We've got a lot o' mail that will be answered as soon as we can get the answers to you."

Or, once when two runners wound up on the same base: "They're tagging each other out down there."

Sophistication cost Dizzy some of his charm in the closing years of his broadcasting career. His image as an ingenuously comical hillbilly was severely damaged during one of his last seasons of broadcasting when he spoke of hors d'oeuvres — and pronounced it correctly, or very nearly so.

Only occasionally did Diz, with obvious effort, say "slood" instead of "slid." He referred to what had been witnessed on "your screen" rather than his old: "You seen it on your camery."

Diz even learned the difference between respectable and respective — well, more or less.

In one of the last Yankee games Dean described for CBS, pitcher Tommy John hit a home run that gave the White Sox a lead. The camera stayed on Tommy after he touched the plate and Dizzy exclaimed: "There he is, going to his respective place in the dugout. He put the White Sox himself out in front."

The English Teachers Association of Missouri once complained to Dizzy's St. Louis radio employer that his mistreatment of the language was a bad influence on their pupils. Dean said at the time that "maybe I butcher up the English language a little. I allus regretted I never had no chance to get much schoolin'. But education is great and my advice to kids is to get as much of it as they can."

There were a lot of kids who would have settled for a formal education as limited as Dizzy's if they could have had the same financial rewards. On his way to baseball's Hall of Fame, Dizzy was the highest paid Cardinal in the 1930s, then became a $20,000-a-year radio announcer in 1941. His TV broadcasting, along with promotional work for a brewery, netted him $50,000 annually.

Sandy Koufax Could Have Been a Basketball Star

SANDY KOUFAX didn't have to start pitching pro baseball as early as he did to get himself a sports reputation. He could have made the headlines as a college basketball player. Sandy would have been a Cincinnati University regular as a sophomore in 1955–1956 if $14,000 hadn't got in the way. That was the size of the Dodger bonus that had more attraction for the Brooklyn youngster, then nineteen, than a basketball scholarship.

"Koufax was quick and clever in basketball," former Cincinnati Coach Ed Jucker once recalled. "He was only 6-2, but he was a good jumper and a fine shooter. Yes, I'm sure Sandy would have become a regular as a sophomore."

Jucker was Koufax's freshman coach in both basketball and baseball. He was among the first to recognize the potential of Sandy's lean left arm. Koufax had never pitched in high school. He was strictly a first baseman as a prep.

"There wasn't much doubt then," said Jucker, "that Sandy was going to be a great pitcher—when he mastered his control."

Actually, the Dodgers were lucky to sign Koufax—they almost lost him to the Milwaukee Braves. The Dodgers, then in Brooklyn, did their dickering with Sandy's father, an attorney, because the pitcher still was a minor. On a handshake, Al Campanis and the elder Koufax agreed upon the $14,000 bonus.

Before Koufax and the Dodgers got down to the formal contract-signing, however, the Braves came through with a much higher offer, reportedly around $35,000. Legally, Koufax's father could have accepted the Milwaukee bonus for Sandy—but he kept his word with the Dodgers.

Brotherly Pride in the DiMaggio Family

EDITOR'S NOTE: Bryson wrote the following column about the pride among the great DiMaggio brothers after attending the annual "Old-Timers' Game" at Yankee Stadium in July of 1966.

JOE DIMAGGIO was in the mainstream of the nostalgia that flowed through Yankee Stadium Saturday, the day of the "Old-Timers' Game," marking the silver anniversary of the first Yankee-Dodger World Series and Joe's fifty-six-game hitting streak. The fans, former teammates, and other players of the DiMaggio era had favorite memories of Joe's exploits in thirteen Yankee seasons (he missed three because of military service in World War II), ten World Series and

eleven All-Star games. Whatever it was that made the deepest impression on these folks, it undoubtedly was not the same one that Joe's brother Dominic remembers most vividly after all these years.

As a rival center fielder, playing for the Boston Red Sox, Dom opposed Joe in almost 200 American League games, was on the same side in five All-Star games, and watched him in the World Series. Yet Dom's proudest brotherly memory is of a day when Joe was a sixteen-year-old stripling and Dom was twelve.

There was a day this spring when Dominic, serving as a part-time instructor of Red Sox outfielders, and Joe had a reunion in baseball uniform. Joe was filling his annual springtime job as a Yankee batting teacher. The Red Sox and Yanks were meeting in an exhibition at Fort Lauderdale, Florida. The brothers posed for pictures and retreated to their respective dugouts.

That was when the question was asked of Dom: "What was the one performance by Joe that made the deepest impression on you?"

The expectation was, of course, that it would be the hitting streak, a vital World Series hit, a stupefying catch or throw, maybe even the three-time selection of Joe as the most valuable player. "It was," said Dominic without hesitation, "the day that Joe came out of the stands to play in the fastest semipro league in San Francisco."

Brotherly pride then was stirred in both Dominic and Joe by Tom, oldest of their siblings.

"What a hitter Tom was!" said Dom. "He didn't have the speed or the arm that Joe had and he wasn't as graceful — Tom was stocky. But he was as good a hitter as Joe, or just about. He could have been a big leaguer, too, if he'd tried pro ball. I guess he figured there was more security in operating a fishing boat."

Anyway, it was Tom that Dom and Joe went to admire in semipro action on that long ago day in Golden Gate Park.

"Two other teams were scheduled in the second game," said Dom, "but one of the teams was a man short. Somebody from our neighborhood suggested they use Joe." It was the first time Joe had played against full-grown men. "And they were good," said Dom. "There were a lot of ex-pros and future pros in that league. You could tell that the manager of the team Joe played for didn't expect much from a skinny kid like that. But Joe hit a double and a triple. That was really a thrill for me."

A year later, brother Vince, three years older than Joe, was a pro novice with the San Francisco Seals of the Pacific Coast League. The Seals ran short of players late in the season. Vince suggested seven-

Joe DiMaggio

teen-year-old Joe as a fill-in.

Joe appeared in only three games — as a shortstop. The next year, he was on his way with a .340 average that included a sixty-one-game hitting streak.

Over on the Yankee side Joe was asked about the day recalled so brightly by Dom. Joe shook his head: "I don't even remember it," he said. "But Dom's memory is very good, and I don't have any doubt it happened the way he said. He was at a very impressionable age then."

And how about Dom's recollection of the prowess of brother Tom? "I can remember that, all right," said Joe. "He was a fine hitter, but there wasn't much money in baseball then. Tom was the one who had to bring in the bread for the family. He couldn't risk leaving his fishing for the uncertainties of baseball."

Red Grange: There's Nothing New in Footba

EDITOR'S NOTE: Red Grange, University of Illinois football star, one of the premier players in the fledgling National Football League and later a TV sportscaster for the Chicago Bears, was a frequent visitor to Iowa. In this column, published in December of 1962, Bryson wrote about Grange's visit to Des Moines for a speaking engagement.

THE RED HAS GIVEN WAY to brown and silver in Harold E. Grange's wavy hair, but his tomato complexion still qualifies him for the nickname "Red."

Grange's face was redder than usual Wednesday, flushed with the effort of pushing his words past the tension of laryngitis. The usual gravelly voice known to television followers of the Chicago Bears was now a sandy whisper.

Red would have been readily forgiven for skipping a reception and dinner at Hotel Kirkwood, even for begging off his speaking engagement at the Dowling Club smoker a little later. Instead, he stood patiently at the reception and husked out answers to every question, serious or idle, flung his way. Red excused himself only for his second medical treatment of the day.

He could have cut his talk at the smoker to a few strained sentences and everyone would have understood. Rather, he spoke for forty-five minutes.

One of the questions was whether Grange had ever encountered Duke Slater, the old Iowa all-America tackle, in pro football. "Yes, I did," rasped Red, "and I never ran into a tougher player. Bronko Nagurski might have been tougher but, thank goodness, I always had Bronko on my side."

Grange paused to sip his throat lubricant. "That Slater was a guy who really put the foot in football—both feet, and two of the biggest ones I ever saw. If he couldn't stop you any other way, he'd stop you by stepping on your foot.

"Duke was playing with Rock Island and I was with the Bears. My brother Garland was at end for us and I got on him for not getting down on passes the way he should. 'I can't,' Garland said. 'That big Slater steps on my foot and pins me on the line of scrimmage.' "

Somebody asked Grange what he thought about the new *I* formation Southern California had begun using. "New?" Grange got out a strangled sort of chuckle. "We used the *I* formation at Wheaton (Illinois) High School in 1917."

Red sipped again and bystanders rubbed their own throats in sympathetic gestures. "Matter of fact," he grated, "I haven't seen a new offensive play in football for thirty years.

"The other day I was going through some old books in my attic and I ran across one written by Knute Rockne in 1919 and one by Bob Zuppke in 1920. They had practically all the plays that everybody is using now. There are only so many ways to hit, tackle, or go around end. It's the defense where the changes have been made. In my day we had only two defensive formations. Now the Bears have eight or ten, with variations of those. It's the same in college."

As expected, Grange spoke of the importance of players who are dedicated, earnest, and serious. "But it also helps," he said, "to have a fellow on the squad who can help relieve the tension.

"Earl Britton was the guy who kept us loose at Illinois. I remember when we played at Iowa in '23. Zuppke called a morning meeting at the hotel, but Britton didn't show up. Finally we found a bellboy who had seen Earl go up to the roof with a big pile of hotel stationery. He was making paper airplanes and sailing 'em down into the street. On each one, he had written 'to hell with Iowa.' "

No One Could Top Old Smoky

SMOKY BURGESS, who yielded to no big leaguer in fatness or friendliness, was telling one day why he didn't accept a promotion to Des Moines of the Western League in 1947. "It was because," he said earnestly, "the summers are too cool there."

There were three in Smoky's audience who laughed at this obvious jest. Two of us were native Iowans. Mace Brown of North English, then serving as Boston's pitching coach, had pitched a year in Des Moines en route to the majors. I claimed long, humid experience with Iowa summers.

Then there was Len Okrie, like Brown, a former Red Sox coach, who sweltered through many a Des Moines ball game when he was sent there from Fayetteville, North Carolina, after Burgess declined to suffer Iowa summertime chills.

Old Smoky was kidding, of course. Wasn't he? "Oh, no," said the all-round (in physical dimensions) catcher.

"Well actually," he amended, "I didn't expect it to be real cool in Des Moines, but I didn't think it would be as hot all the time as it was down in Fayetteville. I figured heat was the main thing I needed to limber up my shoulder. I'd smashed it up in a jeep accident when I was in the army in France in '45 and it bothered my throwing."

So it was Okrie who was promoted by the parent Cubs from Fayetteville of the Class B Tri-State League to Class A Des Moines.

Offensively, this was not good news to Des Moines. Okrie hit a cool .208 for the second-place Bruins, while Burgess kept flailing away toward a league-leading .387 at Fayetteville.

Defensively, though, it was a boon. Instead of the worst catcher in the league (Dick Kemper), Des Moines suddenly had the best. In fact, as a receiving technician, Okrie was the best Des Moines ever had.

"I couldn't have caught for Des Moines anyway," said Burgess. "I still couldn't throw, and other teams would have stolen me blind. I played in right field at Fayetteville because my arm would do the least damage there, and Len did the catching."

Smoky never did have to risk chilblains in Des Moines. In 1948, the Cubs judged him ready to skip an extra notch to Class AA Nashville. He vindicated them with a .386 average in the Southern Association. The next year, Burgess was all the way up with the Cubs for the first of eighteen major league seasons.

The pudgy catcher, his 5-8 chassis overloaded with somewhat more than 200 pounds, has outlasted most of the slim, trim, smoothly muscled men who look more like big leaguers than bartenders.

Few major league companions had more years toward pro baseball's lush pension than Burgess. Yet only an hour or two kept Smoky's career from being even longer. The Cubs were stricken with injuries early in their 1945 pennant-winning season and put in a hurry-up call for Burgess, who was in his second pro year at Portsmouth, Virginia, of the Piedmont League.

"The train was late," said Smoky, "and I didn't arrive in Chicago until that day's game was over. Then the Cubs found a couple of their players had healed quicker than expected and decided they didn't need me after all. So I went right back to the station and took a train to Portsmouth. A few days after that, I was in the army."

The Cubs later kept him only two years, but other clubs were happy to acquire his big bat: the Phils, Red, Pirates, and the Chicago White Sox, for whom he was an excellent pinch-hitter until he retired after the 1967 season.

Leo Durocher: The Mean Guy with All That Charm

EDITOR'S NOTE: In 1966, the Chicago Cubs hired Leo (The Lip) Durocher as manager in an effort to revive a team that had finished in the second division for two straight decades. One of the first things the Cubs did after signing Durocher was to send him and several of the Cubs' top players on a promotional trip in an effort to drum up some attention for a team that had been as interesting as watching a tree grow. Bryson attended one of these promotional news conferences and wrote the following story late in the winter of 1966.

LEO DUROCHER kept talking about what a mean guy he is, but all the while he belied it by keeping the charm, the courtesy, his all-round niceness turned on for reporters at Davenport. Only once was the new manager of the Cubs provoked to snappish retort.

A fuzz-cheeked reporter said that the Dodgers' success with the running game no doubt would be widely copied in the coming season. Would Leo subscribe to this new Dodger philosophy?

Durocher skewered the questioner with an icy stare. "Will I subscribe to the new Dodger philosophy?" Leo began gently, then swung his verbal whip in the heavy style that umpires used to know so well. "My dear young man, I established this philosophy for the Dodgers many years ago. I was more wide open and more daring than these present Dodgers ever think of being."

Durocher was not criticizing, he added, but: "If I had this present Dodger ball club, I'd run more than they do."

A busy bystander said that was all well and good, but it's the Cubs that Leo is managing, and would he turn them into a Dodger-type gang of runners?

"Oh, we'll run, all right," said Leo, resuming the glow of affability expected on a goodwill tour. "But we don't have to run to win — the Dodgers do. Take away Maury Wills and you take away their offense.

"Just look at that power over there," Leo waved toward the other side of the room where some of his players were deep in interviews, "Ernie Banks, Ron Santo, Billy Williams.

"Oh, and there's speed, too. Williams can run. Our two kids in the infield (Glenn Beckert and Don Kessinger) can fly. There's hardly anybody faster in baseball then Ty Cline, our new center fielder."

After Durocher and his bright-eyed players finished painting rainbows about the potential of the hitting, the running, the fielding, and the pitching, everybody wondered how the Cubs managed to stay buried in the second division in 1965 for the nineteenth straight time. Durocher could only suggest a reason. "Maybe they were lackadaisical. But that was prior to my time.

"I know the talent is here. And I think I'm going to find some of the type of ball players I like — the scratchers, the divers, the fighters. I want some mean players."

*   *   *

Leo wound up leading the Cubs to their greatest prosperity in two decades. Chicago finished tenth in his first season as manager in 1966, but the Cubs finished either second or third during the next five seasons — and furnished their fans with one of baseball's all-time great pennant chases when they dueled the New York Mets down to the wire for the 1969 National League pennant.

The Unsung Relatives behind the Heroes

1 0

Sports Became the Hub of the Podolaks' Lives

EDITOR'S NOTE: Bryson was as intrigued with the people surrounding sports stars as much as he was with the stars themselves. Sportswriters wrote hundreds of stories about Ed Podolak when he was a sophomore record-maker for Iowa's football forces in the mid-1960s and later when he was a junior and senior and then became a pro player.

The year Ed was embarking on his junior year at Iowa, Bryson drove down to southwestern Iowa to take a look at the role Ed's family played in helping this young man become a college star.

THERE WAS A DROUGHT in eastern Nebraska in 1940, and that's one of the best things that ever happened to University of Iowa football. The Hawkeye profit from that long-ago dry spell didn't become apparent until last fall, when Ed Podolak ran and passed for more yardage than any Iowa sophomore before him and was second only to Purdue all-American Bob Griese in Big Ten total offense.

That 1940 drought made jobs scarce around Dwight, Nebraska, where Joe Podolak's father had settled on a farm after immigrating from Czechoslovakia. Joe headed east for greener fields and found them near the small southwestern Iowa community of Atlantic. Employed as a farmhand, he also found his future wife, a comely teacher in a country school.

*Ed Podolak (right), with his parents and his sister
and brother, at home in 1967*

Their wedding plans were delayed because tall, broad-shouldered Joe went off to war for four years. They were married when he returned, gaunt from bouts with malaria in the Philippines.

Edward, the first of their three children, was born September 1, 1947. There was nothing in his heritage to hint that he would become an all-state prep in football and basketball. Or a college quarterback who, in the words of former Iowa assistant coach Dick Mansperger, "has a good chance to become a superstar."

Mrs. Podolak, née Pont, was an only child and "can't remember that my father was at all athletic."

Sports were totally foreign to Joe. "I didn't have any desire for athletics in high school," he says. "I wouldn't have been able to participate anyway because I was expected to get home right after school and help on the farm."

Yet sports were to become the hub of the lives of Mr. and Mrs. Joseph Podolak on their eighty-acre farm seven miles south of Atlantic. The two-story frame house, in a parklike setting, is where Mrs. Podolak was born. It's a comfortable, lived-in house.

Joe used to rent an additional 240 acres for farming, with the help of Ed and his younger — but bigger — brother, Charlie. Charlie, six feet, four inches and 200 pounds, is an eighteen-year-old freshman candidate for defensive end or tackle at Iowa.

Now the Podolaks don't even farm the home eighty. Sports were partly responsible.

"When the boys got up to where they were competing in athletics the year around," says Joe, "it got a little difficult for my wife and I to follow them and still be able to do all the farm chores. That's one reason I gave up farming and got a job with the county highway maintenance department five-and-a-half years ago. We rent our land now."

Mr. and Mrs. Podolak can hardly remember the time when their two-acre lawn wasn't used by the boys and their friends for whatever sport was in season. "You can see," said Joe, "that we've still got the swings and chinning bars I put up for them when they were small. They used to have a pole vaulting pit and a place to shoot baskets — their sister Betty was good at that. The yard has been a football field, a baseball field, and a place for track meets."

Betty is a sophomore at Atlantic High School, which she likes fine except for the fact it doesn't have girls' basketball. "I wanted to go to another school where they have it," she said, "but my folks wouldn't let me."

The boys, said Joe, always were good about doing their chores before beginning their fun and games. "Ed was a good farmer," he said. "He was active in 4–H Club work and raised some pigs of his own. One of them won the reserve championship at the country fair."

"They had to help me with the canning every summer, too," said Mrs. Podolak, who still raises much of the food she cooks and serves at a big table in the kitchen. When Eddie's quarterbacking measures up to her cooking, he'll be an all-American.

One of Mrs. Podolak's happiest days was Ed's sixteenth birthday. "That was because he could get his driver's license and my days of hauling were over," she said. "No longer did I have to wait until 6:30 or later to get home and start supper.

"There were hundreds of nights when I sat in the high school parking lot until after dark, waiting for Eddie—and later Charlie—to get through practice for football or basketball or track."

Mrs. Podolak returned to teaching eleven years ago, when Betty began kindergarten. "The school where I teach is in the Atlantic system, but is two miles north of town," she explained. "Rather than drive the nine miles home and then make a round-trip for the boys, I'd stay at school—correct papers and do other work—until it was time to pick them up. But it always seemed that I'd wind up with a wait in the parking lot. Then there was the hauling in the summer, too, for baseball. . . . But it was worth all the time and bother, all right."

Nor did Mrs. Podolak mind waking up to find that overnight guests had arrived after she retired and that she had extra breakfasts to prepare. "Friends of the boys would often stop over—two, four, maybe even six," she said. "We have plenty of extra beds and we like having young people around."

From this wholesome, folksy background comes the young man whose sophisticated skills give Iowa hope for better things this fall.

At the age of twenty, Podolak is beginning his eleventh year at quarterback. And in one of those years, he played regularly for the Atlantic sophomore team on Mondays and as a varsity reserve on Fridays. "Competitive football begins in the fifth grade at Atlantic," said Ed. "The coach let us play whatever positions we wanted and I guess I was the first to yell 'quarterback.' "

Podolak had to adjust to new passing and running techniques as a rollout quarterback in Ray Nagel's system last fall. But there was something even harder to get used to. "Losing," said Podolak, who experienced defeat eight times in ten games.

"The Atlantic football team was undefeated in my seasons as a regular," he said. "We only lost three games in my varsity basketball career. Before that, we had junior high and freshman-sophomore teams that nobody could touch."

The only thing that Ed calls himself "a fanatic" about besides sports is music.

"Listening, that is," he said. "I can't sing three consecutive notes, but"—and a grin brightened the pause—"I try."

"Pop music," he added, "does something for me. I'm a fanatic, especially about the Rolling Stones. Some people need alcohol or tobacco for their kicks, but I get mine from music like that."

184

The Wife Who Couldn't Bear
To See Her Husband's Team Play

EDITOR'S NOTE: The following column was written on February 19, 1968, while the University of Iowa's basketball team was in the midst of fighting for its first Big Ten championship in twelve years.

THERE'S ONLY ONE PERSON in the Iowa Fieldhouse, on the night of a home basketball game, who doesn't know whether the fortunes of the Hawkeyes in the second half are up, down, or hanging excruciatingly in the balance. That person doesn't know, won't let herself know. But that's no sign she doesn't care. Hardly anybody cares more than Jean Miller, the wife of Iowa's coach, Ralph.

In fact, she cares more than her emotions can bear as a witness of the last-half trials and tribulations of the Hawkeyes in their scramble for their first Big Ten championship since 1956. "The first half I can stand," says Jean, "without getting too wrought up. But I'd be a physical wreck if I sat through the second half."

Mrs. Lanny Van Eman, wife of one of Miller's assistants, had mentioned that Mrs. Miller always left her seat at courtside during halftime, never to return.

Mrs. Miller wasn't around at the time of this conversation. Ralph was. He was asked if he was aware that his wife wasn't present to observe his last-half strategy. "Oh, sure," said Ralph. "I know she leaves her seat and goes to my office. But I suspect she sneaks back out to the arena from time to time and peeks in to see how things are going."

"Oh, no I don't," Jean said later. "I don't want to know until it's all over. I don't listen to the radio, either."

Mrs. Van Eman had said that Mrs. Miller "probably can tell how the game is going by the roars of the crowd."

That theory also was dispelled, along with Ralph's suspicion that Jean peeks. After Michigan State made a few threatening gestures, the Hawkeyes reasserted their authority and were turning the game into a slaughter. It was 63–48 with a little over six minutes to go when I sought out the coach's wife under the mistaken impression that she might like to return to see the relaxing finish. Mrs. Miller's scene of seclusion was a contrast to the shrieking exuberance of the arena. There she sat, on a divan covered in green leather in her husband's office, holding a newspaper with steady hands and reading with apparent calm.

Ralph Miller, 1970

The door swung shut again. Not a murmur of sound seeped in from the hullabaloo of the arena. "You can go out and enjoy the game now," I suggested. "The Hawks have got 'em by fifteen points with six minutes left."

"Thanks," she said. "But I'll stay here. I've seen teams make up fifteen points in less time than that."

There was a later trip with the message that Michigan had knocked off Purdue, meaning that Iowa would be alone in first place.

"Yes, isn't that wonderful?" said Jean. "Ray Nagel (then Iowa's football coach) just stopped by to tell me that." But she didn't even ask if Michigan State was hurling a sudden late threat.

Ralph recalls the time that Jean drove from Wichita to Topeka to visit her brother so she wouldn't be tempted to watch an important game in Miller's coaching career.

Ralph was fighting for the Missouri Valley title then as Wichita's coach and the live telecast originated from Cincinnati. It was the famous game that Wichita apparently had won in the closing seconds, only to have the basket canceled after a long delay and an overtime ordered.

Jean learned that Wichita won in the extra period, then was able to enjoy a delayed telecast carried by a Topeka station. "Before the overtime started," said Ralph, "I naturally had a spirited debate with the officials. My brother-in-law told me that when Jean saw the scene on TV, she snapped: 'Oh, quit arguing, Ralph. You're going to win the game.' "

The President Made a Drunk a Hero

11

Reagan Movie Stretches the Fact

A MOVIE, sticky as a candied apple, about the life of Grover Cleveland Alexander has been showing up on TV screens a lot since Ronald Reagan became president, causing vintage baseball fans to wonder if the passing years have twisted their memories.

Old-timers were willing to accept a clean-cut Reagan as an image of the rough-cut old pitcher whose rampant sandy locks always made him look as though he'd just got out of bed. They even tolerated the agitation and grimaces by Reagan, onetime radio sports spieler in Des Moines, as part of any actor's license. They knew, though, that gallons of antifreeze had never thawed out the ice in Alexander's nerves. Alex, who was mostly called "Old Pete," except in the movie, never betrayed an emotional worry in his life, sober or otherwise.

But when Hollywood tinkered with baseball history, that's when the old-timers began writhing.

Alexander, who had won the sixth game for the Cardinals the day before, shambled out of the bullpen to strike out the Yankees' Tony Lazzeri with the bases full and two away in the seventh inning of the final game of the 1928 World Series. Sportswriters later voted this the most dramatic baseball incident of the first fifty years of this century.

Still, it wasn't dramatic enough for Hollywood. The film had Alex fanning an unidentified Yankee for the championship out as the pitcher gallantly fought off some unidentified type of seizure. Historically, that last Yankee was Babe Ruth, who was walked and was caught trying to steal second for the final out.

The screen dripped with pathos when mean old Joe McCarthy fired Alex early in the 1926 season. The Cub manager mistook a blackout from illness for drunkenness.

Nobody in pro baseball (Hollywood version) wanted anything to do with the thirty-nine-year-old bum, who had a 3–3 record at the time after a 15–11 record in 1925 for a last-place club.

Alex couldn't face his sickeningly valiant wife. He ran away and joined the House of David, a bearded team in Benton Harbor, Michigan, at twenty dollars a game. The David manager also got the impression that Alex was a drunk and canned him.

Next scene: Alex brokenly recalling his exploits in a lecture before hecklers at a flea circus, where his sweet little wife (Doris Day, no less) tracks him down. Ever faithful, she has persuaded Frank Lovejoy, an unbelievably sweet Rogers Hornsby, to give Alex one more chance.

All of these things did happen to the crude, friendly old guy who won 373 big league ball games. But the movie evidence was a little out of order.

The Cubs didn't release Alex outright. They asked waivers on him. The Pirates and Cards put in claims. St. Louis got Ol' Pete and he reported immediately and started winning. He did pitch for the House of David, after bowing out with the Phils, then Dallas in 1930—for $5,500 a season. He did give baseball lectures at a flea circus in New York—in 1939, after he had good-timed away all his baseball earnings.

Oh, well, it was a good movie for the kiddies.

Tennis, Anyone?

THE IDEA that tennis is a young man's game is nonsense, of course. But I do wish somebody had told me they made a lot of changes designed to handicap the player who is flirting with middle age.

It had been quite a few years since I'd been on the courts. But tennis, like riding a bicycle or falling off a log, is something that, once learned, is never forgotten.

Such a simple game, too. You hit the ball over the net, the other guy hits it back. But the local park board doesn't know how to lay out courts anymore. They've made them too long. It didn't used to be necessary to run so hard to get from the baseline for a dropshot over the net. It's the extra length they've added to the playing surface.

They've made the net higher, too. I know I was getting up there just as high on tippy-toe as I once did to long-arm a serve. But that extra-high net cut it off time after time.

Baseball pitchers are always complaining about the lively ball. They ought to see how the manufacturers have juiced up the tennis ball.

Your opponent just pats a return and—whoosh!—even though you dash madly toward the proper spot, the ball is past you like it was jet-propelled.

And the playing surfaces they have nowadays! The park board people don't tell you, but they've started using an especially processed surface on their tennis courts. You can't just get a fast start on the stuff. Worse yet, it's the kind of surface that tires the feet and legs.

There's a mysterious paradox about the court topping. Maybe a chemical engineer or some other kind of scientist could explain it. Although it makes for slow and strained running, it imparts extra zing to the ball. The ball bounces quickly and higher than it did in the old days—I mean a few years ago. Even with all the new handicaps, tennis still is a great deal of fun.

We might even have finished the first set if my opponent, another mature young man, hadn't forgotten to bring his cap. He had to quit because his nude scalp was getting sunburned.

The bronzed striplings on the next court must have overheard our querulous comments about the terrible playing conditions that prevail now. They didn't even try to conceal their smirks and snickers. You'd think they would have sympathized with a couple of somewhat older men, obviously returning from long layoffs, trying to adjust to the new rules and equipment.

The youngsters didn't seem to have any trouble covering all that extra space or mastering those sudden, vicious bounces of the hopped-up ball. But they've probably been playing under the strenuous new conditions all their lives. It's all a matter of early environment and training.

Checkers, anyone?

Basketball Tournament Time: A Culture Explosion

THE CULTURE EXPLOSION strikes Des Moines every March. It's a time when the city is teeming with thousands of contributors not only to culture, but also to mental health. They are also called basketball fans.

This is culture, this brouhaha to see which high school team can throw a ball though a hoop more often than another team? The hoopla and pageantry, this sound and fury, this sweaty test of physical skills in state prep tournaments — all these things are pillars of our American culture?

You doggone betcha they are. There's a whole raft of experts who say so. There's even one who approves the boo as a healthful part of the cultural scene.

Clyde Kluckhorn, an anthropologist, wrote in his book, *Mirror for Man,* that "any cultural practice must be functional or it will disappear before long . . . it must somehow contribute to the survival of the society or to the adjustment of the individual."

Two University of California professors, Frederick W. Cozens and Florence Stumpf, have found that spectator sports fit those specifications because of: "(1) The furnishing of socially approved forms of the ritual and ceremony, (2) the emotional release provided for both players and spectators, (3) an appreciation of sports as an integrating force in American democracy."

The two professors also quote from Melville J. Herskovit's *Man and His Work* that every culture has a certain amount of ritual ceremony . . . which is a powerful agent in uniting a people. Whether they are active participants . . . themselves experiencing the emotional force of a rite, or whether they are spectators, the bonds that bind them to their fellows are strengthened by the ceremonialism."

The professors also note that "we are sometimes moved to make disparaging remarks about the display of showmanship exhibited at various sports events and festivals without realizing the cultural function it serves." But, they continue in a book called *Physical Education and Healthful Living*: "As our modern living becomes increasingly standardized and colorless, such cases have increasing importance. The band, the drum majorettes, the drill team, the card stunts, the color guard, and the playing of the national anthem, all of these create an atmosphere of oneness and belonging which is too seldom achieved; they create a sharing of a common interest — they are indispensable to the culture."

Veterans Auditorium during tournament time is the state's biggest drainage area for pent-up emotions. That's good, according to the psychologists and psychiatrists (the late William C. Menninger is the most famous) quoted in *Physical Education and Healthful Living.*

And anthropologist Kluckhorn finds that in America ". . . tensions can be drained off more effectively than most human societies have done in the past through socially useful competition, through socially harmless releases for aggression, as in sports."

So be socially useful—go drain off your emotions and aggressions at the basketball tournaments. You can release those nasty old emotions whether you boo or boohoo or yell in jubilation.

Professors Cozens and Stumpf say "the point of view of one psychologist is the most interesting," to wit: "Booing is only applause turned inside out. A fellow cheers at a game to express his emotions—his emotions that follow approval. Why should he not boo to express his emotions that follow disapproval? They are just as genuine. They are just inevitable. And they are quite as much in place.

"Few of us go to see games to study them. And disapproval is as much a part of enjoyment as approval is."

Serendipity

Serendipity, a word I once found while looking up something else, has led to the discovery that sports have contributed more than muscle and mania to our American way of life. Now I know that serendipity means a word, or something else that turns out to be desirable, found by accident while looking for something else.

For example, it's fitting and proper that one of sports' most radical creations, the Houston domed stadium, is crowned by a plastic roof.

Because the sports world was responsible for the plastics industry in the first place, that's why.

That's where serendipity comes in. What I really was trying to find was an explanation of why the English don't say *english,* the way we do when we talk about spin on a billiard ball, but instead call it *side.*

The *Encyclopedia Britannica* didn't answer that question, but it answered one I hadn't asked when a paragraph about the game's history caught my roving eye. "In 1868, John Hyatt, in his search for a better billiard ball," it related, "discovered that a mixture of nitro-cellulose, camphor and a small amount of alcohol when properly prepared becomes thermoplastic, i.e., soft when heated, and can be molded in a hydraulic press. After cooling at ordinary atmospheric pressure, it becomes hard and strong. This discovery heralded the beginning not only of the composition billiard ball but also of the plastic industry."

Other cases of serendipity have revealed that sports have been responsible for additional vital inventions and developments (in addition, of course, to the catcher's mask, the double armlock, the football helmet, the basketball hoop, and parimutuel betting).

Radio wasn't invented for the benefit of sports, but it was helped along by sports. When Marconi sought money to perfect his wireless, James Gordon Bennett, Jr., paid him $5,000 to report the finish of the America's Cup yacht race to Bennett's New York newspaper in 1899.

If it hadn't been for a sports argument, the movie industry wouldn't have sprung up as early as it did. The first motion picture was made of a trotting horse. Leland Stanford, an early railway tycoon and breeder of harness horses, in 1872 wagered an affluent friend $25,000 that all four of a trotter's hoofs leave the ground simultaneously during its gait. Stanford gave the photographic problem to John D. Isaacs, a mechanical engineer. Isaacs contrived a battery of twenty-four cameras with electrical shutter controls.

His first sequence pictures of rapid motion won the $25,000 for Stanford, set Thomas Edison and other inventors to work refining the process, and laid the groundwork for the future wealth of actors and popcorn growers.

Another sport provided the first commercial movie ever shown on a screen. It was a six-round fight between Young Griffo and Battling Barnett in May of 1895.

The first efficiency expert in business and industry, Frederick Winslow Taylor, devised many of his theories about how man should work by watching men play. Taylor, known as the father of scientific management, discovered in golf and tennis the value of analysis of motions, the importance of methodical training, and the worth of time studies.

Taylor knew about tennis from personal experience. He was an efficiency expert there, too. Paired with Clarence M. Clark, he won the national doubles championship in 1881.

As the first of the consulting engineers in management, Taylor speeded up production for many companies but still lamented that "the workmen don't display the same fervor in the factory that they do on the athletic field."

Basketball Is a Glum Sport

HEARD ANY FUNNY basketball stories lately? It hadn't occurred to me what a solemn sport this is until a fellow posed that question. He was a banquet speaker looking for material. I couldn't help him out.

"This basketball must be pretty grim," he said. "I hear jokes all the time about baseball and football. Boxing and golf, too. But basketball—almost never. Oh, there's a gag still going around about the star who could do everything with a basketball except autograph it."

The search for enduring basketball humor turned into research.

There are lots of books with such titles as *Joe Blow's Favorite Football Stories,* or *Best Laughs from Baseball.* Golf funny books abound. But I couldn't find one on basketball.

Next came a look into the anthologies, whose blurbs promise the funniest happenings in all sports. One had eight Yogi Berra stories. There was only one basketball yarn: "At a college noted for its basketball team, there was a sign outside the office of the coach that read: 'This door is specifically constructed to the height of six feet, four inches. If you can walk through it without ducking—DON'T.' "

The late Frank Menke, a specialist in athletic history, once put together a book titled *Sports Tales and Anecdotes.* The tales are numbered. There are 266 of them. Two are about basketball, or five fewer than there are about hockey. One soberly relates how Dr. James Naismith invented the game. The other tells how a coach in Kansas City kept protesting until the referee had given the opposition seven successive free throws for personal fouls.

Anyway, if you know a lot of hearty har-har basketball stories and want to write yourself a book, the field's wide open.

Golf (Ugh!)

THERE'S NO ONE more insufferable, except possibly the person who tells how he gave up smoking, than the golfer who mentions casually how many strokes he chopped off par. It's characters like these, with their grating nonchalance, who take all the joy out of breaking 100—make that 120—for mature beginners like me.

Just strolling in the golden sunshine, caressed by a wandering breeze; hearkening to the lark, or listening to the gurgle of the brook that hides your wayward ball—that should be pleasure enough for anybody.

Swinging a club here and there with carefree zest should be only incidental exercise. To tone up the muscles, you know. But, no, there has to be this eternal preoccupation with lower mathematics.

What do you mean, did I take a nine on that last hole? I got down in three putts didn't I? That only makes eight!

There's a good side to being a bad player. Cap Timm, the former Iowa State University baseball coach, made this observation when we assaulted Iowa State's monstrous course one day. "Pity the good golfers," said Cap, hacking at the tangled wildwood with a No. 7 iron. "They never get to see anything but the fairways. Why, we've seen wilderness beauty today they don't even know exists. Just look at those beautiful wildflowers."

It must be unexciting to have every shot go just about where you expect it to, with a little rough grass and a sandtrap as the only challenge. What kind of adventure is that? Give me the test of busting out of a clump of bushes, splashing a shot out of a limpid lagoon, or trying to reach the No. 3 green from the No. 9 fairway. That's stimulating golf.

It is a bit embarrassing, though, to lose holes to your ten-year-old son.

Everybody told me I should take lessons. And, for goodness sakes, please get some clubs of my own.

I took two lessons and the teaching pro said to go out and play a few experimental rounds. "If you don't mind," he said, "please don't mention my name if anybody asks who's teaching you."

Time came for the 1,000-mile checkup—overhauling the stance, changing the slice, greasing the strained muscles.

"Let's see," said the pro, "you shot a fifty-six on the first nine you played. How many nines have you played since?"

"Five or six," I told him.

"And what did you shoot today?" he asked.

"Fifty-nine," I said.

"H-mmmmmm," he said.

"Well, back to the fundamentals," the pro said. "Now, it's all very simple. These are the only things you have to remember: Relax your knees — no, don't sag . . . hold your head still . . . pivot your hips — no, don't bend your back . . . keep your left arm straight — straight, not stiff . . . right elbow close in to your side . . . left arm above the right.

"Now bring the club head back — wide arc . . . hold your head still! . . . now pull your club down like you were pulling a rope to ring a church bell . . . collapse your right knee . . . hold your head still! . . . hit from the inside out . . . you're cocking your wrists too soon . . . hold your head still!

"So it only went twenty-five yards — you hit it straight, didn't you?"

Weathermen Would Have a Ha of a Time without Golf Bal

PRO WEATHER OBSERVERS should give a thunderous cheer for golf and baseball. Where in the hail would they be without these sports to provide such quickly recognized comparisons? What would hailstones be as big as if they weren't as big as golf balls or as big as baseballs? For the record, a golf ball is 1.68 inches in diameter, a baseball is just under 3 inches.

In case hail of intermediate size should fall and the weather experts need a quick comparison, here's a reference table in the interests of meteorological precision: Squash racket ball, 1¾ inches in diameter; handball, 1⅞ inches; jai alai pelota, 2¼ inches; tennis ball, 2½ to 2⅝ inches; cricket ball, 2¾ inches.

The Game's Only a Minor Activity at the Rose Bow

THEY HAVE THIS AFFAIR out in Pasadena, California, every January 1 called the Tournament of Roses, and one of the minor attractions is a football joust between a Big Ten team and one from somewhere around the West Coast. Around the lushly landscaped hotel where the Big Ten's prize football livestock, along with attendants and admirers, is stabled, you get the idea that the football game is the main event of the holiday festival. It is also where the football writers hang out. So do the publicity people who are fond of comparing attendance in the Rose Bowl (100,807) with lesser crowds drawn by imitators in various southland bowls.

Yet everywhere else in Pasadena, the football game is only the No. 2 topic of conversation. The rank and file of citizens can't tell you the name of the Big Ten coach, but they can tell you who's grand marshal of the parade.

Oh, sure, the football game offers a nice bit of extra recreation on hangover day. But something of an anticlimax, you know, to *the* event: the parade.

Mention that there will be 100,000 fans at the football game and the average Pasadena citizen will look pained or bored. "Yes, a fine little gathering," you'll probably be told. "That's about one-fifteenth the size of the crowd that will watch the parade. In person, that is. They say 98 million will see it on TV—a lot more than will watch the football game."

Pasadenans thought of football as a New Year's Day recreation in 1902 when they invited Michigan's football squad out to frolic in the sun. They kept right on frolicking in the game, over Stanford's feeble dissuasion, 49–0.

But there had been parades for twelve years before that, beginning when members of the Valley Hunt Club drove around on New Year's Day in buggies and surreys decorated with flowers from their own gardens.

The first football game was such a thumping failure that chariot races, in the old Roman style, were substituted as the sports attraction until 1916. The return of football then was no rousing success, either.

There was no Rose Bowl then. Stands seating about 8,000 were borrowed from a circus. They were far from filled on a rainy day. Receipts were $7,000 for Washington State's 14–0 victory over Brown. The deficit was $11,000.

REMEMBER WHEN football players were plain old ends, tackles, guards, centers, quarterbacks, halfbacks, and fullbacks? Now a leader risks eviction from the coaches' union if he makes the language so uncomplicated.

An end can no longer be simply an end. The means have to justify the end. He must be tight, split, wide, lonesome, strong, weak, or heads-up, and so on to the bitter end of verbal invention. Halfbacks are rare. They are tailbacks or running backs, wingbacks or floaters or flankers, slot or short backs. And, in the coach's despairing private thoughts, maybe drawbacks.

Chuck Studley of the University of Cincinnati is the inevitable winner of the award for "coach who has done most to confuse the public." When copies of the lineups were handed out before Drake's game at Cincinnati one year, Paul Morrison's consternation brought him as close to profanity as he ever came.

"Holy cow!" he yelped, "I thought I'd seen everything in the lineups, but what in the world is this?" The Drake sports publicity director pointed to the Bearcat listings: WE, ShT, ShG, C, LgC, LgT, TE, QB, WB, HB, FB.

We were toying hopefully with speculations that these might mean "shiftless tackle" and "lumbering guard" and "wrong end," when a code-breaking expert came by.

"Very simply," said Hod Blaney, Bearcat press agent, "the ends are wide or tight. The linemen on the side of the wide end are short guards and tackles. On the side of the tight end, they're long."

The mental strain of devising these names obviously exhausted Studley before he got to C, QB, HB, and FB. Otherwise, he surely would have called Zippy Al Nelson his high, wide, and handsome back.

There's a suspicion eating me that football coaches could make their sport even more popular if they wouldn't carry the esoteric language of field and locker room into public areas. They must think they'll lose their reputation for genius-type strategy if they merely say a halfback ran off tackle or a quarterback faked a run and threw a pass.

So they go on radio or TV and talk about how "their big rush took away our long pass, so we went to a roll comeback action with a double-hook action by the receivers."

Or: "They took away our traps and their monster beat our out-side counters, but we caught 'em on the slant with our belly action. And we moved the ball some on counters with diving action."

The coach's cult of confusion can't be unplanned. Their associa-tion must have a private meeting on linguistics every year. "Look fellows," the president probably says, "the public is beginning to catch on to things like 'monster' and 'flip-flop' and 'stunt.' I even heard one of you guys say 'red-dog.' The fans have been familiar with that one for years. Now 'Z-outs' ain't bad and 'bloody-nose defense' is good. But we gotta come up with some new ones that'll really throw the fans." And they do.

What the Outsiders Had To Say about Baseball

PEOPLE FAMOUS in baseball are always being quoted about their game. So, for a change of pace, or maybe a change of venue, let's see what some people famous outside of baseball have had to say about it:

Bruce Catton, historian —

> Baseball is the American game, great or otherwise, because it re-flects so perfectly certain aspects of the American character that no other sport quite portrays.
>
> It has few of the elements of pure sportsmanship, as that dubious word is commonly accepted, and it is not notably a game for gentlemen. But it does embody certain native-born fundamentals, including above all others the notion that the big thing about any contest is to win it.
>
> It also is built upon the idea that anything you can get away with is permissible, and it is the only sport . . . that puts an invitation to homi-cide in one of its enduring sayings: "Kill the umpire!"

Laraine Day, actress and ex-wife of Leo Durocher —

> Baseball is a serious thing in this country, and if that reveals our immaturity, I suppose there is little we can do about it until we grow up.

Mark Twain —

> Baseball is the very symbol, the outward and visible expression of the drive and push and rush and struggle of the raging, tearing, booming century.

George Bernard Shaw, British dramatist and novelist —

> Baseball has the advantage over cricket of being sooner ended.

Ken Hubbard, homespun philosopher—

Knowin' all about baseball is just about as profitable as bein' a good whittler.

Russell Maloney, author—

Most males who don't care about big league baseball conceal their indifference as carefully as they would conceal a laughable physical deficiency.

Jacques Barzun, college professor and historian—

Whoever wants to know the heart and mind of America had better learn baseball, the rules and realities of the game. . . .

Accuracy and speed, the practised eye and hefty arm, the mind to take in and readjust to the unexpected, the possession of more than one talent and the willingness to work in harness without special orders—these are the American virtues that shine in baseball.

There has never been a good player who was dumb. Beef and bulk and mere endurance count for little, judgment and daring for much.

. . . baseball has something sociable and friendly about it that I especially love. It is graphic and choreographic.

Herbert Hoover, former president and a Dodger fan until the club left Brooklyn, then a frequent spectator at Yankee home games until his death—

I began playing baseball on the sandlots when I was about eleven years of age.

When I went to college (Stanford), I thought I could play, so I tried out for shortstop. . . . But after a while, the student manager informed me that I'd make a better manager than I would a shortstop, so I took his job and he became the shortstop.

Sinclair Lewis, novelist—

"The game was a custom of his clan, and it gave outlet for the homicidal and sides-taking instincts which Babbitt called 'patriotism' and 'love of sport.' "

Thomas Wolfe, novelist—

The scene is instant, whole and wonderful. In its beauty and design that vision of the soaring stands, the pattern of forty thousand entranced faces, the velvet and unalterable geometry of the playing field, and the small lean figures of the players, set there, lonely, tense and waiting in their places, bright, desperate solitary atoms encircled by that huge wall of nameless faces, is incredible.

And more than anything it is the light, the miracle of light and shade and color—the crisp, blue light that swiftly slants out from the soaring stands and, deepening to violet, begins to march across the velvet field and toward the pitcher's box, that gives the thing its single and incomparable beauty.

What Did He Say? What Did He Say?

EDITOR'S NOTE: While covering the 1966 World Series between Los Angeles and Baltimore, Bryson took a couple of hours off one afternoon to attempt something that no other sportswriter had ever achieved—an understandable interview with Casey Stengel, who had retired from baseball two years earlier. The following column, which was printed in October 1966, is the result of those bewildering two hours with the master of mangling the language.

NOW WHAT IF THEY'D ASK ME what kind of a man Casey Stengel is, and I looked at my notes and saw that there was this insane asylum back of the outfield fence at Kewanee in 1910, and that ol' Case is proud of Hank Bauer, but Bauer didn't like him on the Yankees, and what if Stengel had had Blair in center field instead of the fifteen men he discharged—or that discharged themselves?

And what if they'd ask me what Casey thought caused the collapse of the Dodgers in the World Series? Well I'd have this quote: "If you looked it over, you'd still say it couldn't happen."

And what if they'd ask me what Casey's baseball duties are now, as vice-president of the club he called "the amazin' Mets"? Then I could refer to another quote: "I saw the Angels and Dodgers play a lot and I would say that Willie Davis is a great baserunner, not stealing, but going from first to third or three bases. But they told me I'm not supposed to be a regional scout. What if they asked me if four of our ballplayers is as good as one of the Dodgers?"

Don't ask why, but the next note I had was about how Cookie Lavagetto got his nickname.

Well, I should say that Stengel has a deep well of sympathy for those listeners he has confused; an understanding that he has defied understanding.

Casey limped across to the door of his handsome hotel suite to grin a farewell after I had spent two giddy hours spinning back and forth on the wave of Stengel's reminiscences. *"The Saturday Evening Post* paid me $155,000," said Casey comfortingly, "and they later made it into a book, and it didn't sell, and it took six stenographers to take it down, and *they* couldn't figure it out."

Then, he went on: "They said I was crazy for platooning and using all those relief pitchers.

"Bauer didn't like me because I wouldn't let him play every day and platooned him in right field. But," Casey added about the man who managed Baltimore to the world championship in 1966, "I liked him because he ran out every ball he ever hit."

The Blair mentioned by Casey was Paul, the center fielder who beat the Dodgers with a home run in the third game of the World Series and gloved a homer away from Jim LeFebvre in the fourth game. Stengel was chagrined that the Mets' front office failed to protect Blair from the draft when he was on one of their farm clubs. "The Orioles stole him from us for $8,000," said Casey, referring to the draft price. "But," he added, his seamy features brightening, "they also stole that left fielder—what's his name?—yeah, Curt Blefary—from the Yankees for $8,000."

Casey doesn't come right out and say he's happy over the collapse of the Yanks, the club that fired him after the 1960 World Series because he was "too old." He can't hold back the grin, though, when he remarks: "Those men in the Bronx, it burns 'em up that the amazin' Mets are in ninth place and they're in tenth, and they didn't draw as many people as we did even when they were still up and we were in tenth."

The Time of Year When Parent Start Acting Childis

WHEN THE LITTLE LEAGUE SEASON gets under way, you kids playing for the first time are going to have to learn to make allowances for your parents and other adults. Don't forget, the grownups are at an impressionable age. They're likely to get more riled up than you are over errors, unfavorable judgments by the umpire, and especially by defeat.

National Little League headquarters has had psychologists conduct surveys that show that you kids eight to twelve bounce back quickly from setbacks. The psychologists use bigger words. "Emotional resiliency," they call it. It just means you snap out of it in a big hurry.

But you'll have to remember that parents sometimes don't have that resiliency. Their emotions are more easily wrenched out of shape and it takes longer for them to calm down. You'll just have to be patient with them.

You know, of course, that the main reason you're playing the game is to have fun. Naturally, it's more fun to win than it is to lose, but losing isn't the calamity that some adults seem to think it is.

There are parents and other spectators, you'll find, who don't know that one of the first things pointed out in the organization's code is: "To win *is not* the prime objective in Little League baseball." They may not be familiar, either, with the advice that "spectators must realize that the youngsters in the game are children and, if they make an error or a bad play, they feel worse than anyone. Make cheering positive."

Speaking ill of Little League is equal to insulting motherhood or spitting on the flag. Still, disapproval is sometimes voiced, and national officials admit that "deportment of parents at Little League games has many times caused criticism of the program."

"It is," headquarters admonishes, "a deplorable exhibition of incivility or plain ignorance to boo a youngster who is learning to play the game, or his league leaders (all volunteers) who are trying to help him."

Let's hope you don't wind up as a sub under a manager who won't take the regulars out unless victory is assured or the team is hopelessly beaten. We hope your manager knows that you can build morale by developing all of the players — not just the nine or ten best players. And, we hope that your manager can remember some advice from Dr. Arthur A. Esslinger, who was a member of the Little League board of directors:

"An overly serious atmosphere takes the fun and happiness out of Little League. After all, it is a GAME! It isn't Little League if it isn't fun."

*   *   *

A degree in psychology isn't a requirement for Little League, but leaders of the kid baseball program want managers who can apply psychology to a certain degree. Managers can't give all their players the kind of "security blanket" Linus clutches when he fields the baseballs boomed off Charlie Brown. But they are urged to help their players "gain acceptance and satisfy the need for emotional security."

The manager is supposed to know, for example, that the ten-year-old is developing great independence and is beginning to clash with his or her parents.

A person has to know these things in order to be a successful manager? The national officials of Little League think so. They have quoted from six books on child psychology in their manual for managers on the care and handling of players who may range from little darlings to little monsters.

The manager is expected to be aware that, at Little League age (nine to twelve), the players are "sensitive to the subtle pressures of acceptance and rejection." It is important, therefore, that the manager "gives everyone on his squad a chance to play."

Managers should be able to deal out firm discipline when necessary (for talking back to the umpire, rough play, and so on) and still let the culprits know they like them.

Managers have to cultivate a poker face to disguise true feelings when a kid srikes out with the bases full. They are warned to remember that "children respond readily to solicitous encouragement and to recognition of small successes they achieve."

Managers, it is further pointed out, will, in some cases, "be working with youngsters deprived of love and affection; they will work with highly overprotected children and come in contact with the out-and-out rejected child. Leaders must do their utmost to help these children, and if they are unable to help them, the least that can be done is to attempt to understand them."

Like, say, understanding the urge for small success in the player who is out trying to steal home, ending the game in a one-run defeat with the team's leading hitter at the plate.

Managers will learn when they study the manual that they're not wasting breath in talking about honesty, justice, and moral codes to ten-year-olds and eleven-year-olds. Under "some characteristics of the twelve-year-old," it is noted: "Abstract ideas such as 'honesty' and 'justice' are now within the realm of understanding."

The typical eleven-year-old still likes to play rough, as they did a year earlier, but now they're fascinated by "hazardous activities," accentuating the need for supervision. At eleven, too, they begin to "put an emphasis on excellence in the performance of physical feats, and are willing to work hard at acquiring physical skills." From sluggard to slugger.

A Triple!!!

THE LITTLE LEAGUER put all of his sixty pounds into a ferocious swing and connected—barely. The ball, scraped by the bottom of the bat, jiggled straight back to the pitcher, who groped and fumbled a moment. There was still plenty of time to nail the batter at first. The pitcher's throw soared high over the first baseman's head. The slugger flew on toward second.

Somebody retrieved the ball. The next throw sailed into left field. The hitter swaggered into third, puffing through a man-sized grin.

"Oh, boy!" he said. "That's the first triple I ever hit in my whole life!"

To preserve such innocent childish illusions, the Raccoon Valley Little League in Des Moines, and perhaps others, didn't reveal batting averages to the players. The averages were figured, but were kept secret from everyone except league officials and managers, who used them mostly to help determine All-Star selections.

The Raccoon Valley at one time didn't have enough people to score the games, and the call went out for volunteer scorekeepers. Thirty-two mothers responded, though some of them had never so much as seen a scorebook.

"But," said one, "I don't want to score any games that my son is playing in." Afraid she'd be prejudiced? "Oh, no," she said. "But I'd get so excited watching him that I'd forget everything else that was going on."

They asked me to conduct a scoring clinic, but they didn't say it was to be mostly for mothers who had never put pencil to scorebook. That frightening information came later. The imagination reeled at the thought of the naive and silly questions that would spring from feminine fancy.

Some of the mothers had to begin from scratch by learning the position numbers: 1 for pitcher, 2 for catcher, and so on. Some had never even heard of a fielder's choice or a sacrifice fly.

But forebodings were groundless. The questions were sensible and to-the-point. The mothers caught on quicker than a lot of men who have been playing or watching baseball most of their lives.

Some of the tots may be skeptical at first. They'll soon find out that Mom knows what the score is.

One mother had her scoring baptism a couple of days before the clinic and ran into a problem that veteran scorekeepers have never faced. "I'd never even seen a scorebook before," she said, "but I figured I could at least get the number of runs right. The managers filled in the starting line-ups and one of them put down fourteen names without any positions listed.

"He told me: 'After those fourteen boys bat, start over again at the top of the batting order. I'll pick out the nine boys to put in the field as we go along.'

"Somehow, that didn't seem right to me, and I told him I didn't think he could do it that way. He said: 'Yes I can. I've been doing it for two years.'

"I couldn't keep up with all the changes he made in the field, but I'm sure the other manager must have kept track.

"Anyway, I'm sure I got the score right."

Did Ted Williams Deserve To Be
Elected to the Hall of Fame?

TED WILLIAMS, who had the world's worst public relations counsel — himself — has received a generally favorable press since his 1966 election to the Baseball Hall of Fame. "Give the devil his due" is the attitude of most sports fans.

Even the many who knew only the touchy, sulky, abrasive facets of Williams's complex personality, who never forgave him for his spitting tantrums or the profane insults he shouted at booing fans — even these have admitted Ted deserves enshrinement as one of the greatest of all hitters.

There are still a few critics, though, who begrudge Williams a place in the Hall of Fame on the grounds that his .344 career average was an individual exhibition that paid off in just one Red Sox pennant. "One pennant for his team in nineteen years," one writer said. By this reckoning, Williams was responsible for Red Sox failures in 1952 and 1953, as well as in all his other seasons except triumphant 1946.

True, Ted wore the Boston uniform in those two years — on each side of a tour in a marine uniform while flying thirty-four missions in Korea.

Williams played six games in 1952 and thirty-seven in '53. No wonder the Red Sox didn't win the 1953 championship. They were in fourth place, sixteen games out, when Ted returned. He damaged the pennant drive by hitting .407 in his thirty-seven games. Boston there-fore stayed in fourth place.

It's an old refrain, the carping at Williams's personal failure to lift the Red Sox to the top "because he was a selfish individualist and not a team player."

That complaint was heard when Joe Cronin was general manager of the Red Sox and Williams was at the peak of hitting efficiency. "How," demanded Cronin, "can a man who hits .350, with 35 home runs and 140 to 150 runs-batted-in, be anything but a help to you? Even if he didn't want to help you, how could he be anything but a help to you?"

When Williams was playing, the Red Sox ranked from fourth to seventh in pitching efficiency—fourth in 1946 when they won the pennant. Only the slugging of Williams and his robust mates let the Red Sox get as far as a losing playoff with Cleveland in 1948. Boston pitchers gave up 720 runs that year; Indian hurlers allowed only 567.

So Williams doesn't belong in the Hall because he could help generate only one pennant surge? O.K., then kick out Nap Lajoie, George Sisler, Harry Heilmann, Luke Appling, and Ted Lyons. Of course, Lajoie was the best combination fielder-hitter of all the second basemen. Sisler was a virtuoso at first base who hit .420 one year and .407 another. Heilmann, four-time American League batting champion, was .342 for his career. Appling and Lyons were long-time stalwarts.

But not one of them helped any club win even a single pennant.

Today's Ballplayers Are Better Than the Old-Timers

FRANKIE FRISCH, "The Fordham Flash," created a stir some years ago when the Hall of Fame second baseman labeled modern baseball play-ers as sissies. "They do not have the same old urge, the fighting spirit that characterized the ballplayers of what I call the old-timers' era. Everything is made easy for them. Training camps are country clubs without dues," said Frankie, adding that "the old fire and snap has gone out of baseball."

The Flash said today's fielders rely upon "snaring nets they call baseball gloves," contrasted to the "leather pancakes" of his day (1919–37). And he complained over hearing "modern sissies moan" about how the slider has ruined batting averages.

*[OVERLEAF] Bill Bryson, second from left, watches
Ted Williams take batting practice, 1946*

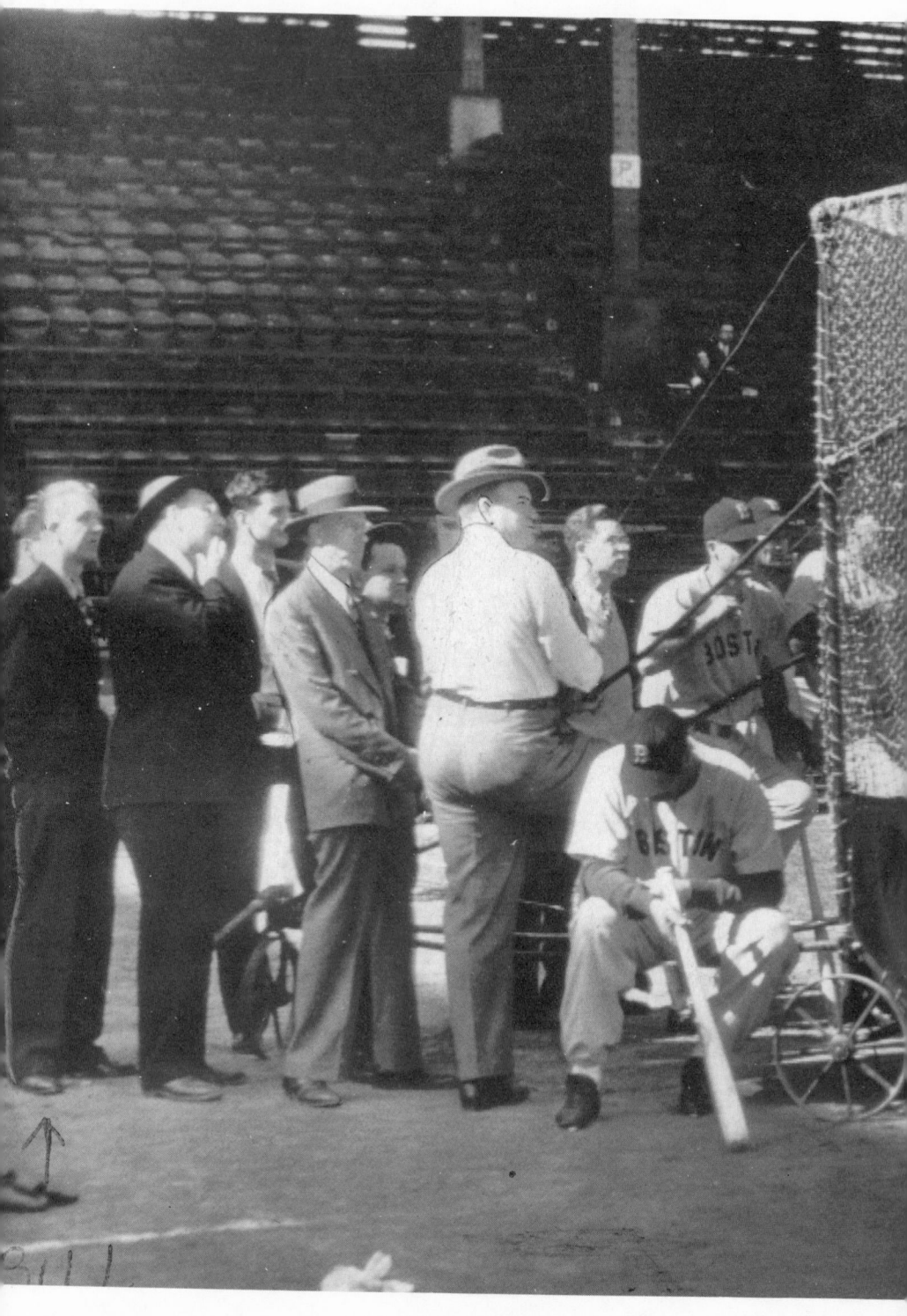

Oct 15, 1946   Ted Williams

But you'll get a different story from many of Frisch's playing contemporaries. Casey Stengel and Al Lopez, who were more successful as managers than Frisch, were two. Fresco Thompson was another, at least as far as fielding goes. "Neither Frisch nor any of the rest of us old-timers," said Fresco, a former vice-president of the Dodgers, "could make the double play with the speed and precision these fellows do today."

Lopez, a former Cleveland and Chicago White Sox manager, once told me he thought present-day ball players are smarter, faster, stronger, better-conditioned, and better-coached than those of any of the past era. "And don't let anybody tell you," said Lopez, "that the pitching isn't tougher than it was thirty or forty years ago.

"When I broke into the National League in 1930, the only knuckleball pitchers were Freddy Fitzsimmons and Jes Haines. Now every club has at least a couple of knuckleballers. A good knuckler is just as hard to hit as the old spitball was.

"Four or five pitchers had the slider in the early thirties — Waite Hoyt, George Blaeholder, Johnny Babich, Bill Lohrman. Now everybody throws it — and it's a tough pitch. It comes up without spin, looking like a fastball, then breaks quick and practically saws off your bat at the handle. There are more good pitchers now, too, and lots more good relief pitchers."

Two or three times I've heard Stengel surround the subject of changes in the game since his days as an outfielder. It pretty much filters down to: "I could build up the methods they used to play by in baseball and show you that half of them aren't worth a quarter today — the sacrifice, the steal, the hit and run, and those things. Now they'd say, 'Why are you trying to play that kind of a game? You're going to finish fourth instead of first.' And you possibly will, with those big hitters on other teams going for home runs and murdering you.

"They go for the loft hitter now. It used to be the pitcher would pitch to make them hit a ball in the outfield. That's too dangerous now with everybody slugging. A pitcher has to bear down all the time. He goes out there and puts something on every pitch. He doesn't try to pace himself for nine innings. He goes as far as he can, and then you take him out and put somebody else in."

A Tribute to Sec Taylor

EDITOR'S NOTE: Garner W. (Sec) Taylor was as well-known to most Iowans as any of the country's major athletes. Sec was sports editor of the *Des Moines Register and Tribune* for more than half a century, and it was an Iowa tradition to sit down each morning with a cup of coffee and read Taylor's popular "Sittin' In with the Athletes" column. Taylor and Bryson teamed for decades to cover the World Series, All-Star games, and other major events. When Sec died unexpectedly of a heart attack while attending baseball spring training camps in Florida, Bryson wrote the following column dated March 2, 1965.

THE FIRST THING OF MINE that ever appeared in a newspaper was a letter I drafted and redrafted, copied and recopied, pecked out on my dad's old Oliver typewriter and mailed to Sec Taylor. Wonder of wonders, it showed up a few days later in Sec's "Sittin' In" column, which was as much a part of my morning nourishment as bacon and eggs.

Talk about thrills! For a thirteen-year-old kid, growing up in an Iowa village of 800, this was like knighthood, a medal of honor, and a Pulitzer Prize rolled into one.

But that was only part of the excitement. Not long afterward came a letter from the greatest man in Iowa. He thanked me for my contribution, some obscure statistic I had dug up about Lou Gehrig. This, I was to learn later in long years of cherished friendship, was typical of the man.

Now and then, he'd ask me to do a spot of research for him, or I'd leave him a trifle or two for his column. And he always would leave me a note of appreciation and thanks.

Nobody ever wrote more letters of congratulations, condolences, and gratitude, to all types of people, in sports and out (or to their widows), to public relations men and hotel managers for accommodating him, or to managers and coaches for their courtesies.

Having recovered briskly from two earlier heart attacks, he wrote cheery and encouraging letters to any friend or acquaintance fighting back from similar distress.

Sec answered every letter and card, even the ones from the cranks, the crackpots, and the churls, no matter how moronic or scurrilous they might be. He was not a man who suffered fools gladly, but if they were unavoidable, he suffered them with courtesy and tolerance.

Sec had certain prejudices and admitted them. He also admitted his errors in reporting, which didn't occur often. But if it was a matter of opinion — and his opinions were carefully thought out — he'd stick to his convictions. "Events have sometimes proved me wrong," he once said, "but I've never written anything that I didn't sincerely believe was right and fair at the time."

Once I wrote a magazine article in which Sec was quoted extensively. I referred to him as "a revered sports authority."

The editor wrote back that *revered* was a word that hardly applied to people in sports and journalism; that his first reaction was to cross it out. "But," he added, "having known Sec for many years, I've decided to let it stand. I can't think of anybody else in our business, though, that I'd put into my magazine as revered."

Two things Sec never lost: his enthusiasm or his tendency to blush like a schoolboy when someone paid him a compliment. I never saw him take a more lively interest in his favorite sports event, the World Series, than he did at his last in October. It was the eighteenth in which I sat next to him in the pressbox.

Sec liked nothing better than to sit with a convivial group in press headquarters until the wee hours, reminiscing and arguing. He liked to talk, to argue, but he was also a good listener.

In recent years, doctors' orders sent him to bed at ten o'clock. When we were traveling together, usually I'd awaken him through some bit of carelessness when I came later to our room.

He'd never complain. "Let me switch on the light for you," he'd say. Then: "What did you write for the *Tribune?*" or "What earth-shaking decisions did you fellows arrive at after I left?" And we'd talk for an hour.

He was the best "roomie" anybody ever had.

A Great Sports Fan — and a Wonderful Da

THE FIRST TIME I played hooky, my dad caught me.

Any truant stupid enough to stand out on a sidewalk on Winfield's Main Street in the heart of the business district (its unpaved length a full two blocks) deserved to be caught. He probably also deserved to be punished, either by the customary instrument of torture, the razor strop (nobody called it strap), or by the withholding of the weekly twenty-five-cent allowance.

It should have occurred to me that Dad would be driving his Model-T much faster than usual so he could finish his rural mail route in time to listen to Graham McNamee's thrill-throbbing voice telling how the Yankees and the Cardinals were doing in the World Series.

Dad didn't seem shocked, or even surprised, to see his sixth-grade son in the cluster of grown men entranced by the electronic marvel of the age, there in front of Rukgaber's hardware store.

All Dad asked me was "What's the score?" then he stood there with me while McNamee's resonance vibrated the Atwater Kent radio loudspeaker that looked sort of like the big end of a tuba painted black.

We rode home together and replayed the game all through supper (dinner was at noon in the country). Truancy wasn't mentioned. The razor strop stayed on its hook. But I knew better than to ask Dad to write me an excuse for school, or to ask him to ask Mother to write one. Subterfuge was as foreign to his nature as vanity or sloth. It cost me several sessions of "staying in" after school.

I didn't even know Dad had been a semipro pitcher of considerable ability, beginning at the age of fourteen, until one time I ran across an old scrapbook his mother had kept. He was embarrassed when he found me showing it proudly to the neighborhood kids.

* * *

We were envied because we had a team of horses, something already rare in town, and a jaunting cart. Best of all, there was also a sleigh, for winter frolics.

Great fun, yes — for the kids. For Dad, they were the only means of transportation when not even the Model-T could groan through the mud or snow over twenty-eight miles of dirt roads — gumbo flats and clay hills.

Well, there were a couple of other means of transportation. Sometimes he'd walk across the fields when the roads were drifted high or hub-deep in mud. And a couple of winters, after freezing rains left the countryside a glare of ice, he skated long stretches of his route, the mail sack on his back.

Dad didn't miss a day, or a patron's mailbox, in forty-four years except for the brief times he grudged for treatment of tuberculosis of the bone in one shoulder. For two years, he worked, made a big garden, and played ball with us kids one-handed. His shoulder was immobilized in a monstrous eighteen-pound steel cast that required yards of wrapping to help keep it in place while the shoulder bones fused.

Even in those years, after ten or twelve hours over roads clotted with mud or frozen into boneshaking ruts, he wouldn't come right in to his own supper. Always, the horses had to be fed first, then curried and brushed by the light of a lantern.

He found time to foster my interest in sports and my regard for sportsmanship. If he was disappointed that his only son didn't inherit his ability in baseball, tennis, billiards, and other pursuits, he never showed it. He taught us all—children, grandchildren, and a great-grandchild—that the main thing was to do your best, play by the rules, and have fun.

Dad's own interest in sports never flagged. He was very happy the spring that he was within TV range of White Sox', Cubs', and Twins' networks. On the last weekend of his life, my mother told me, he watched four baseball games on TV.

Award Winners and Favorites

12

The Upset of the Decade

EDITOR'S NOTE: It was a warm and sunny late October afternoon in 1952 when Iowa's football team, then a tribute to outrageous futility, clashed with powerful Ohio State, considered a leading contender for the Big Ten championship. The Hawkeyes, who hadn't won a Big Ten game in nearly two years and were huge underdogs, pulled off an 8–0 upset that was labeled one of the greatest Big Ten games of the decade. Bryson's report of the game was selected by a panel of sportswriters for *Best Sports Stories—1953 Edition,* an annual anthology of the tops in sportswriting.

IOWA CITY, IOWA — Iowa's gallant Hawkeyes, scorned and derided, scaled the rocky heights of football greatness Saturday.

Here was a team that didn't have a chance, a team that had suffered through ten straight games without a victory, a team slaughtered by Purdue and Wisconsin.

Yet this was the team Saturday that roused itself from the depths of frustration to whip—and whip decisively—mighty Ohio State, 8–0. When it was over, the 44,659 homecoming witnesses sat in stunned disbelief for a moment before loosing a roar that boomed and echoed against the slanting walls of Iowa Stadium.

Forest Evashevski, the new coach who contrived this greatest upset of the year, was carried from the bench all the way across the churned turf to the dressing room by his hilarious Hawkeyes.

There have been greater Iowa teams — the Big Ten champions of 1921 and 1922, the legendary 1939 Ironmen, and others. But never has Iowa conquered such overwhelming odds as these brave, brash Hawkeyes did on a bright, homecoming afternoon.

The Hawks walked with the gods Saturday. They played the heralded Buckeyes off their feet. Their aggressive, savage tackling gave them a safety in the second quarter. They could have made that skimpy lead stand up, too, so relentless were their charges and counter-charges.

But they added insurance to the trembling advantage by scoring a fourth-quarter touchdown that grew from Bernie Bennett's amazing forty-four yard punt return to the Ohio State twenty-five-yard line.

It was safer then, but it was still perilous, for there remained twelve minutes and forty-three seconds for Ohio State to generate the terrifying offense that had humbled Wisconsin and two other vaunted foes earlier this season.

The Buckeyes' John Borton was beginning to find the range with a pinpoint passing assault that put him close to a Big Ten individual record.

The tall, talented sophomore completed eighteen passes in a day of tremendous activity that saw him pitch thirty-seven against a Hawkeye defense that never faltered when the danger zone was reached. The Buckeyes, favored by three touchdowns, were expected to send their fleet and furious backs almost at will through an Iowa line that had been riddled in four straight losses this season.

Borton, who had averaged two touchdown tosses a game, figured to do at least that well against a leaky Iowa pass defense. Yet not once did the Buckeyes pierce beyond the Hawkeye thirty.

Iowa's lightly regarded line stopped them once at the thirty-three-yard line in the first half after Ohio State had ripped all the way from its own seven. Again the Hawkeyes stopped the blustering Bucks at the thirty-two, and again at the thirty-one in the first half.

Nobody expected the Iowa defense to continue such savagely stubborn resistance through another two periods. Only Purdue, a team that mauled Iowa, 41–14, had been able to hurl back the challenge of Ohio's lashing backs. Surely the Hawks' pitifully thin defensive ranks would wilt under the pounding influence of eighty-degree heat and Ohio blasting.

They didn't. Instead, they seemed to gather strength and inspiration. Just once in the last half could the now-desperate Buckeyes surge into Iowa territory. That was right after the touchdown.

A fake punt on fourth down, with Bill Peterson's pass catching the Hawks asleep, moved Ohio State thirteen yards to the Iowa forty-seven. Then Borton fired three successful passes in a row, short and sharp. The Bucks were at the thirty.

Now came the plays that put the crusher on Ohio State, a team that humiliated the Hawks, 83–21, two years ago, and beat them 47–21 last season. Borton threw to Bob Joslin at the northeast corner. Bennett broke it up close to the goal and Coach Woody Hayes of the Bucks came charging from the bench to bellow a protest. The official ruled it was not interference.

Borton tried again and this time Don Chief, the Iowa left tackle, burst through and spilled him for a ten-yard loss. It was fourth and eleven. Borton switched his target from Joslin, who had hauled in nine passes, to Bob Grimes, the other end.

Lyle Leinbaugh, whose clever and aggressive defensive work balked the Buckeyes all afternoon, kept this one out of Grimes's eager paws by batting it down at the goal.

Ohio State had two more chances, but both came after Binkey Broeder's powerful punts put the bewildered guests deep in their own territory. The rebellious Hawks kept them there both times and made them punt.

It was a story of a magnificent defense by a team that had been feeble and inept all season in that phase of the game. Ohio State's heralded Fred Bruney, Hopalong Cassady, and its other fancy backs could hack only forty-two yards against the Hawks. Iowa itself, the team that was supposed to be reliant upon passes, roared along the turf for 194 yards.

Two new starters, halfbacks Bob Phillips and Juggler Hatch, flared through the Buckeyes' bulky line for forty of the sixty-eight yards in the Hawks' opening drive. Burt Britzmann, who was a masterful director until he was injured late in the third quarter, and Bob Stearnes, Dusty Rice, and Broeder were others who lacerated the Buckeye defense.

It was Broeder, his stubby legs chopping through a hole at right guard, who scored the touchdown with two minutes and seventeen seconds gone in the last quarter. Binkey had only inches to go after the desperate Buckeyes held three times within their own one-yard line. His short journey climaxed Iowa's first Big Ten victory since the Hawks won at Minnesota, 13–0, on November 4, 1950.

The Hawks' first points came with seven minutes and twelve seconds left of the second period. Doug Goodsell of Ohio State fielded Broeder's punt on his own two-yard line and fumbled it over the goal. A horde of Hawks were upon him as he retrieved the ball and tried to circle back to safety. The defense snapped on him like a steel trap—three Iowans burying him in the end zone for two points.

Iowa previously had twice shuddered to a halt with a touchdown in sight. The gears that meshed so beautifully in the opening march finally squealed and clashed, and Ohio State took over on downs on its own thirteen. A little later, Britzmann fumbled at the Buckeye fifteen and Marts Beekley recovered for the guests. Again the Hawks were balked at the Ohio State thirty-one-yard line.

Opportunity came knocking for the Hawkeyes at the start of the second half, but the door quickly slammed shut. Cassady fumbled on the first play after the kickoff, under the powerful persuasion of Iowa Captain Bill Fenton, and Andy Houg recovered at the Buckeye thirteen-yard line.

With fourth and four on the eight-yard line, Britzmann was swamped on a "keep" play. Punting exchanges kept the action out of the danger zone until Bennett seized Peterson's kick at the Iowa thirty-one.

Bernie faked a hand-off to Rice. That fooled only a few defenders as Bennett headed toward the east sideline, the ball held against his right leg. There was a large and eager reception committee in that area, but Bernie tucked the ball under his arm and busted right through six tacklers at midfield.

Stunned Buckeyes were bouncing in all directions from the piston-like legs of the Mason City blaster. Only frantic bursts of speed by Tony Curcillo, the last Ohio State defender, kept Bernie from going all of the way. Curcillo dragged him down at the twenty-five-yard line.

Britzmann then crashed to the Buckeye twenty-three-yard line. A running southpaw pass from Stearnes connected with Britzmann at the nineteen, but Burt had to dive to make the catch and injured his shoulder.

With Jackie Hess now at the helm, the Hawks became extremely fancy. Broeder took a pitchout, headed around right end and lateraled to Rice. Dusty barged on to the thirteen for a first down. Stearnes plowed off right tackle to the eight. He cracked the same gap and the quarter ended with Iowa at the six-yard line.

Rice's try, again at right tackle, left the Hawks a yard and a half shy of a first down. Dusty darted through a quick opening at left guard to make it to the one. The Buckeyes demanded measurement, but it was a futile request; Iowa had a first down.

Dusty tried to drive across the goal line, but the Buckeyes stopped him a foot short. They stopped Stearnes too, and Rice again — six inches away. But Binkey made it.

Stearnes was the workhorse of the Iowa ground attack on this day of miracles. He netted forty-seven yards in nine tries. Hatch, who hadn't played before the Wisconsin game the previous week, also had a forty-seven-yard yield. He carried thirteen times. Britzmann contributed forty-one yards in eleven attempts, Broeder thirty-one in eleven, and Rice sixteen in seven.

The Ohio State pass defense, featuring Beekley and double-duty Bruney, was so alert and aggressive that Iowa was limited to eighteen yards in the department that usually hogs its offense. The Hawks all but abandoned the airways in the second half after completing just one of ten first-half tosses for nine yards. They tried only two in the closing periods — and made them both good.

But Iowa didn't need passes Saturday, the way its fiery backs were twisting and lashing and pounding Ohio State's line. As Evashevski said, it was strictly a team victory and certainly the entire defensive cast was heroic.

Leinbaugh and Fenton were perhaps the most conspicuous — but nobody can overlook the inspired play of such stalwarts as Don Cheif, Phil Hayman, Andy Houg, Dick Frymire, Lou Matykiewcz, Emmett Sawyer, Ed Lindsey, Dan McBride, and all the others who made the line as stern and unyielding as a mountainside. They rushed Borton so savagely that the Ohio State sharpshooter was smeared for losses totaling forty-two yards. John's thirty-seven attempts came one shy of the listed record of thirty-eight by Indiana's Lou D'Achille against Ohio State in 1950.

The Hawks restrained Bruney to forty-four yards in eleven tries; they curbed Cassady, the celebrated freshman runner, to thirty-two yards in fourteen trips. The Bucks' offense was not at full strength because John Hlay, their pile-driving fullback, was hampered by a groin injury and hauled the ball just once.

But nothing can detract from this first Hawkeye victory since they turned back Pittsburgh, 34–17, on October 13, 1951. The only redeeming factors in ten intervening games were 20–20 deadlocks with both Minnesota and Notre Dame last year.

Mazeroski's Last-inning Homer Beats Yankees

EDITOR'S NOTE: One of the most dramatic finishes to a World Series was Bill Mazeroski's ninth-inning home run in the seventh game of the 1960 classic that enabled Pittsburgh to topple the mighty New York Yankees. Bryson's story again was one of the best sports stories of the year and was included in *Best Sports Stories—1961 Edition*.

PITTSBURGH, PA. — The most hallowed piece of property in Pittsburgh baseball history left Forbes Field late Thursday afternoon under a dirty gray sports jacket and with police escort.

That, of course, was home plate, the pentagon of rubber where Bill Mazeroski completed his electrifying home run while Umpire Bill Jackowski, broad back braced and arms spread, held off the mob long enough for Mazeroski to make it legal.

One of the 36,683 jubilant maniacs stole the plate, and a cop hauled him off.

Pittsburgh's steel mills couldn't have made more noise than the crowd in this ancient park did when Mazeroski smashed Yankee Ralph Terry's second pitch of the ninth inning. Hysterical patriots were leaping out of box seats and onto the field even before Bill's drive rocketed over the head of left fielder Yogi Berra.

By the time the ball sailed over the ivy-covered brick wall, the rush from the stands had begun and these sudden madmen threatened to keep Maz from touching the plate with the run that beat the lordly Yankees, 10–9, for the title. Two hours after this seventh World Series game, dozens of fans were walking in a happy daze around the scene of Pittsburgh's first world title victory since 1925.

This was the area where, through a sunny afternoon, joy and despair alternated at tearing the emotions of the witnesses. Joy came early with a 4–0 lead against the tyrants who had so long dominated baseball's autumn classic. Rocky Nelson's two-run homer set the foundation in the first inning.

The first sinister touch was Bill Skowron's lonely homer for the Yankees in the fifth inning. But there was no real despair yet. After all, it was only the third New York hit off precision-throwing Vern Law, and the Mormon preacher promptly disposed of the next three Yanks.

Distress bordering on terror struck in the sixth inning. The Yankees, so accustomed to winning under pressure, not only chased the tiring Law, but fell upon Roy Face, the emergency expert. Face had saved all three previous Pirate victories in this series with his forkball.

Mickey Mantle smacked Face for a run-scoring single. Yogi Berra crashed a three-run homer, jumping up and down on the first-base line as he watched his towering fly soar just inside the foul pole and into the stands.

Now, the Yankees, eighteen-time world champions, were in front, 5–4, and Pirate fans shuddered at the thought that this might turn into another rout. They had sat through two fearful drubbings in Forbes Field, 16–3 and 12–0. The other Yankee victory, in New York, was almost as humiliating — 10–0. It was no rout, but it looked like security for the Yankees when a walk, two singles and Clete Boyer's double boosted the Yankeee margin to 7–4 in the eighth inning.

By this time, stubborn little Bobby Shantz had kept the Pirates helpless for five innings. Despair was almost as apparent as the haze that hung over the nearby hills. Pirate fans must have wished for the type of Yankee power that had blasted ten homers in this Series. The Bucs had just two.

The Pirates vanquished the gutty Shantz when pinch hitter Gino Cimoli and Bill Virdon and Dick Groat clipped him for singles and a run with nobody out. Virdon's smash, which might have been turned into a double play, took a weird bounce and hit shortstop Tony Kubek in the throat. Kubek had to leave the game and was taken to a hospital.

In came lanky Jim Coates. There were mutterings when Manager Danny Murtaugh wasted Bob Skinner's power potential by having him bunt the runners along. Luck joined the Pirates after Rocky Nelson's fly. Roberto Clemente topped a roller to the right of Coates.

First baseman Bill Skowron had to field the maddening trickler. By the time he scooped it up, there was no chance for a play. A run scored.

Once again, though, Murtaugh was open to criticism. When the Bucs were behind by only 5–4, Danny had substituted skillful Hal Smith as his catcher in place of Smoky Burgess, a left-handed power — just the man for this vital spot against the right-handed Coates. Smith swings right-handed. And Smith, an ex-Yankee, swung right indeed — but only after looking about as bad as possible on his second strike. Hal missed the high fast ball by almost a foot.

The count was two balls, two strikes when the drive sailed over the wall. Bedlam broke loose and the Pirates led, 9–7. But the fans who had come to bury the Yankees stayed to praise them — grudgingly, despairingly—for a comeback of their own.

Bob Friend was entrusted with the fresh lead but was no more reliable than he had been in two losing starts. Little Bobby Richardson and pinch hitter Dale Long each singled. Reed-thin Harvey Haddix, who had beaten the Yanks in the fourth game, was beckoned to face the Yankee gargantuans—Roger Maris and Mickey Mantle.

Harvey got past Maris, who popped an easy foul to Smith, but Mantle singled for another run. Then it was Mickey's artful dodging that let the tying run score. Nelson was playing tight to the line to keep Mantle close to first base. His position was ideal for Berra's bouncer.

Rocky seized the ball, touched the bag, and turned to stab at Mantle. If he had tagged Mickey, it would have been a game-ending double play, completed before pinch runner Gil McDougald could cross the plate. But Mickey slid under the tag and the Yankees had a new opportunity. Skowron was a dangerous threat to bring Mantle around. Haddix was his master, though. Bill Skowron bounced to Groat at short and there was an easy force on Mantle at second.

So Ralph Terry, who had retired Don Hoak to end the eighth inning, went out to defend the tie. Instead, he became the twenty-sixth victim of a last-inning Pirate rally in Pittsburgh's most glorious baseball year since the Pirates won the world championship in 1925.

The Big Giveaway

EDITOR'S NOTE: In the era before post-season baseball playoffs were a yearly ritual, the two bitter West Coast rivals—Los Angeles and San Francisco—finished in a dead heat for first place at the end of the 1962 regular season. A best-of-three playoff was held to determine which team would represent the National League in the World Series, and Bryson's report on the third game of that playoff appeared in *Best Sports Stories—1963 Edition*.

LOS ANGELES, CALIF. —Opportunity finally got tired of knocking for the collapsible Los Angeles Dodgers Wednesday, so San Francisco will have its first World Series game today. Los Angeles, trying to give away the National League pennant for two weeks, succeeded in the dying gasp of the longest of all seasons.

222

In the biggest giveaway since the Indians peddled Manhattan Island for a little booze and a few trinkets, the Dodgers thrust the championship upon the Giants in a sickening ninth inning, 6–4. The pennant wasn't won. It was lost.

The Dodgers tried to give it away early with errors in this third playoff game, but Tommy Davis wouldn't let them. The new league batting champion whaled a home run after Duke Snider singled in the sixth for a 3–2 Los Angeles lead. Maury Wills compelled a bit of charity from the Giants in the next inning. He got them so giddy with two stolen bases that a wild throw sent him home.

For the first time since mid-September, Dodger patriots in the crowd of 45,893 were able to settle back with some security. The atmosphere was still serene when Ed Roebuck, the Los Angeles rescue expert, strode out to deliver the clincher in the ninth.

Who wouldn't be confident? A two-run lead—and fearsome Willie Mays probably wouldn't even get to bat. Willie was fifth in line. But Mays did prance out after the bases were loaded on Matty Alou's pinch single and two walks. A force play had yielded one out.

Willie, twice walked intentionally, ripped into Roebuck's first pitch. The vicious drive flared straight back at the pitcher, bounced off his up-flung glove, and scattered away for a run-scoring single. That was the last hit the Giants needed to complete a desperate championship journey that found them four games back with only seven to go in the regular season.

Stan Williams, whose relief work corked the Giants Tuesday to even the playoff, came in to try to end it. Stan got the second out, all right, but it was a fly ball by Orlando Cepeda long enough to permit the tying run.

From there on, San Francisco was a charity case. Williams's intentional walk to Ed Bailey reloaded the bases. Five pitches later, four of them off course, the Giants were, to all intents and purposes, National League champions and foes of the New York Yankees in the World Series. Williams's walk to Jim Davenport made it 5–4. The gigantic giveaway program ended when second baseman Larry Burright, installed for defensive reasons, muffed Joe Pagan's hopper for a surplus run.

Billy Pierce, shutout winner in the playoff opener, easily disposed of Los Angeles' dying bid in the ninth, guarding a victory for Don Larsen. Don answered a minor emergency call after starter Juan Marichal walked Tommy Davis to start the eighth. A sacrifice and a strikeout left Don one out from escape, but Davis stole third as Frank

Howard fanned. So Manager Al Dark ordered the bases filled with walks. Dodger Manager Walt Alston then surprisingly and unexpectedly decided against using a pinch hitter for Roebuck. The pitcher bounced weakly to Davenport at third.

Roebuck had earned the skipper's confidence by pulling the Dodgers out of the worst kind of jam in the sixth — bases full, nobody out. Roebuck had a dazzling defensive ally in Wills, whose offensive work wasn't bad either. Maury punched four singles.

In the sixth, the Giants loaded the bases on hits by Cepeda, Bailey, and Davenport. Roebuck came in to relieve Johnny Podres — and Wills went to work on defense. First, he took Pagan's hard grounder and threw to home for a force-out, then started a double play on Marichal's grounder. This was a vivid contrast to the Dodger defense in the third inning, when errant throws by Podres, catcher John Roseboro, and Jim Gilliam got the Giants to a 2–0 lead.

Marichal was first wounded in the fourth after Snider doubled. The slow-footed Duke had to stop at third on Tommy Davis's single to left. He got home only because Tommy cut down Chuck Hiller on a force play at second and prevented Hiller from doubling Howard at first base for the third out. Davis homered in the sixth inning to put Los Angeles on top, 3–2.

The fourth Dodger run was entirely the work of the lone bandit: Wills lined his fourth single and promptly stole second. The blazing brigand, urged on by the "Go-Go-Go" from the fans, then took off for third. Catcher Bailey hurried his throw. It dipped into the dirt in front of third and skipped into left field. Maury scored and his reception in the Dodger dugout was almost as jubilant as the celebration that greeted his winning run Tuesday.

The rejoicing was premature. Madville soon turned to Mudville.

EDITOR'S NOTE: Bryson witnessed more than two hundred World Series games during his career. In later life, he said that in addition to his award-winning World Series stories, his favorite stories included the sixth and seventh games of the 1975 World Series, considered one of the best and most thrilling of the post-season classics, and the New York Mets' World Series championship in 1969.

Red Sox Win on Fisk's Twelfth-inning Homer

BOSTON, MASS. — The best catch Sparky Anderson ever saw kept the enemy Boston Red Sox alive for Carlton Fisk's early-morning home run that squared the World Series, 7–6, in the twelfth inning Tuesday night.

Fisk's drive was barely fair above the towering left-field wall. So it traveled only 304 feet, not the 315 listed on the fence sign. But it was high enough and long enough to send a crowd of 35,205 into mass mania that has surely never been surpassed for loudness and lustiness in quaint Fenway Park.

"I was afraid it was going to curve around in front of the pole and go foul," said Fisk. "The wind had already carried it fifteen feet out of fair territory. All I could do was hold my breath till I saw the ball hit the foul pole. Then I let it out with a big yell."

The rangy Fisk, who has slimmed down too much for his nickname of Pudge, completed the tension-tortured game that was "homer-or-no-count" for the Red Sox against favored Cincinnati. Fred Lynn rocketed one with two passengers in the first inning. Bernie Carbo's second pinch home run of the Series scored three to bomb out the Reds' 6–3 lead in the eighth.

The National Leaguers slammed only one beyond the outfield that had been a swamp before Tuesday's glorious sunshine ended the streak of three postponements. That lone Cincinnati homer was enough to offset Carbo's drive into the center-field seats and send the electrifying competition well past midnight.

Except for right fielder Dwight Evans's catch that astonished Manager Anderson and stunned Ken Griffey into immobility, the Reds would have become world champions in the eleventh inning. Evans, whose only hit went to waste, more than made up for his offensive weakness with a display of defense that will go down as one of the greatest and most crucial in World Series history.

The wall in right field is only three feet high at the point toward which Evans was fleeing in a mad race with Joe Morgan's smoking liner.

"I've made catches like that before — I mean where you have to turn and sprint back in the general direction of where you think the ball will be," said Evans. "Once I saw I'd guessed right, I thought I'd get it."

To get it, Evans had to keep pell-melling toward the barrier, leap and make a cobra-like stab as the ball steamed into his glove. "He really crunched it," said Evans. "It would have gone three or four rows into the stands if I hadn't grabbed it."

Evans may have expected to make the catch, but Griffey saw no way the drive could be clutched. Ken was so confident of scoring the championship run, he had dashed from first base well around second. When the out was called to Griffey's attention, he did stutter steps.

So it didn't matter that Evans, off balance after he bumped the fence, threw far wide of first base. Alert Carl Yastrzemski, moved from left field to first in the ninth inning, retrieved the wayward throw, and there was still lots of time to double Griffey as second baseman Denny Doyle covered first.

Fisk whacked "a sinker down and in" for the hoist that sailed to victory on Pat Darcy's second serve of the twelfth inning. Darcy became the loser as the eighth Cincinnati pitcher. He helped set a record of twelve hurlers employed in a World Series game.

The Reds began the game with homer-prone Gary Nolan before Boston called in a replacement for Luis Tiant, two-time conqueror of the Reds, who lost his bid to become the first pitcher since Red Faber of Cascade, Iowa, to win three of six games in a Series. Faber did it for the Chicago White Sox against the New York Giants in 1917.

Tiant, perhaps the first Series pitcher to receive a standing ovation before the game, tried the patience of Manager Darrell Johnson through two Cincinnati outbreaks. The first wrought a 3–3 tie in the fifth inning. Two runs scored when Lynn suffered a back injury as he crashed into the center field wall in a desperation try for Griffey's caroming triple.

The next cannonading of Tiant pushed Cincinnati ahead, 5–3, on George Foster's double after singles by Griffey and Morgan in the seventh. Johnson stuck with the clever, chunky Cuban until Cesar Geronimo homered into the right field customers in the eighth. Rick Wise became the winner by overcoming the menace of singles by Tony Perez and Foster in the twelfth. It was Wise's only inning after shutout emergency work by Rogelio Moret and Dick Drago.

Except for Johnny Bench's run-scoring single that dented the tin above the scoreboard in the fifth inning, the Reds shot for much deeper targets. Foster's double was off the center field wall, over the head of Lynn. Fred was able to stay in the game after first aid following his collision with the cement wall earlier.

Now it comes down to a game that begins on the same date on

which the dramatic sixth contest ended. Anderson has saved his ace, Don Gullett, for this one against Boston lefty Bill Lee, who was infuriated because he was passed over for the sixth game.

Cincinnati Rallies To Win 1975 Series

BOSTON, MASS. — Sparky Anderson's ace in the hole turned out to be a deuce, but the Cincinnati Reds still came up with the winning hand in a ninth-inning World Series showdown Wednesday night, 4–3.

"We had a full house going for us," said winning hitter Joe Morgan amid the popping of champagne corks in the Reds' first world championship festivities since 1940. "It was like a poker game. I felt we had the eight best men in baseball and good pitchers going for us."

At first it appeared that the fleet Reds would be "walking away" from their title chance against Boston in this seventh game of the fall classic. Don Gullett, the ace Anderson had saved for the finale, was overwrought for resumption of a drama that began early Wednesday morning with Boston's twelfth-inning victory.

Gullett's nervous pitching thrust two runs upon the Red Sox in the third inning. Don's two walks with the bases full completed a three-run inning that began with a pass to Bernie Carbo. Denny Doyle, the only player to hit in every game, and old reliable Carl Yastrzemski inserted singles.

Doyle's halo was tarnished in the sixth when the Reds began to display their typical resilience with Tony Perez's two-run homer. "Sure, it looked bad when we were down 3–0," said Pete Rose, voted the most valuable player in the Series. "But we never quit. We had been coming from behind all year."

Fifty times the Reds had dug out of ruts, twenty-seven times in their last turns at bat, before they did it again with thousands of extra dollars in the pot. Morgan did it this time. He didn't hit where he intended to deposit the ball. The direction and distance turned out to be just right, though, when the Reds were one out from being stuck with a tie.

"It was a good pitch," said Joe, a left-handed swinger, "down and away. I wanted to go to the opposite field with it — to left. I almost did it a couple of pitches before on that line drive foul into the stands."

Instead, the ball flared into the wide open space of short center field, the same landing area of Rose's tying single in the seventh. Ken Griffey walked, then ran for both the tying run and the winner that turned misshapen little Fenway Park into a place of mourning for the 35,205 spectators.

Griffey progressed when third baseman Rico Petrocelli threw out the bunting Cesar Geronimo from a sitting position. Rookie Jim Burton, groping for the escape hatch, came closer on pinch hitter Dan Driessen's grounder. That put Griffey on third, waiting impatiently as Burton walked Rose. Then Morgan's misdirection sent the Reds on the right road.

It's traditional to have a goat in every World Series. Doyle will bear that stigma because of his throw into the Boston dugout on what should have been a double play ending the sixth inning. But Denny was under the influence of Rose's fierce slide that bumped his leg and forced him to jump high to launch his throw after the force at second. That opened the door for Perez to become the first Red who could take really productive advantage of the nearby towering target in left field. "Peter made it possible," said Perez. "No chance if he didn't break up that double play."

Perez said he was looking for that off-speed pitch from Bill Lee, the eccentric left-hander who was striving for his sixth shutout inning. "He fooled me with that slow pitch earlier," Tony added, "and I was sure he would throw it again."

During batting practice, the blithe Lee had gibed: "After this game, Don Gullett will go to the Hall of Fame and I'll be going to a saloon." Lee was free to visit a grog shop before the game was over after developing a blister on his thumb while walking Griffey with one out in the seventh. Reliever Rogelio Moret let that become the tying run. He walked pinch hitter Ed Armbrister after getting the second out.

Rose's single and a pass to Morgan turned a bases-loaded complication over to Jim Willoughby. Carlton Fisk prevented further damage by reaching into the box seats for Johnny Bench's foul pop for the inning's third out.

Ragamuffins Achieve Their Impossible Dream

NEW YORK, N.Y. —The Miracle Braves of 1914. The Red Sox realizing their Impossible Dream in 1967. The Yankee-killing Pirates of 1960. And all the other World Series astonishers of the past. Put them down as impostors. Their claims to the most incredible deeds in baseball were rendered fraudulent Thursday.

The ragamuffins have overrun the palace. The most derided club in major league history through seven previous ridiculous seasons is now the most successful and admired.

The Mets are champions of baseball. Impossible dream? Not even a pot-smoking visionary could have entertained such a fantasy last April, when the New Yorkers were 100–1 shots in the National League.

Only the most giddy dreamers gave them a glimmer of a chance against the overpowering Orioles in the World Series. But by mid-afternoon Thursday, the Orioles were groveling on the turf of Shea Stadium, 5–3, dazed and crushed in five games, beaten by Ron Swoboda's eighth-inning double.

It was a turf that later had enough holes in it to bury the Orioles individually. Patches of the sod now occupy hallowed places in homes all over this madly hilarious megalapolis.

The climax was as incredible as the pennant drive that flamed after the Mets trailed the Chicago Cubs by nine-and-a-half games in mid-August.

The wonder workers wallowed in futility for five innings, down, 3–0, on home runs by Frank Robinson and Dave McNally, their pitching master in that span.

Often-discarded Donn Clendenon gave them their first worthwhile hit with a two-run homer in the sixth. That was Donn's third Series homer, so it wasn't totally unexpected. But the next one, the one that made it a 3–3 game, was as astonishing as most Met heroics.

The most unlikely homer-smasher of all delivered it to lead off the seventh. Little Al Weis has averaged one home run for each 241 times at bat in eight big league seasons.

Weis is a Punch-and-Judy hitter. He chokes up on the bat and specializes in loopers over the infield. But now he was like a giant with a sledgehammer, crunching McNally's pitch over the green wall in left near the 371-foot marker.

McNally escaped further damage, but left for a nonhitting pinch hitter in the eighth. The rescuer, Eddie Watt, could not stand up against the mystique, magic, and mastery of the New York incredibles. Watt, born in Lamoni and resident of several other Iowa towns before he left the University of Northern Iowa to turn pro in 1962, was made the guardian of the 3–3 tie.

Watt, who had pitched two shutout innings in Wednesday's ten-inning Baltimore loss, floundered into immediate trouble with a 3–0 count to Cleon Jones. Cleon took a strike. Eddie tried for another and made it too good. Jones whaled it over the head of back-tracking Paul Blair in center. It hopped against the wall at 396 feet for a double.

Watt lured an easy grounder from Clendenon. Then came Swoboda, a figure of scorn for both his fielding and hitting in four previous years with the Mets, a man benched in the middle of this season when his average shriveled to near .200.

The Met mystique, which even included shoe polish Thursday, cast its spell on Watt after his first serve to Ron was a ball. Swoboda's drive on the next pitch was neither long nor fierce, but the Met hex put left fielder Don Buford in a daze just long enough to make it the crowning blow.

Buford, often bewildered by fly balls in Shea Stadium, didn't get a jump on this one. The ball looped down along the foul line and could have been an out with a quick start by Don.

Buford got to the ball—but on the first short hop. Larry Napp, the umpire on the left-field line, semaphored the safe sign, meaning that Buford had trapped the ball. Jones was home free with the championship run.

It would have been only the tying run if the Mets hadn't pointed to shoe polish on the ball and persuaded plate umpire Lou DiMuro to award Jones first base in the sixth. That made Cleon a passenger for Clendenon's howling swat into the second-deck customers near the left-field foul pole.

It was another Jones, known as Nippy, who first made shoe polish famous in a World Series—for the Milwaukee Braves in 1957. The stain on the ball persuaded the umpire that Nippy had been hit.

It was the same with Cleon. DiMuro first called a ball on McNally's low, inside pitch. The Mets squawked and won the argument by showing the black polish on the ball.

The Orioles lost a similar debate in the sixth on a foul tip by Frank Robinson, who had cracked out a 390-foot homer in the third. Manager Earl Weaver, evicted for protesting a called strike Wednesday, made a moderate approach to the umpire this time. Robinson was more vigorous in this argument that the pitch had hit him in the side. The Orioles had no shoe polish as evidence. The game was delayed while Robinson went to the clubhouse for treatment. Frank was roundly booed the rest of the afternoon.

Frank knocked in his first run of the Series with his homer after McNally stole the Mets' amazing thunder. The pitcher, an .086 hitter with one homer all year, belted one to left after Mark Belanger led off the third with a gentle single to right.

Robinson homered two outs later. But the Orioles were to drive just one more hit off the slashing curves of Jerry Koosman in his second victory.

That was a blow on which Boog Powell tried to check his swing in the sixth. The accidental jab sent the ball past shortstop Bud Harrelson with a deceptive hop. Swoboda, Wednesday's defensive dandy, took a prospective double from Blair in that inning with a backhand stab while running lickety-split toward center.

The Mets' second run in the eighth was an anticlimax and an outright gift. First baseman Powell fumbled Jerry Grote's simple grounder. Boog recovered, but Watt was tardy in covering first. Eddie compounded the mess by dropping the throw and Swoboda scampered home.

Koosman, who stopped Baltimore on two hits in the second game, allowed five this time. Jerry faltered at the start of the ninth with a five-pitch lead-off walk to Frank Robinson, but Powell forced Frank at second.

Then, Brooks Robinson and Dave Johnson hoisted soft fly balls—and the maniacs began tearing up the scene of triumph.

Index

Russo, Jim, 55
Rutgers University, 95
Ruth, Babe, 7–8, 16, 100, 139

Sager, Sam, 74
St. Louis Browns, 39, 64, 84, 138
St. Louis Cardinals, 39, 40, 64, 69, 99,
  109, 111, 112, 113, 114, 115, 163,
  169–70
San Francisco Giants, 36, 37, 115, 222–
  24. *See also* New York Giants
Santo, Ron, 179
Saperstein, Abe, 102–3
Savold, Lee, 61
Sawyer, Emmett, 219
Saydel, Iowa, 44
Schmidt, Joe, 53
Schoendienst, Red, 112
Sczeny, Matt, 115
Seminick, Andy, 50–51
Shantz, Bobby, 221
Shaw, George Bernard, 199
Sheridan, John B., 71
Shocker, Urban, 39
Shotton, Barney, 109–10
Sibley, Iowa, 39
Sinatra, Frank, 18
Sioux City, Iowa, 42, 60, 84, 117, 118,
  127, 157
Sisam, Dave, 129–30
Sisler, George, 207
Skinner, Bob, 221
Skowron, Bill, 220, 221, 222
Slapnicka, Cy, 21–22, 58, 59, 63, 165
Slater, Duke, 103, 176
Smith, Hall, 221, 222
Smith, Reggie, 114–15
Snider, Duke, 223, 224
Somers, Iowa, 127
Spahn, Warren, 40
Spalding, Al, 74, 84
Spirit Lake, Iowa, 127, 150
State College of Iowa, 54
Stearnes, Bob, 217, 218, 219
Stengel, Casey, 11–12, 129, 130, 144,
  201–2, 210
Stern, Bill, 17–19
Storm Lake, Iowa, 78–79, 128
Stovey, George, 72
Strode, Woody, 104
Studley, Chuck, 198
Swoboda, Ron, 229, 230, 231

Taft, William Howard, 18
Taylor, Garner (Sec), 211–12
Teague, Charlie, 117–18
Tebbetts, Birdie, 50–51
Tener, John K., 75
Terry, Ralph, 220, 222
Texas Rangers, 36
Thompson, Fresco, 153, 210
Thompson, Gus, 31
Thorpe, Jim, 8–9, 50
Thurston, Hollis (Sloppy), 141
Tiant, Luis, 226
Timm, Cap, 52, 135
Tinker, Joe, 19
Tipton, Iowa, 127
Trosky, Hal (Harold Troyavesky), 23–
  24, 52
Twain, Mark, 199
Twogood, Forrest (Toogy), 42, 44

University of Chicago, 105
University of Illinois, 176
University of Iowa, 49–50, 61, 72, 77,
  81, 82, 105, 124, 215–19
University of Kansas, 82
University of Michigan, 42
University of Minnesota, 81, 104, 147
University of Nebraska, 82, 104

Van Meter, Iowa, 58–59, 61
Veeck, Bill, 102–3, 121, 122
Veil, Bucky, 31
Vinton, Iowa, 26, 83
Virdon, Bill, 221
Vogel, Otto, 34, 40–42

Walker, Moses, 72
Wallace, Jack, 137
Waner, Lloyd, 123
Waner, Paul, 123
Ward, John Montgomery, 72
Washington, Kenny, 104
Washington Redskins, 128
Washington Senators, 26, 76, 149
Waterloo, Iowa, 26, 85, 113, 114, 127,
  150
Watt, Eddie, 54–55, 230, 231